A Pan-American Life

A Pan-American Life

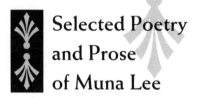

Selected Poetry
and Prose
of Muna Lee

Muna Lee

Edited and with biography by
JONATHAN COHEN

Foreword by
AURORA LEVINS MORALES

The **UNIVERSITY** of **WISCONSIN PRESS**

The University of Wisconsin Press
1930 Monroe Street
Madison, Wisconsin 53711

www.wisc.edu/wisconsinpress/

3 Henrietta Street
London WC2E 8LU, England

Library of Congress Cataloging-in-Publication Data

Lee, Muna, 1895–1965.
A pan-American life : selected poetry and prose of Muna Lee / Muna
Lee ; edited and with biography by Jonathan Cohen ; foreword by
Aurora Levins Morales.
    p. cm. — (The Americas)
    Includes bibliographical references and index.
    ISBN 0-299-20230-5 (hardcover : alk. paper) — ISBN 0-299-20234-8
    (pbk. : alk. paper)
    1. America—Literary collections. 2. Spanish American poetry—
Translations into English. 3. Poets, American—20th century—
Biography. 4. Translators—United States—Biography. 5. Feminists—
United States—Biography. 6. Women—Literary collections. 7. Lee,
Muna, 1895–1965. I. Cohen, Jonathan. II. Title. III. Americas
(Madison, Wis.)
PS3523.E3448A6   2004
818'.52—dc22   2004012626

 For Ellen

Let's find ourselves before we leave today
for where only you and I know the way

Can there be more than one Muna Lee? more than
the one whose verse I have known since a long time?

— WILLIAM FAULKNER, *in a letter
to Muna Lee dated June 29, 1954*

Contents

→ Verse Translation

Foreword

1

What I keep thinking is: why didn't I know about you? I have needed you and I didn't know. I grew up in the Puerto Rican independence movement, in a home full of books, speaking English and knowing other families who did, pacifists, university people, circles you would have moved through. I am a poet, a translator, a feminist historian studying women's resistance, women's voices, and I never heard that Luis Muñoz Marín had a first wife, far less one like you.

But of course I know the answer. I understand how we are disappeared from history, from literature, from print. It fills me with fear, with rage, with grief, with a righteous fury of intent that you be known. Your life is too close to mine for this to be some academic exercise, a cool assessment of your place in the various scales of importance. You are important to *me*. That is the story I am going to tell.

2

People who are intending praise say that you became Puerto Rican, that you were Puerto Rican in your heart, that you were, for all practical purposes, native, but I know you are something more rare. There are people who move into the cultures of others with such grace and respect that the friction of foreignness virtually disappears, who can un-self-consciously love the unfamiliar as if it were the most natural thing in the world. It is clear in the way people speak of you, and in the tracks of the life you lived, that you were one of them. You entered Latin America this way again and again, through political action, through marriage, through poetry, through the paid work of communication. It is a gift of relationship that requires a certain boldness of affection, and a generosity and curiosity toward the variety of humankind.

I grew up embedded in two entwined stories of "Americans" who also had this gift, who married into Puerto Rican politics and made children, richly woven lives, deep-rooted alliances. The first, Jane Speed, was a white woman and radical from Alabama who married communist labor leader and journalist Cesar Andreu Iglesias and came to Puerto Rico with her mother, Mary Craik Speed, in 1937. She had long red hair that she wore in a braided crown on her head, straightforward strong good sense, and she was an organizer with the originality and nerve to become a

Tampax sales rep because the moment she mentioned her reason for visiting a rural household, the men disappeared and she could talk to the women alone.

The second was my Brooklyn Jewish father, Richard Levins, who married my Spanish-Harlem-and-the-Bronx Puerto Rican mother in 1950 and came to the island the following year, where Jane and Cesar became their close friends and political comrades. And my father, who knew only a few words of Spanish, decided that his high-school Latin would be close enough and unabashedly blundered his way into fluency, drinking unbelievable amounts of coffee in the cause of organizing coffee workers and small-scale farmers in the wilds of Yauco and Maricao.

I grew up in the house Jane and her family had built on our farm, and because she and her mother loved flowers as you did, I grew up among the forget-me-nots and gladioli they planted, which persisted among the upthrusting spears of ginger and tangled hibiscus decades after they were gone. But most of all, I grew up within a legacy of joyous border crossings, of knowing we have the right to love anyone, to learn any language and speak it, to offer ourselves wherever we choose. And this makes you my kin.

3

I also grew up in a house full of books, with parents who read poetry aloud, in English and Spanish, and those rhythms saturated my earliest sense of language. Most of them were men, but men of many countries, writing in many languages, translated into our reach. I read Bertolt Brecht and Nazim Hikmet, Pablo Neruda, Antonio Machado, and the *Eighteen Laments* of Tsai Wen Chi. Bad translations irritated me almost physically. I was still a child when I began revising the English versions of Neruda in the bilingual editions we owned and ached to know what might have vanished from the German of Brecht's poems in order to preserve their rhythm and rhyme. I recognize your need. You had entered our world. Once you had read and loved the poems, the itch to make them audible to others, to bring something back, must have been irresistible. I remember vividly my discovery, in college, of the first good translations of Neruda, my relief that someone had done the work, that I could share the beloved poems unfrustrated, and that I didn't have to learn the difficult art myself.

I know what it takes. That talent for relationship, akin to listening. A keen awareness of subtlety in language. A touch that is sensitive and bold. Respect for the poet, honest intent, meticulous faithfulness, reckless daring, acknowledgment that that task is ultimately impossible, and joyous in the attempt. Both accepting and refusing defeat, you wrote of translating from Spanish that the poetry "is only partially translatable—that is, so much of its beauty depends upon the intricately braided jet and silver of its cadences that a great deal is necessarily lost by translation into a less liquid tongue." Your work is exquisite, your translations breathtaking in their own right, each one a pleasure, another aspect of your talent for love.

You were always hungry to know more, share more, kindle excitement in others. You describe your anthology of Latin American poets as a cage full of birds from every climate, a mere suggestion of the vast richness you found in the poetry of a language you acquired in two weeks (in order to get a government job as a translator, which turned out to be censoring letters) and came to know as intimately as your own skin. I am full of gratitude for your skill and dedication, for the way you loved our poets and took them home with you, for doing what I lack the patience for, for using yourself to open the border wider, to make gates and doorways and windows through which sounds and images of these other lives could flow. To listen to the other is the beginning of possibility.

4

Like you I devoured books and was devoured by them, scribbled poems from an early age, was encouraged by my parents, struggled for belief in myself, translated the poems of others, was a passionate feminist, disrupted congresses and conventions to make a collective voice heard, loved men who could not rise to the occasion and broke my heart, kept writing anyway, kept finding ways into the work, not only wanted the peace of nations but believed it possible. I look at the good strong bones of your face in these photographs and wish you had been my teacher; wish I had not been eleven when you died; wish we were friends and I could call you, any one of those hundred times a day when I go out against despair with only poetry, personal joy, and collective faith and find them too small for the task. So I invoke you instead.

5

I am standing beside you. It is Havana, 1928, the Sixth Pan-American Congress at which the men of the Americas have gathered to make policies and deals, thinking about the fact that you, a white girl born in Mississippi, raised in Oklahoma, are here representing Puerto Rican women, your arms locked with those of Cuban, Peruvian, Brazilian, Costa Rican, Mexican, Argentinean women, all of you insisting on a place at the podium. I can imagine the elation, the rage, the energy, knowing the balconies above, the streets outside, were crowded with Cuban women. Arguing, holding out, pushing harder, finally, after a month of agitation, winning the chance to speak and a mandate to study the legal condition of women in every member state. I remember what it's like. Walking out of the endless monologues of men, teaching birth control in our living rooms to the outrage of male medical monopolies, shouting out loud with thousands of other women filling up hitherto off-limits public space, seeing our own words roll off hand-run printing presses. I am with you, eating together afterwards, laughing, talking fast, exhausted.

I am thinking of the year I tried to teach the history of Western feminism on a North-South axis—U.S., Latin American and Caribbean feminism, not U.S. and European—and first heard the names of these women you rubbed shoulders with, Bertha Lutz, Clara Gonzalez, Elena Torres, Minerva Bernardino, Amalia de Castilla Ledón, Paca Navas, Irma de Alvarado.[1] No one in my class had ever heard of any of them, not a single one. Not the Latin American delegates who put women into the U.N. Charter and saw to the creation of the Commission on the Status of Women; not the women who openly balked at the militarization of the continent in 1947; not any of the writers, thinkers, and agitators who had struggled not only for suffrage (which came far later to them than to women in the United States and kept them militant through the lull between our first and second waves) but also for divorce and child custody, nationality independent of a husband's, national self-determination, and living wages, and against dictatorships and fascism and the arming of the Americas.

But you knew. You had become part of this transnational agitation of women whose loyalties were to each other and not to borders, who were cynical about the political conduct of even their nations' most progressive men, who held meetings, drafted proposals, created commissions, traveled all over the continent, worked out of offices from which hostile men kept stealing the furniture. Who raided scientific conventions, political congresses, the League of Nations, shoving their way into the places where treaties were being made, because they believed this was their best shot at shaming and pressuring governments into making women citizens of their own countries, full human beings under the law, with human rights.

This was not some exotic side trip you made. You were right in the center of something most women in the United States knew nothing about, laying foundations for what we were to inherit, for labor laws that were not passed until the year of your death, for the long, unended struggle for the Equal Rights Amendment, for legal and economic rights established after you were gone. You stood in that meeting hall in the winter of 1928 and said, "Every enlightened woman of this hemisphere desires for her sister of another country, the same good which she craves for herself." Your ardent band of delegates to Havana planted the seeds of the United Nations Decade of Women, of Mexico City and Beijing, of global alliances beyond your reach but within your vision. There is nothing as sustaining as legacy, as foremothers on whose lives we can build. I understand your life. I understand what you made of it. It gives me another place to stand.

6

Then there is the mirror of sorrow. Of being bright, creative, strong-minded, generous-hearted women in love with men who are first entranced by and then cannot tolerate our brightness, who treat us badly, for whom we grieve in spite of ourselves, for whom we are heartsick. It only takes a glance at the outlines to guess that he must have been unable to handle your independence of thought and action, the fact that you had your own priorities and didn't follow him, were never his shadow. That you went to Washington for the summer to work for the Inter-American Commission of Women, your feminism carrying you into different spheres of politics than his, instead of being the handmaiden to his destiny. I reconstruct from long, bitter memory the sulkiness of offended male ego; the souring of your passion in contempt for his personal smallness; his writing to you from New York asking for money when you are scraping to feed the children in San Juan; the ache for the sweet lost bond; the small reconciliations and spurts of hope; the certain knowledge of the other woman; the unbearable pain that you nevertheless bear, first loneliness and then solitude; the putting of one foot in front of the other; the moments of ferocious joy: "I wake to exult that the world is changed—is vivid and salt because we are estranged." I can imagine each gesture of it, the slow earthquake you wrote of, tilting your bedrock into the abyss. I am weathering my own cataclysmic rupture of the heart.

The history of strong women, of writers and revolutionaries, is full of these shattered places made by loving men incapable of loving us as we are. The women I look to most are often heartbroken. It's a condition of history, a moment in evolution, that those of us who act most powerfully, who are artists and activists, who take up space and show ourselves to the world, and whose lovers are men, rarely find loves who can stand to be our matches. Emma, Rose, Luisa, Alexandra, Rosa, Jane—when I look at the lives of the women before me who give me strength, I see them mostly torn with grief or stoically alone, powerful and articulate and in pain, unable to have it all.

But you didn't die of it. You didn't join the ranks of our suicides or start drinking or stop writing poems or shrivel away into obscurity. You wrote and translated and organized and worked for a living, and went on alone.

> Since this hour is the worst, since I have found
> The doom long-dreaded, and found it can be borne,
> For all that hope is trampled to the ground
> And the force in which I trusted fled and torn:
>
> Why, I am still what I was one hour ago;
> What I was then, with this knowledge for new power—

> Though ruin is swift and resurrection slow,
> This hour being worst, I shall be better in an hour!

> "Dies Irae"

So I have mounted your photographs on a thin piece of wood, with a print of wildflowers, and set you to watch over my desk, because you denied neither love nor pain, neither politics nor poetry, and I am still reeling from my own recent losses, trying to remain whole. So I will learn from you the slow resurrection, the strength in solitude, the writing through, and remember that you were not defeated. We have the poems to prove it.

7

Meadowsweet, Verbena, Spiderwort, Johnny-Jump-Up, Foxglove, Lavender, Columbine, Wild Rose. Choctaw, Creek, Arapaho, Cheyenne, Wichita, Caddo, Ponca, Pawnee, Seminole, Kiowa, Apache, Ottawa, Shawnee, Comanche, Chickasaw, Potawatomi. You grew up reciting the names of Oklahoma wildflowers, but if you spoke of the nations being destroyed around you, no one has recorded it. It was Indian Territory the year your family came, the most Indian place in the country, full of exiles from the Southeast, refugees from the northern forests and lakes, people of the plains. It was the year the railroad came, and behind it the flood of white settlers came pouring into "empty" lands. I know that you saw Choctaw faces in the streets of Hugo every day, but I don't know what that meant to you. The nations don't appear in your poems, but the flowers do:

> Uninventive child of dust,
> The flower, responding as it must,
> Even under skies of doom
> Finds no other way than bloom . . .

> "Apology for All That Blooms in Time of Crisis"

Fierce organizer, tireless in the cause, it was poetry, after all, that meant most to you. The delicate shade of rose among the tall grass. The startle of blue. The violets of a first love betrayed. The flamboyánes of San Juan, blazing against the sea. You didn't write agitprop. You wrote about love and heartache and blossom, the early sentiment ripening into a clear, strong voice, acquiring edges, an iron tang. You fought for laws as concrete and mundane as soup on the table or not, and you wrote of the roses, of acacia, of trinitaria against a wall. You said that poetry was as much the daily bread as the white hyacinths of life, insisting that it was necessary, not a luxury, more powerful, in its electric spark, leaping across the gaps between us, than any other form of speech. You used it to heal your broken heart and to make bridges and pathways between peoples, and it was as essential to you as breath.

8

Even those whose lives have touched mine most nearly have thought last, if at all, of my poetry.

Oh, this is the place I can least bear to meet you, the place I dread in myself. That what meant most to you was least thought of. That you could write to your mentor, H. L. Mencken, "You are, I think, the only person who has ever considered my verse seriously." The more I talk with other women who write, the more I know what that deprivation costs us, the leaching of spirit, the way malnourishment leaches minerals from our bones and teeth and makes them brittle.

"I do not think it would have changed the aspect of the world for anyone else if I had not written," you told him, although you knew it would have changed it for you. Yes, I know you loved the work of translation and saw its importance as a different kind of political action. Yes, I know you published your poems in many periodicals that were widely read, that you got good reviews, that reviews you wrote were published in prestigious places, that you made a living writing, editing, reviewing, working as a cultural diplomat, a woman with children, on her own in the 1940s and 1950s. All of this matters.

But I also know the corrosive, intruding, deadly voice that whispers in the ear of every woman writer I know, belittling, criticizing, stripping, mocking, poisoning the creative moment. You published one book. In 1923. And lamented when it was out of print. You could see to it that Andrade was known, that Storni was recognized, that Mistral was revered, and write, of your own work, to Mencken: "I can only add my hope that you will find it worthwhile."

This is not a society that honors poets or respects women. I must celebrate that you had the recognition you did, that you survived your battles, that you were not poverty stricken to the point of silence, that your poetry is there to be found, that this book is possible. But I cannot find it enough.

Sitting alone with my writer's block and the rent due, my e-mail box and date book filled with the endless clamor of obligation, of invitations to give away my time or sell it cheap, with the urgent disasters of the world crying out for eloquence and spirit, it takes a strength I don't always have to let myself bloom in a time of crisis and do what means most to me. I am a different poet than you. The flowers and politics coexist in my poems. I write of war and heartbreak, blossom and atrocity, and I take my poems to the street as often as I speak them from a lecture hall podium. But my struggle is no different from yours. I have not published the half of what I've written, or written a fraction of what I could. It is far easier for me to fight for the voices of others than for my own. I am underpaid and tired, and though I can raise the hairs on people's arms with the passion of my defense of poetry and of hope, I don't always believe it matters that I write.

Here is the final gift of this encounter. What is not enough for you is not enough for me. I have needed you as another Anglo-Rican living in the tidal zone between cultures and as a foremother to my radicalism, my Latina feminism, another strand to add to my sustaining sense of history. I have needed you as a woman surviving the loss of love through her own strength of spirit and a woman artist carving a public place for herself in an earlier time, when fewer of us did. I have needed your mix of militancy and prairie wildflowers, your defense of simple blossomings, your willingness to engage the intricacies of love and keep stealing back the desk and chairs from which you agitate for women's lives within the law. I have needed your expansive sense of "we," so desperately absent from the evening news, the Pan-Americanism of your day that would have been a global sense of mutual responsibility today. I have needed this sense of companionship across time. And I have needed what I know right now, writing of you at two in the morning while rain drums on the roof.

I hope that future generations of women writers will have lives so much easier than mine that they will instantly perceive barbarities of my situation I don't see, because I can't imagine their absence. Perhaps it will be inevitable that some future woman, writing of me after I am dead, will feel the grief for me I feel for you and be angry that I didn't have more. But I am looking back at you and thinking that this is how I will honor you. I will say that my writing matters, and I will write, before laundry, before phone calls, before editing jobs and lectures, through grief and worry and distraction, whether I am intimately loved or not, and I will publish every way I can, so no one will have to hunt through out-of-print periodicals and attics full of boxes to find me. Militance is easy for me, but blooming without apology is hard. The world is full of opportunities to be of use, but I believe with you that poetry has a special power to reconnect our severed bonds, and I will practice it, because for myself and also for the world, you have reminded me that poetry is bread.

Aurora Levins Morales

NOTES

1. Most of this history is drawn from Francesca Miller's wonderfully comprehensive history, *Latin American Women and the Search for Social Justice* (Lebanon, N. H.: University Press of New England, 1991).

Preface

This book started as a curiosity about Muna Lee and became an adventure. During a previous study of the Pan-American literary tradition, I read a very savvy book review that she had written about a translation of Pablo Neruda's poetry, which appeared in the *Saturday Review* in 1947. Who was she—this most intelligent woman who spoke of him as a poet "closer to blood than to ink"? She understood him so well, and was well ahead of her time in this regard. Nothing much about her was available when my investigation began in the late 1990s. Her significance became clear early in my search for pieces of the puzzle of her life. My library work led to impressive publications by her that I found scattered in magazines and anthologies, then to lively phone calls and correspondences with scholars and, ultimately, to close friendships with members of her family. All told me that she was truly important and worthy of my energies. My trip in May 2003 to Puerto Rico, where I explored trunks of her papers and personal things kept in a jungle cottage, further confirmed what I had discovered about her.

The purpose of this book, therefore, is to tell the story of Muna Lee's extraordinary life, and also to present the first collection of her diverse writings—poetry, translations, essays, journalism, public addresses—in an effort to recover her work that is replete with lyricism, brilliance, and progressive ideas. These writings form a record of her personal history as much as they contribute to the literary and social history of the Americas. Collectively, they embody her vision of Pan America, an old concept that remains new and meaningful today.

I wish to express my gratitude to the following people who in various ways contributed to the realization of this book: Elaine Hughes for her biographical sketches of Muna Lee, which gave me the first glimpse of my subject; Esther Sue Wamsley for her work and conversation about Pan-American feminism; Carmen T. Bernier-Grand and Gladys Jiménez-Muñoz for sharing their knowledge of Lee's relationship with Puerto Rico and for giving their encouragement; Joseph Parisi, editor of *Poetry*, for providing information about Lee's history with the magazine; Lemuel Coley, Daniel Deutsch, and David Unger for their helpful criticism of early drafts of the biography; Graham Everett for his review of the final manuscript of the entire book; Luis Muñoz Lee (1921–2003) and Frances Klafter, Lee's son and sister, respectively, for their clarifications and their strong support; Margarita Rosado Muñoz, Lee's granddaughter (second daughter of Munita), for providing wonderful stories and photographs and encouragement; Gloria Arjona, Lee's daughter-in-law and devotee, for sharing her amazing archives and memories; Virginia Reppy, Lee's niece (daughter of sister Virginia), for a full day of Lee family history and photographs; Blanche Wiesen Cook for her powerful support and for opening doors; Jean Barman for a photograph; Frank Parman for essential documents from Oklahoma; Lawrence Rodgers for clarifying the "Oklahoma manner" (Mencken) and Vincent Fitzpatrick, curator of the H. L. Mencken Collection of Baltimore's Enoch Pratt Free Library, for help in locating the source; Jennifer Ford, of the special collections at the University of Mississippi, for her special support and for Lee's page in the Ole Miss yearbook; Julio Quirós, archive director of the Luis Muñoz Marín Foundation, for historical clarification and photographs; Beth Holler, of the Florence Bayard Hilles Feminist Library of the National Woman's Party, for her search through the NWP's *Equal Rights* for Lee's publications in it; J. Enrique Ojeda for the dates of Luis Aníbal Sánchez; Jason Torre, of the special collections at Stony Brook University, for documents from the Jorge Carrera Andrade Collection; the staff of the Interlibrary Loan Office of Stony Brook University's Frank Melville Jr. Memorial Library for providing many of the needed works by Lee and others; Danielle Lewis for typing much of the manuscript; Marjorie Agosín, Hertha Essman, Margaret Sayers Peden, David Sheehan, and Asa Zatz for their special support and encouragement; Ilan Stavans and Irene Vilar, editors of The Americas series of the University of Wisconsin Press, for their enthusiastic response to the manuscript; Aurora Levins Morales for embracing Muna Lee; Jean Franco, for providing astute critical comments and suggestions for revision; Edith Grossman for translation consultation; David Sheinin for discussion about the Pan-American movement; Daniel Cohen (Harvard '03) for helping me to keep my mind alive; and Kathryn Cohen—for always believing in the value of my doing this book.

A Pan-American Life

Muna Lee

⇥ A Pan-American Life ⇤

THIS EXTRAORDINARY WOMAN

Muna Lee's name no longer rings a bell with readers of American poetry. Her once-celebrated work as a lyric poet who embraced both North and South America has been forgotten for decades and remains ignored by scholars for reasons largely due to the fragmented humanities of today's universities. Her work as a translator and essayist in the Pan-American literary tradition and her activism in the early decades of the Pan-American feminist movement both figure prominently in their respective histories. Moreover, as a distinguished leader of the cause to further cultural relations between the Americas, Lee can be credited with important advances in the Pan-American movement, which embodied her lifelong vision of our achieving what she called "Pan-American character," a multicultural American ethos composed of "aboriginal copper, carbon of Ethiopia, Latin dream, and stark Anglo-Saxon reality."[1]

Indeed, the lasting contributions made by Muna Lee to both American literature and society remain as impressive as this extraordinary woman was herself: a petite (five feet three inches), dark-haired, dark-eyed lady from Mississippi, with striking intelligence and charm—and a graceful southern voice, which toward the end of her life the Library of Congress recorded for posterity in a reading of her poetry.

FROM MISSISSIPPI TO OKLAHOMA

Lee was born on January 29, 1895, in small-town Raymond, Mississippi, to Benjamin Floyd Lee, a self-taught druggist who was the son of a wealthy plantation owner, and Mary Maud (McWilliams) Lee, the daughter of a physician in nearby Blue Mountain. They named her Muna not after anyone in particular but because they liked the uniqueness and the sound of it and because it derived from the poetic Latin word *munus*, meaning gift. The descendants of early British settlers, her parents were both college graduates, and from the start they nurtured their daughter's intellectual curiosity and, later, her idealistic spirit. Muna was the eldest of nine children (five girls and four boys), three of whom died in infancy. The family enjoyed a modest yet genteel life in the quiet town of Raymond, about which she later said, "That old dream-like memory of Raymond has always stayed with me, [and] remained a reality when so often tangible things have seemed unreal."[2]

During the years of her early childhood, Lee showed a remarkable taste for, and interest in, poetry, drama, and all types of literature rarely relished by children. This passion of hers was encouraged especially by her mother, who had published poems occasionally in her own youth. Not surprisingly, from the time Muna could write, she composed verses.

In 1902, enticed by business opportunity, her father boldly moved the family to what became Hugo, Oklahoma, then part of Indian Territory (now the county seat of Choctaw County, in the southeastern corner of the state), with its vast, open expanses of land. Oklahoma, whose name was derived from two Choctaw words, *okla* (people) and *humma* (red), was then the home of more Native Americans than any other state in the country: the Chickasaw, Choctaw, Seminole, Cherokee and Creek; Cheyenne and Arapaho; Kiowa (Apache, Comanche, Kiowa, Wichita, Waco, Tawkoni, Caddo, Kichai, and Delaware); Pawnee (Pawnee, Ponca, Nez Perce, Ottawa, Confederated Peoria, Quapaw, Seneca, Eastern Shawnee, and Wyandot); and Sac- and Fox-Shawnee. Living in Hugo, she would have seen Choctaws in town every day.

The year the Lees arrived was the year the Saint Louis–San Francisco Railway built an east-west line from Hope, Arkansas, to Ardmore, Oklahoma, creating the territorial town—"a straggling town of tents"—later named Hugo (after the French novelist, whom a local surveyor's wife admired).[3] Almost overnight with the completion of these two strategic rail lines, Conestoga wagons converged on the new territory. The town's rail depot was the center of attention with trains coming and going all day long. The Harvey House Restaurant in the depot grew in popularity. There were dance-hall girls, hustlers, and gunfighters. And the "Harvey Girls"— the women who worked as waitresses in the Harvey House—who greeted each train that arrived.

There in Hugo with its frontier atmosphere, surrounded by wilderness, Lee spent the next seven years of her life, growing into her adolescence. Coming from the circumscribed, genteel southern Raymond to Hugo's Wild West, she was immersed for the first time in a very different ethos—one in which gentility did not work; only strength and daring would make it. "In that incredibly ugly and incredibly beautiful Indian Territory," she later recalled, "murder and sudden death were of frequent occurrence—seemed in the natural order of things. The streets were unpaved and the mud [. . .] a thing to be dismissed from one's mind as a grotesque exaggeration."[4]

In contrast were the prairie flowers—great billowing masses of color and fragrance—that enchanted her (and later would help give a distinctive character to her poetry: meadowsweet, spiderwort, johnny-jump-up, foxglove, lavender, and columbine). There was the never-ending fascination of her father's drugstore, where long rows of blue glass jars were filled with strange substances—such as "linden leaves in dried bunches with tiny flowers still clinging to the stem"—labeled in abbreviated Latin that suggested to her the world beyond the prairie. And it was there in her father's store that Lee would take fiction from the rack of books and magazines, go curl up inside an empty packing case, and read for hours—"anything," she said, "literally thousands of books": George Eliot, Victor Hugo, Charlotte M. Braeme, G. A. Henty, Sir Arthur Conan Doyle, Alexandre Dumas, and numerous other popular authors.[5]

Lee's childhood was filled not only with literature but with politics as well. Her father, an ardent Democrat who served as a member of the 1907 Oklahoma Constitutional Convention, often held political gatherings in a room above the store. Politics was a much-discussed subject in her family, and what she absorbed also contributed to the development of her intellect, preparing her for her future political life.

Moreover, her experience in Oklahoma no doubt helped take her beyond the bounds of conventional southern femininity and opened her eyes to new possibilities of womanhood. It nurtured her independent spirit, as surely did word of the time's reawakened suffrage movement.

In 1909, at the age of fourteen, Lee returned to Mississippi for a year to attend Blue Mountain College, her mother's alma mater, a small privately owned liberal arts college for women. Already unconventional and indifferent to schoolgirl activities, she spent much of her time with her English teacher, David Guyton, reading Browning and discussing Plato on the porch of her maternal grandfather, known as Dr. Mac Williams (who knew Faulkner's family). Guyton, himself a poet and blind as Homer, encouraged Lee to write, and soon she was bringing him large numbers of poems she had secretly written amid her studies of English literature, Latin, French, physics, chemistry, and botany.

Guyton later recounted that "most of her college-day verses were amateur in type, but there were hints and flashes of genius even in those early attempts at writing."[6] He also noted that "Robert Browning was her breath of life even in her early teens; she read him then with the skill and sympathetic understanding of a master."[7]

Browning, who believed that the incarnation of divine love was necessary to guide human love and that art was rooted in the ethical nature of human beings, gave her a model of religious and artistic convictions. He brought Christian beliefs to the test of experience, discarding orthodox dogma such as original sin, and gave her the idea that men and women cannot be judged merely by their acts but by their quality of character fashioned in the act of living. In stressing the importance of intellect in moral affairs, he defined for her the approach to life that she would follow. Furthermore, his earliest published verse exhibited the poet's most private feelings, as her own lyrics would do as well.

In June 1910, Lee returned to Oklahoma to live at home in Hugo and then help her family move to Oklahoma City, the capital of the new "Sooner" state. Originally settled in a single day in the Great Land Run of 1889, it had become a thriving commercial center with new oil money flowing like adrenalin and stimulating the city's development. It offered her family a relatively richer life compared with their frontier life in Hugo. Just eighteen miles south of the city was the young University of Oklahoma, in Norman, where Lee enrolled in the fall of 1911.

After a full year including summer school there, during which she fell in love for the first time, she returned again to Mississippi and entered the University of Mississippi, from which she graduated with a Bachelor of Science degree in June 1913 at the age of eighteen. Little is recorded about her year at Ole Miss, where she took classes in English literature, Italian, history, mathematics, psychology, and geology. The school's yearbook has only a couple of sentences beneath her name, which identify her as "fraught with learning [. . .] a person with brains. We are glad that she came to us in time for Ole Miss to claim her as one of her daughters."

STARTING OUT AS A POET

After her graduation Lee returned to Oklahoma. Her career ambition at the time was to be a schoolteacher, that traditional job of educated single women. She started her first position in September, teaching third grade (for fifty dollars a month) in the public elementary school of Sulphur, Oklahoma, in the hilly south-central part of the state. For the first time she was living on her own, working with children during the day and with words at night, to express herself in verse. She would soon start submitting her poems to a variety of literary magazines.

During the summer after that school year in Sulphur, Lee returned to the University of Oklahoma to take graduate courses in English literature and education. She had accepted a better teaching position at Mission High School in Mission, Texas—in the southern tip of the state, a region called the Rio Grande Valley. It was a small town originally founded by the Oblate Fathers, who had built a mission there in the early nineteenth century. When Lee was there, it was not much more than a railroad stop, with the recent advent of the Missouri Pacific Railroad. She taught classes in English literature and grammar, composition, and rhetoric, as well as four courses in Latin.

Although she had obtained a Texas teaching license, she moved back to Oklahoma the following year to teach high school in Lawton, in the southwestern corner of the state, by Fort Sill (where Geronimo had been held prisoner just a few years before; his grave lies close to Lawton). The town itself had been founded at the turn of the century when the Kiowa-Comanche reservation was opened for white settlement, and it was growing rapidly with the influx of settlers. Lee's new teaching job not only gave her a better salary (eighty-five dollars a month, compared with seventy-five), it enabled her to be closer to her family in Oklahoma City. At Lawton High School she taught classes in English literature and in composition and rhetoric.

While in Lawton, Lee made her first significant public appearance as a poet in the January 1916 issue of *Poetry: A Magazine of Verse*, with a sequence of nine poems titled "Footnotes." The opening poem, "Magdalen," establishes the tone of the sequence:

> God made my body slim and white
> To be men's torture and men's delight.
>
> God made my heart a wayside inn,
> And there the guests make merry din.
>
> God left my soul a lamp unlit—
> But only God ever thinks of it.

The poems focus on her personal experience with love lost. Composed in the aftermath of her first great love involving a young poet named John ("Jack") McClure, whom she had met at the University of Oklahoma, they express her pain and sorrow, anger and regret.[8] Like most of her poetry, they are short subjective poems in the lyric tradition—poems with a songlike outburst of her innermost thoughts and feelings:

> I shall not sing of love—
>   I weary of the old unrest.
> (But like a hangman, love has burned
>   His crimson emblem on my breast;
>
> But, like a hangman, love has set
>   A crimson scar my heart above.)
> Yea, I am wearied with old pain—
>   I shall not sing again of love.

The poetic sequence of "Footnotes" ends on an ambivalent note of recovery, which shows the conflict of inner forces that persisted in her for years:

> Now have I conquered that which made me sad—
>   The bitterness and anguish and regret.

Yea, I have conquered it. And yet—and yet—
The moaning of the doves will drive me mad.

This initial publication of Lee's in *Poetry* was soon followed by others in this influential magazine from Chicago. During this period she spent a summer there working in its office and strengthening her relationship with the publication (subsequently, the salutation of her correspondence with *Poetry*'s founding editor, Harriet Monroe, was "Dear Aunt Harriet," since Monroe, not a blood relative, had become her patroness and thus "poetry aunt"). The time in which Lee was starting to gain recognition for her verse happened to be a good one. Indeed, the founding of *Poetry* in 1912 had heralded a great revival of interest in poetry throughout America, and poets and poetry abounded everywhere.

Nineteen sixteen was Lee's debut year as a poet, for that year she entered the world of publishing with multiple publications in a variety of literary magazines. Also in January, she published in *Smart Set* the first of several lyrics, most written about her great love of the time, to appear in this self-proclaimed "Magazine for the Civilized Minority." It was one of her so-called love songs, "The Unforgotten":

> I can forget so much at will:
>   That first walk in the snow,
> The violet bed by the April rill,
>   The song we both loved so;
>
> Even the rapture of Love's perfect hour.
> Even the anguish of Love's disdain—
>   But never, but never, the little white flower
> We found one day in the rain.

In the February issue she published another short lyric, "Bereavement," and in the April issue she published "Arcady," which to her joy was featured on that issue's opening page:

> It was such April weather
>   As a lover never forgets,
> When I and my love roamed together
>   Looking for violets.
>
> The breeze laughed straight in our faces,
>   And joy laughed straight from our hearts,
> While grasses lisped in the marshy places
>   Where the johnny-jump-up starts.

> And the violets were joy in plenty,
>> With the dark, cool leaves between,
> To my love, who was not twenty,
>> And me, who was just seventeen.

Alluding to her early days in Oklahoma City, where she had found by the streams and in the hills outside of town a bucolic world suited to her romantic passions, she translated the classical Greek Arcadia into the landscape of the American Southwest. By using images of the nature around her, instead of importing them from abroad, she had found a way to be original with an American voice and thus enhance the appeal of her poetry.

Published in New York, *Smart Set* at this time was featuring the brilliant criticism of H. L. Mencken (who in 1914 had joined George Jean Nathan as the magazine's coeditor); his bold ideas were helping to clear the way for the tremendous flowering of new writing in America, to which Lee would contribute in the decades to come. And the magazine was gathering laurels for its poetry. For the young schoolteacher, the excitement of her initial publications in *Poetry* and *Smart Set,* which both had wide circulations here and abroad, was nothing less than inspirational and helped motivate her to keep writing verse for her new-found audience. Moreover, through her correspondence with Mencken, she found a long-time mentor and stimulating force (Appendix A). His generous praise of what she had already produced—and what she later called his "contagious belief" in her ability to keep producing good work—spurred her continued poetic development.

Later in the spring of 1916, Lee published a sequence of seven short lyrics in the combined May-June issue of *Others: A Magazine of the New Verse* from Grantwood, New Jersey, just outside of New York. This new magazine, launched in 1915, was edited by Alfred Kreymborg (his friend and fellow imagist, William Carlos Williams, would be guest editor of the magazine's next issue). Lee's verses in this publication had no titles and were simply numbered. Again, they focus on her experience with love and its loss, as in number III:

> Do not chafe at your bonds, dear.
> It is only my heart that holds you;
> That is easily broken.

And number VI, which presents an image of her loneliness in the separation she endured:

> In our town
> There are painted wooden houses, one dusty park,
>> and I.
> We grow more faded each year,

More hopeless,

More alike—

The houses, the park, and I.

Others had been created, in Kreymborg's words, "to print the work of men and women who were trying themselves in the new forms."[9] He thus welcomed Lee's experiment with free verse. She later polished four of the seven lyrics and presented them under the title "Imprisoned" in her future book.

In July 1916 she published "A Villanelle of Forgetfulness" in *Contemporary Verse* from Philadelphia, another new poetry magazine, which first appeared in January. With the flourish of her publications that year, which paralleled the flowering of new journals devoted to poetry, Lee was establishing her identity as a poet, while still struggling with the daily realities of her life in the Southwest.

When an even better teaching job was offered her for the next school year— to teach at a young junior college called University Preparatory School (now Northern Oklahoma College) in Tonkawa, Oklahoma, in the north-central part of the state—Lee gathered her books and moved herself once more. Another small town on the plains but not far from the capital city, Tonkawa had sprung up after the historic land run of the late nineteenth century. The school had been created by an act of the legislative assembly of the Oklahoma Territory. Again, Lee taught English literature as well as composition and rhetoric, but the young men and women in her classes were relatively more sophisticated than the children she previously had taught.

In August 1916 in *Smart Set*, Lee published a brief statement in prose titled "Like a Tale of Old Romance," which served as an explanatory note seemingly taken from her correspondence with the editors: "In all things my story has been like a tale of old romance. First love in April weather. Kisses snatched in fear of impending disaster. Midsummer madness and madness of twenty years. Heart-breaking farewells. Gray cities. Wild love-songs from over sea. Tears. Bitter immutability of time. Quarrels. Reconciliations. Dragons, jousts, and gaping wounds. In all things my story has been like a tale of old romance [. . .] except the happy ending."

This statement in itself, along with the series of poems Lee published in *Smart Set* starting in 1916, perfectly reflects the magazine's editorial policy: "Our stories need not strive to point a bourgeois moral [. . . and] there must not necessarily be a happy ending, for the great moving stories of life often end in disaster." Although the story of Lee's first love had ended in disaster for her, the growing success she was enjoying as a poet became a certain salvation. In the fall of 1916, while teaching in Tonkawa, she won *Poetry* magazine's first Lyric Prize. The monetary prize was one hundred dollars and equaled a month's pay at University Prep. But more important to her than that, she was not only a published poet but also a prize-winning one.

The poetry that she was writing in the Southwest shows the influence of the prevailing mode of love lyrics, as well as her relationship with McClure. His manner of heartfire was much inspired by the lyric style of the Elizabethan poet Thomas Campion, whose airs McClure always had in his pocket during the days of their romance. The verses of the two Oklahomans were often part of a dialogue between them. Her poems written then were simple lyrics done mostly in rhymed quatrains, with occasional experiments with free verse, and the point of view was decidedly feminine. Nonetheless, when she departed from the fragile voice and the predictable sentiment—a feminist departure that grew in force in her mature work—her poetry demonstrated the strength and daring that life in the Southwest demanded of her.

In "Compensation," published in *Poetry* in August 1917, Lee again focuses on her heart's misfortune, but with a strong-willed song to her metaphorically "dead" lover, which opens:

> I shall not grieve that you are dead.
>   I sing to you when the stars hang low;
> And though I sang till dawn were red,
>   You still must hear, you could not go.

A few years later she revised this lyric, toughening it with a new opening (and closing) line, "I am so glad that you are dead," which she then used as the poem's new title. She also deleted the original third quatrain:

> Ah, once you wandered far and long.
>   And left me waiting hopeless here.
> Though I sent you my breaking heart in a song,
>   You were too far—you could not hear.

These early lines, subsequently abandoned, reveal the lingering grief that still burdened her in Oklahoma. Life was testing her, toughening her, and compelling her to draw on her inner strength.

Adding to her personal dilemma, Lee's promising teaching career was cut short when the Oklahoma governor temporarily closed down the junior college. Unable to secure another teaching job on short notice, the question of what to do next confronted her like a dust cloud. She fell back on her family, returning to her parents' home, and she started to work in the retail cooperative grocery for farmers—the Southwestern Commercial Company—that her ever-enterprising father had organized and managed; he had been forced to abandon his pharmacy business for lack of the formal education required for a state license. This job gave Muna room and board, but no income. She took charge of the store, acting as cashier, handling correspondence and ordering from wholesalers. After work, exhausted by the day's business, she spent a little precious time with poetry.

The year was 1917. At twenty-two, there she was with her intellectual brilliance and literary aspirations in Oklahoma City, amid the sultry plains, working in a lonely grocery store and living at home with her parents and young siblings. All the while, as always, she was devouring literature, including the work of contemporary poets. It took her to a better place. Reading the monthly issues of *Poetry*, *Smart Set*, and *Others* to which she subscribed, she heard the worldly voices of Modernism calling to her.

Isolated and stifled, Lee needed to change her life. She wanted so much more for herself—for her intellect and her ambitions. When the opportunity to work with her linguistic skills presented itself to her in the spring of 1918, she pursued it with all her vigor. She applied for a federal job as a translator, and she landed a position as "confidential translator" for the U.S. Secret Service, specifically, the Postal Censorship Division. With Germany's aggressive use of espionage during the First World War that was then in its fourth bloody year, the U.S. government felt compelled to impose itself on the free flow of international mail.

Lee's work involved translating and censoring mail written in Spanish, Portuguese, and French. She had qualified for this civil-service job, she said, by teaching herself Spanish in two weeks. Her solid foundation in the Romance languages, together with her burning desire to improve her situation, made this possible.

Lee had originally expected an assignment in border service. To her surprise, though, she was assigned to work in New York City, where a new life awaited her. The prospect of living in New York appealed to her very much. She was drawn from the plains and isolation of Oklahoma to New York's cosmopolitan and intellectual excitement, like a hungry flower to the sun. It was there that she soon found the community she needed to flourish as a writer and woman of ideas.

IN THE WORLD OF NEW YORK

Arriving in Grand Central Station with its bustling multitude of people and its ecstatic high ceilings, Lee was captivated by the energy of New York. She had never seen such a great metropolis. Fifth Avenue seemed like a royal carpet rolled out just for her. She boarded in the home of a woman named Gabriela Delgado, on West 72nd Street, close to Central Park. Working downtown on Washington Street, she felt at home among the bohemian artists and writers of Greenwich Village, whom she was meeting; and, as an extension of her work with Spanish, she was developing a keen interest in the Pan-American movement, of which she was destined to become a distinguished leader.

Initiated by the United States in the late 1880s for largely commercial and political reasons, this movement aimed (in theory) at mutually beneficial cooperation and had stimulated an interest in cultural relations between the Americas. During the First World War, when much of the business of the Pan American Union, established in Washington in 1890, was put on hold, translations of poetry—English renderings of South American voices, and Spanish of North American ones—enjoyed a certain popularity in books and magazines.

Lee had already gained a reputation as a talented new poet. Two dozen of her poems had appeared in *Smart Set* by the time she arrived in New York, and while there she continued to publish her love songs in it; in fact, during this period she was the magazine's second-most-frequent contributor of verse, second only to John McClure. Following the Lyric Prize, her "Songs of Many Moods," a sequence of five poems, had been published in *Poetry* in 1917. In July 1918, the month after she started her government job, two of her poems appeared in the *Pan-American Magazine*, along with Spanish translations of them: a love poem, "When We Shall Be Dust," and a related lyric from her "Footnotes" titled "I Who Had Sought God," which depicts her sense of being abandoned and thrust upon herself to survive, with only "the heart of the yellow flower with the scent / of citrus clinging to its pointed leaf" to turn to for comfort in her grief.

These publications changed her life dramatically, for they brought her work to the attention of Luis Muñoz Marín, a poet and journalist at the time (and future governor of Puerto Rico)—the son of Luis Muñoz Rivera, the most prominent Puerto Rican statesman of his time, a leader of the movement for political autonomy from Spain, a journalist and poet, and founder of the opposition newspaper, *La democracia*. In February of the following year, the dashing young Muñoz (three years her junior) presented himself to Lee, carrying with him a letter of introduction and a sheaf of her poems, which he had translated into Spanish with the hope of publishing them in his new—but short-lived—bilingual magazine "devoted to Pan-American culture" called *Revista de Indias* (Indies Review).

Two exceptionally bright and passionate intellectuals, both restless and ambitious to make their marks, they fell wildly in love with each other, almost at first sight. They took long walks together in Central Park, talking about the rich literature of Latin America. Each step they took led swiftly to the next, and she started writing verses to express her new-found joy, as in "A Song of Dreams Come True":

> My love was born on a tropic coast
>   And I, far from the sea;
> But the ardent eyes of my lover
>   Know the dreams that came to me
> When I longed for wide blue waters
>   And great winds flung out free.

And the magic words of my lover
    Are the songs I tried to sing
When my heart grew sick for green hill-tops
    In the midst of the arid spring
That brought no rain to the wheat-stalks,
    Nor brought me anything [. . .]

After knowing each other for only a few months, Lee and Muñoz were married on July 1, 1919 (six days after her government job ended); her married name was Muna Lee de Muñoz Marín, though she continued to publish her work under Muna Lee. Now, living together in Greenwich Village, they vigorously pursued their individual writing and publishing ventures and soon became a well-known—"most interesting"—couple in the literary world of New York.

A luminary in this world, Sara Teasdale, the celebrated lyric poet and friend of Lee's, had just said to Harriet Monroe in a letter written in May: "I'm awfully glad that Muna Lee has found happiness—at least let's hope it will be happiness. She talked a lot about wanting to find 'a rock' and I told her men are never rocks. [. . .] And if she has a Latin-American, heaven keep her."[10] But at the time, Lee had never been happier.

The newlywed poets went to Washington, D.C., and Philadelphia for a belated honeymoon; Lee's writing commitments had delayed it. Having hardly any money, they hitchhiked (and sometimes walked) from New York. In Philadelphia, when they ran out of funds, Lee called *Poetry* magazine, which had not yet paid her for some of her work. They were stranded. Sitting in a park in the rain, they waited for the telegram with the money to come. It finally arrived after a few wet hours and enabled them to make their way back to New York—back to reality.

Later that year, Lee and Muñoz were forced by their limited finances to move to a less costly house on Staten Island. Big changes were at hand: by the third month of their marriage, Lee was pregnant with the first of their two children. In the spring of 1920, Muñoz was pulled back to Puerto Rico, his true destiny, and took her with him; he wanted to devote himself to bettering the lot of the island's poverty-stricken masses. She knew his socialist attitudes quite well and translated into English some of his political poems, such as his "Pamphlet":

I have broken the rainbow
against my heart
as one breaks a useless sword against a knee.
I have blown the clouds of rose color and blood color
beyond the farthest horizons.
I have drowned my dreams
in order to glut the dreams that sleep for me in the veins

of men who sweated and wept and raged
to season my coffee . . .

. . . .

I am the pamphleteer of God,
God's agitator,
and I go with the mob of stars and hungry men
toward the great dawn . . .

Their daughter, Muna (Munita), was born in Puerto Rico in May. Busy as a house-wife and mother, Lee still pursued her professional interests, and in September she took a job at a high school in San Juan, teaching English. She also continued writing and publishing her poetry.

One poem composed during this year in Puerto Rico, titled "The Flame-Trees," depicts the "sea-change" occurring in her life that moved her beyond the haunting grief of her previous love affair and refocused her passions. A recurring image in her poetry, the Caribbean flame tree—an umbrella-shaped tree—blooms in the summer months and dazzles the landscape with its flaming red blossoms:

For I have reached a fairer place
  Than I had hoped to find,
With all the life that I had known
  A scroll cast-off behind;

And changed into a slighter thing
  The torrent of old grief
Than heavy waves that break in spray,
  White on the outer reef;

And love so sure and joy so strong
  That pain and sorrow are thinned
To a little mist that cannot blur
  The flame-trees in the wind.

Six months after the birth of her daughter, she was pregnant with her second child, Luis (Luisito, who was blond haired). Muñoz moved his small but growing household, which now included his mother, back to the New York area during the summer of 1921 so that he could regroup from his frustrating year of political activity with the Socialist Party. Thanks to the money from a building his mother mortgaged in Puerto Rico, the Muñoz's were able to make a down payment on a house in Teaneck, New Jersey, just outside of New York. This would be Lee's home for the next four years. Muñoz found a job writing book reviews, and Lee likewise earned money by writing.

With the birth of their son in August, Lee's duties as mother and housewife again claimed her time. Describing her work during these years, she recounted: "From May 1921 until January 1927 I was again not employed, since my duties as housewife and mother kept me at home. However, during this period, I did considerable free-lance writing and translating, published my book of poems, edited and translated the Spanish-American anthology number of *Poetry*, and reviewed books for the *New York Herald Tribune*, *New York World*, and *New York Times*."[11]

Lee's experience living in Puerto Rico had opened her further to the vast cultural landscape of Latin America. She started calling Puerto Rico her "rich port" (the literal translation of the island's name), and it eventually became the place she called home. She said she loved its "remoteness and completeness and intensity of life." It was during this period that she developed her passion for, and expertise in, contemporary Latin American poetry.

PUBLISHING HER *SEA-CHANGE*

Having established herself as a gifted writer in New York and having the advantage of access to good publishers there, Lee set out to publish a book of her poetry. One of her motives, as she explained to Mencken in a letter dated January 15, 1922, was related to her new interest in promoting the poets of Latin America: "I have decided to print a book of poems if I find a publisher. My opinion as to the folly of books of poems hasn't changed, but if I'm to carry out my plan of integrating South American poets, a book of my own is advisable as a starting-point, it seems."[12] She gathered her old and new lyrics—a total of eighty-two poems, mostly love songs—into a manuscript she called "Sea-Change." This title unified the different emotional and geographical landscapes depicted in the work written over the past decade of her life. Her efforts to find a receptive publisher were successful, not surprisingly, since her poetry had already gained a wide audience and some critical acclaim, and in April 1923, Macmillan published her *Sea-Change*.

Poetry celebrated the book in a review titled "Words That Fly Singing": "We have been waiting several years for this book. Long ago we read in *Poetry* sensitive, sharp-outlined lyrics signed by Muna Lee, and longed to see them under covers of their own. [. . .] The book is probably the better for its long delay. It opens with some lyrics so good the reader warns himself that it will be hard for the rest of the book to live up to them, then fools the reader by quite consistently maintaining a high quality and thereby winning for its writer a place among our four or five best lyricists."[13]

Among the lyrics in *Sea-Change* is a sequence of twelve sonnets that, among other things, express Lee's poignant realization of the impossibility of denying love. It was a deeply personal vision that took her back in memory to the Southwest, where she had first fallen in love and then endured its loss. But in a short lyric she contented herself with this:

> I remember you because of a grassy hill
> Where the violets grew thicker than the grass,
> And through my memory flames and whistles still
> A flock of red-winged blackbirds we watched pass.
>
> Because of a rain-filled night I remember you,
> And a tree we came on suddenly in the fall,
> And a vague horizon that broke and foamed in blue,
> —But I do not remember any words of yours at all.

The *New York Times*, however, was not as enthusiastic as *Poetry*. It placed her in that school of lyrists led by Teasdale, saying that she "displays finish, a captivating rhyme, and she achieves a certain poignancy. But there is nothing new; there is no unique personality developing itself here."[14]

The criticism in the *Times* suggests that her poems are imitative and that is sometimes true. Unlike the popular *Love Songs* (Macmillan, 1917) by Teasdale, however, Lee's poetry uses imagery of the Pan-American landscape with its unique geological and botanical features, which gives her work a distinctive character. Her verse shows the quality of enlightened regional consciousness that Mencken would soon celebrate as the "Oklahoma manner" of poetry.[15] She expands it. She draws on her knowledge and awareness of natural history to depict the different scenes in her romantic drama and thus locates her lyrics in American nature. Lee also has a habit of seeing the less usual image or seeing it in a slightly different way, which imparts a freshness to her poems. Beyond that, her lyrics have a sophisticated music of their own and, as the *Boston Evening Transcript* noted, "there is always something sharply individual in her vision."[16]

The closing poem of *Sea-Change* reveals her quest for continued development both as a woman and poet. Originally one of the lyrics in her "Footnotes," it is the same poem she had published in the *Pan-American Magazine* under the title "I Who Had Sought God." Its new title, "The Seeker," emphasized a more mature understanding that her salvation was something to be expected not from above but rather to be found through her own experience and free will.

Mencken's encouragement of Lee was essential to her poetic success. Soon after the publication of *Sea-Change*, she sent him one of the first six copies she had received from Macmillan. With her characteristic self-deprecating humor, she signed it: "For H. L. Mencken, to whose persistent encouragement of young writers is due the publication of a great many unnecessary books; this one among them." In her letter to him she elaborated:

A good deal of the responsibility for the book lies at your door undeniably. You are, I think, the only person who has ever considered my verse seriously. Even those whose lives have touched mine most nearly have thought last, if at all, of my poetry. As it happens, I am absurdly responsive to appreciation—hence your responsibility.

I can only add my hope that you will find it worthwhile. For though I do not think it would have changed the aspect of the world for anyone else if I had not written, I know that it would have changed it for me. And I have always felt grateful to you.[17]

With the publication of *Sea-Change* and the subsequent flourish of her poetry appearing in a wide range of magazines—*American Mercury* (Mencken's new monthly), *New Yorker, Current Opinion, Saturday Review of Literature, Literary Digest, New Republic, Commonweal, Poetry*—Lee would establish herself not only as an important poet on the scene of the new American writing, but also as a major voice in Mississippi and Oklahoma verse. Her uncollected poems, which would also appear in various anthologies, show her greater maturity as a writer.

Sea-Change remains the only book of her own poetry that she ever published. She was content with contributing poems to the periodical literature, for it allowed her to reach a wide audience. And since the early 1920s, her poetic endeavors had begun to expand with her new commitment to serving others as a translator of Latin American poets. Nonetheless, some twenty years after the publication of *Sea-Change*, she would lament that the book was out of print "since it is my poetry that means most to me."[18] Indeed, she always thought of poetry "as daily fare [. . .] as being as much the daily bread as the white hyacinths of life."[19]

The publication of her book in the spring of 1923 was a joyous occasion for Lee, but soon after her marriage took a distressing turn when Muñoz left her and their children (as well as his mother) in Teaneck so that he could return to Puerto Rico to compile his father's unpublished works and participate more actively in the island's politics. She chose not to follow him into an unstable life again. Her sense of responsibility as a mother of two young children kept her at home in Teaneck, and close to New York and the publishers there on whom she depended for income. He lived in Puerto Rico without his family for almost two years, before returning to them after his disenchantment with the outcome of the November 1924 general elections there.

In March of that year, while visiting her family in Oklahoma City, Lee gave as a gift to an old friend a copy of her *Sea-Change*, in which she inscribed: "The days that make us happy / make us wise."[20] Her life had certainly changed dramatically— for better or worse—since her Oklahoma days, and she lived in a completely different world, the one she needed in order to thrive as a writer. Now, moreover, she had embraced two causes that would become central to her career, namely, feminism and Pan-Americanism.

For Lee, these two causes were intimately connected. Her marriage brought them together. Her later choice of Puerto Rico as her home would nurture them. Throughout the 1920s, by which time recent U.S. intervention in Latin America and strong nationalist movements there had lessened the attraction of Pan-Americanism, she remained true to the cause. Her Pan-Americanism, at heart, was always romantic and idealistic. Initially, it had much to do with her campaigns for women's rights, as well as her dream of political harmony between the Americas, where Latin American critics had come to view the United States as the imperialist "Colossus of the North."

She would dedicate the rest of her life to creating various forms of inter-American cultural relations, especially literary ones ranging from poems to programs, intended to help build bridges between the different nations for mutual acquaintance, understanding, and respect—what she considered basic ingredients for a better world.

IN THE PAN-AMERICAN LITERARY TRADITION

In 1925, as a translator and advocate of Latin American poetry, Lee made her first major contribution to the Pan-American literary tradition that dated back a century to the pioneering work of William Cullen Bryant, the premier translator of Latin American poetry in his day. Her achievement was an expression of everything she was and had become by 1925, the year that *Poetry* published a special issue in June called its "Spanish-American Number," of which she was guest editor. This landmark publication, the first of its kind in the history of twentieth-century literary magazines, presented poems by thirty-one contemporary authors (all but three living) whose work Lee had selected and translated into English.

Lee's earliest translations from Spanish had appeared in 1920 in Thomas Walsh's *Hispanic Anthology,* a collection of verse translations made by "some of the greatest poets of England and America," in which Bryant's work is amply represented (including his famous rendering of José María Heredia's "Ode to Niagara"). Lee's contribution consisted of three translations, one short lyric by the mid-nineteenth-century Spanish poet Gustavo Adolfo Bécquer and two short lyrics by contemporary Latin American poets, Fabio Fiallo of the Dominican Republic and Rufino Blanco-Fombona of Venezuela. All three poems are natural extensions of the love poetry she herself had been writing, for example, Blanco-Fombona's "At Parting":

My love had known fifteen springs—
    I kissed, and I pressed to me
Her lips like a flower, her chestnut hair,
    Beside a lyric sea.

"Think of me; never forget,
    No matter where I may be!"
—And I saw a shooting star
    Fall suddenly into the sea.

Her other two translations are equally poetic in their attempt to re-create the poetry of the original Spanish.

Four years later, in May 1924, Lee published an essay in the *North American Review* titled "Contemporary Spanish-American Poetry," in which she provides an overview of major trends; it was done while preparing her project for *Poetry*. In attempting to answer two "fascinating" questions she poses—"What of the voices that sound most clearly above the chorus? What is their method, and what its results?"—she states: "A poet may express his environment in either of opposite ways: by an interpretation of it or by a reaction against it. Certainly the best contemporary example of the former method is José Santos Chocano; of the latter, Rubén Darío." She then discusses their work, providing as examples her translations of selected poems. In addition, she addresses those poets who revolted against the "shining and honied things" produced by Darío and the followers of his *Modernismo*.

Lee's feminism led her to consider Latin America's women poets as well: "the mystic who prefers to be known as Gabriela Mistral," who "is more often concerned with the invisible than with the visible world," but in whom is still found "the awakened social consciousness"; "that lovely and dauntless and irresistible seventeenth-century Mexican nun, Sister Juana Inez of the Cross"; Uruguay's "most popular and very talented woman-poet, Juana de Ibarbourou"; and Alfonsina Storni of Argentina.

Comparing the poetry of the last two poets, Lee says, "Alfonsina Storni's work, while sometimes carelessly finished, seems to me of firmer texture and more original quality than Juana de Ibarbourou's." More significant is Lee's comment that "both, however, show a new insight—new, at least, in the literature of their race [ethnicity]—into feminine psychology; the young Argentine speaking characteristically in 'Running Water'":

Yes, I move, I live, I wander astray—
    Water running, intermingling, over the sands.
I know the passionate pleasure of motion;
    I taste the forests; I touch strange lands.

Yes, I move—perhaps I am seeking
    Storms, suns, dawns, a place to hide.
What are you doing here, pale and polished—
    You, the stone in the path of the tide?

This lyric would be the opening poem in the Spanish American anthology she produced for *Poetry.*

In concluding her essay, Lee acknowledges that she had "simply offered a footnote to a richly interesting literature of which we think too seldom." She ends by saying that "this ferment of creation to the south of us, in conjunction with our own quickened interest in poetry, is perhaps helping in the achievement of the Pan-American character." This character, she adds, requires a multicultural fusion—"a vision worth pondering."

Poetry's 1925 publication of its special issue devoted to the work of Latin American poets enabled Lee not only to pursue her new passion for the literary landscape of Latin America, but also to embrace the art of translation and its poetic challenges. In "A Word from the Translator," following the presentation of the poetry, she explains: "In making the English versions of these poems, my intention has been to reproduce, as nearly as possible in our very different vocables, the meaning, sound, and atmosphere of the Spanish. Our scarcity of feminine rhymes, as opposed to the Spanish abundance, has sometimes prevented an exact counterpart in rhythm, but I believe the rhythmic *effect* is always, to a fair degree, the same. [. . .] In every case the original form has been reproduced with its pattern of rhyme, assonance, or unrhymed lines."

Acknowledging the limitations of her anthology, she says that it is "a suggestive collection, a cage in which humming-birds and parroquets, flamingoes and blackbirds are represented, as well as the condor and the tropic nightingale. It does little more than suggest, faithfully and gratefully, something of what readers of the poetry of our sister republics may expect to find." Nonetheless, this modest anthology gave many readers for the first time a strong introduction to the poetic brilliance and innovation of voices little known in North America.

Lee selected work by a wide range of poets, many of whom would later establish themselves as major figures; they represented fourteen Spanish-speaking countries of South America, including the Caribbean. In most cases, she offered one poem by each author. She presented work by most of the poets she had discussed in the *North American Review:* Darío, Chocano, Storni, Mistral, Ibarbourou, Enrique González Martínez, Luis Palés Matos, Leopoldo Lugones, and José Asunción Silva.

Her translation of Silva's "Nocturne" shows how well she herself could work with free verse, re-creating his poem with its expressive cadences and haunting music. At the same time, she understood the impossibilities of translation and elsewhere said that "it is only partially translatable—that is, so much of its beauty depends upon the intricately braided jet and silver of its cadences that a great deal is necessarily lost by translation into a less liquid tongue." But also recognizing the poetic possibilities of translation, she added that "it has strength enough, however, to remain a poem even though some of the music vanishes—a poem which, even in translation, more than any other that I know, really chills the listener, across whose consciousness seems to blow the cold wind of mortality":[21]

> One night,
> One night filled with murmurs and perfumes and the music of wings,
> One night
> When fantastic fireflies blazed in the moist nuptial shadows,
> By my side slowly, clasped to me, paler and silent,
> As if a presentiment of infinite bitterness
> Agitated the most secret depths of your heart,
> Over the blossomy path through the meadow
> You wandered;
> And the full moon
> Scattered white light over bluish skies, boundless and deep.
> And your shadow,
> Frail and languid,
> And my shadow
> By the rays of the moon projected
> Over the gloomy sand,
> Joined together
> And were one,
> And were one,
> And were one,
> And were one long shadow,
> And were one long shadow,
> And were one long shadow. . . .

Concerning Silva's voice, she was quick to perceive the inter-American connection he had with Edgar Allan Poe; her essay, "Brother of Poe," published in the July 1926 issue of *Southwest Review,* is one of the earliest studies on the subject of Poe's influence on Silva.

All told, Lee's brief anthology successfully offered an impressive glimpse of the robust poetic activity in Latin America and showed that, in the words of *Poetry's* editor, Harriet Monroe, "the Spanish-American style in poetry is more expansive than the modern fashion among our own poets has encouraged. One finds little of that stern compression which has been our discipline during most of the present century, and a more eloquent elaboration of motives than is instinctive in the Anglo-Saxon mind or customary in English speech."[22] (The subsequent growth of North American poetry, in the decades immediately following the Second World War, would thrive on lessons learned from the vitality of this "Spanish-American style.")

In the preparation of this issue of *Poetry*, Lee was assisted by several Latin American poets and critics, including of course her husband. Muñoz contributed a commentary titled "A Glance at Spanish-American Poetry," appearing at the end of the issue. A brief account of major contemporary trends, his essay includes a remarkable statement about the significance of poetry written by women: "Perhaps the most interesting departure within the *modernista* movement—itself the most interesting of all departures in Spanish poetry since the century of Góngora and Quevedo—is the recent release of the lyrical tongues of women, which had hitherto spoken either not at all, or else with prim conventionality. Militant femininity—not feminism—has broken down formidable barriers of social prejudice with a sweep of glory."

With his well-known *macho* disposition, Muñoz had surely had his eyes opened to this new phenomenon by his wife who, by 1925, was becoming increasingly involved with American women's struggle for equal rights in society. Lee always challenged his thinking about women and their social roles. Just as her marriage with him was also a marriage with the literature and culture of Latin America (the one that never ended), his was a marriage with the ideas of the bold "new" American woman.

The Spanish American issue of *Poetry* closes with Lee's review of the first book by Mexican poet Jaime Torres Bodet, in which she points out the "graphic quality in his phrases" and provides as an example of it her translation of the following image: "Silence, in some women, / Is a bough heavy with birds." Her selection of this particular image reveals more of her own concerns and temperament than the author's. It is, moreover, the final poetic image encountered in the entire issue which, as noted above, opens with her rendering of Storni's female voice. Like Storni, in whose works at the time the themes of love and feminism predominated, Lee would soon raise her powerful voice to champion women throughout the Americas, not in poetry but in the political arena.

The *Bulletin of the Pan American Union*—"believing that the road to that real understanding between nations which is the very essence of all Pan American ideals will be found in cultural rather than commercial or political contacts"—opened its July 1925 issue with an editorial tribute to *Poetry*'s "Hispanic American edition," followed by a group of Lee's translations taken from it. Lee was described as "the ardent young Hispanist and poet who served as translator," and her achievement hailed as "a distinct contribution to Pan American letters and inter-American friendship."

In August 1925, Lee and Muñoz sold their house in Teaneck and moved back to New York. Together, they established their West Side apartment—on Riverside Drive above 100th Street—as a gathering place for literary figures, such as poets Horace Gregory, Marya Zaturensky, Sara Teasdale, William Rose Benét, and Constance Lindsay Skinner. Indeed, their well-known Sunday night "open house" parties included these writers, among others, as well as teachers, explorers, diplomats, dilettantes, artists, revolutionaries, and mercenaries, even Spain's famous bullfighter, Juan Belmonte. Skinner, a close friend of Lee's, who then was working in New York as a literary critic for the *New York Herald Tribune*, was often cohostess of these lively soirees, which had two firm rules: no invitation required and no recitation of anyone's poetry.

"Why," a poet friend asked Lee at one of them, "do you insist so on wildflowers and rain?" She replied: "Because of a childhood on a prairie without trees, without mountains, far from the sea—but alive and joyous with foxglove and wild rose and verbena and California traveler and a hundred more. A childhood amid dust and glare and heat—and the sudden great floods of rain—even the dullest spirit must be thrilled by rain over parched prairies."[23]

In his autobiographical work, *The House on Jefferson Street*, Horace Gregory recalls the Sunday night parties he attended at the home of Lee and Muñoz:

> Their guests were an extraordinary combination of Arctic explorers, European journalists, young New York writers, Spanish American military men, and soldiers of fortune: talk was of revolution, the wisdom of the Eskimos, reindeer meat, the novels of D. H. Lawrence and James Joyce, the poetry of Robinson Jeffers. Political, military, and literary arguments ran their continuous course throughout the apartment in whispered manifestoes of political discontent; with them flowed the names of Marx and Unamuno, Bertrand Russell and Croce, Freud and Veblen, and over these warring factions weaved the host, handsome, witty, a delightful mimic, and ineffably tactful, a forefinger vertical at his lips, silencing a raised voice by giving its owner a fresh tumbler of bathtub gin.
>
> No less successful at keeping order among their social fauna was his matronly young wife, who wore a Spanish shawl in swirling reds and blacks and orange tossed over her shoulders and a dove-gray evening dress. Her large brown eyes dispelled all rudeness, and the lightest touch of her tapered fingers on the sleeve of a guest's jacket would be sufficient warning to lower voices.
>
> To sustain arguments, slogans would be quoted, phrases and sentences trembling in air: then perhaps, the recital of a few lines of verse.[24]

Gregory adds that on those Sunday nights, he felt part of "a more recent, more 'serious,' somehow more *responsible* generation than that which drifted off to Paris soon after World War I." This seriousness was an everlasting quality of Lee's character.

The daily realities of her present life demanded it, with motherhood and household duties, reading and writing work, not to mention marriage. Furthermore, her politics compelled her to take life seriously and take part in society.

The period of the mid-1920s also saw Lee expand her work as a literary translator to include prose from Latin America—the translation of which was a labor of love she pursued throughout her life. In the spring of 1926, her critically acclaimed rendering of (General) Rafael de Nogales's *Four Years beneath the Crescent* was published by Scribner's. The war memoirs of a Venezuelan soldier of fortune serving with Ottoman forces in Turkey and the Near East during the First World War, the original Spanish had just been published in Spain in 1924. The author's observations of the massacres in the Near East made him distinctly persona non grata in the official quarters from whence issued the laconic order to burn—demolish—kill. Luckily he escaped assassination and, receiving honorable discharge from the army, returned to Venezuela to write these memoirs.

The publication of Lee's translation of his adventure story created a sensation among critics. Highly favorable reviews appeared everywhere. The *New York Times* said that "the book, delightfully and feelingly written, would be worth its weight in thrills, if every page weighed a ton, as a tale of chivalry in the age of iron." The *Review of Reviews* said that "one should not dismiss it as merely a narrative of a soldier of fortune. It is that and much more." The *Boston Evening Transcript* called it an "engrossing volume"—and at 416 pages it was a sizeable volume. Acknowledging the literary feat of Lee's translation, the *New York Herald Tribune* said: "There is present in this military Don Quixote always the Latin love of beauty. [. . .] And the picturesque imagery, the vivid objectivity which his style often achieves is so perfectly rendered by Muna Lee's translation that the reader finds it difficult to realize that he is not reading Nogales in his own Spanish idiom, or that Nogales has not told his tale in English."[25]

Indeed, giving a strong voice to others, whether by means of translation and other forms of writing or by use of the podium, had become the focus of Lee's career.

SPEAKING OUT FOR PAN-AMERICAN WOMEN

In the summer of 1926, Lee moved back to Puerto Rico with Muñoz. He had been offered the directorship of the prominent newspaper his father had founded in San Juan, *La democracia*. He also wanted to "go home" in order to engage more actively in the politics of Puerto Rico, where glaring inequalities in wealth contributed to sharpened social and political tensions. He was bent on helping to bring about the economic reform needed to improve the lives of the island's forgotten working class. Such reform had become a major issue in the new climate of freedom in

Puerto Rico that followed the U.S. Congress's enactment of the 1917 Jones Act, which gave it a measure of political autonomy from the United States.

Signed into law by President Woodrow Wilson, the Jones Act extended U.S. citizenship to Puerto Ricans for the first time. It also established a locally elected Puerto Rican Senate and House of Representatives, modeled after the organization of the Congress in Washington. The local political leadership continued to be obsessed with the status issue. This issue loomed large in Puerto Rico, with arguments about the ideal form of autonomy it should have, while the United States maintained that it could not give Puerto Rico statehood or independence until the island lowered its illiteracy rate. Muñoz believed that independence should always be in the program of a serious political party, and at this time, in the mid-twenties, he was an outspoken supporter of Puerto Rican independence.

Energetic as always, Lee ran their large household. The paper prospered under his directorship, and for the first time the family was financially secure. Nonetheless, in January 1927, in addition to her responsibilities at home and her continued literary activity, Lee started to work for the University of Puerto Rico as director of its bureau of international relations. This position appealed to her interest in Pan-American cultural affairs. It gave her a position of her own in the world as well, outside of the home. She held it for more than a decade, with the exception of a two-year leave of absence in the early 1930s to work for the feminist National Woman's Party (NWP) as director of national activities.

As the university's lead publicist, she prepared daily press releases in both Spanish and English; wrote a daily newspaper column on international, educational, and cultural relations (about which she would lecture widely); and acted as liaison with educational and cultural representatives in the United States, the other American republics, Spain, and England. She also wrote and edited numerous special publications for the university and found time to teach English literature there. In the years to come, she prepared and supervised radio programs as well as inter-American literary conferences. It was a position that challenged her intellectually and creatively. It also kept her close to the literary scenes in both South and North America.

Soon after arriving in Puerto Rico in 1926, Lee became actively involved with the women's suffrage movement there, which had been gathering momentum since the turn of the century. She had long been a supporter of the suffrage movement in the United States and the young NWP founded by Alice Paul, who spearheaded the movement's drive to victory in 1920. When Paul led pickets on the Wilson White House and brought thousands of women from across the country to march for equality, Lee was always cheering for them, for it was her cause too.

Having fully identified herself with the struggle of women for equal rights in a democratic society, Lee naturally embraced the cause of her sisters in Puerto Rico. Throughout the island, she gave speeches and wrote articles defending their right to vote; the island's legislature, in 1929, would finally pass a law granting "literate" women the vote (universal suffrage was not won for all Puerto Rican women until six years later).

During the course of her feminist activism in Puerto Rico, Lee formed close ties with the leadership of the NWP. Since the passage of suffrage, the party's primary goal had been (and still is) to educate the public about the Equal Rights Amendment. Education was the tool the party used to create change—an approach in which Lee had undying faith. Just five years before Lee returned to Puerto Rico, Paul had authored the Equal Rights Amendment to the U.S. Constitution, guaranteeing "equal justice under the law" for all citizens, regardless of their gender. This proposed amendment articulated what Lee had long believed was a social right of not only the women of the United States but also of all women in the Americas and the rest of the world.

Lee's unique position as both an adopted daughter of Puerto Rico—a virtual native in many people's eyes, given her marriage—and a born citizen of the United States, combined with her brilliant political mind and her rhetorical powers, gave her the credentials to speak out on behalf of Pan-American women. She had already established herself as a leading member of the Puerto Rican branch of the NWP.

In January 1928, as the delegate representing the women of Puerto Rico, she went to Havana to join forces with a large group from the NWP led by Doris Stevens, chair of the party's committee on international action. This group, composed of women from the United States as well as other nations of the Americas, had gathered to confront the Sixth Pan-American Conference (of the twenty-one member nations of the Pan American Union), and demand an audience for women's rights. Specifically, Lee and her sister feminists wanted the members of the conference to ratify a treaty giving equal rights to men and women before the law in all twenty-one countries of the Pan American Union; drafted by Paul of the NWP, the proposed treaty was intended to move the consideration of women's rights into political debates throughout the hemisphere.

In her published report of the event, which later appeared in the *Nation* as a letter to the editor titled "Pan-American Women," Lee recounted: "Sandino [whose guerrilla army in Nicaragua was then battling the U.S. Marine Corps sent to maintain imperialist policy] was kept out of the Sixth Pan-American Conference at Havana, but the Woman's Party of the United States got in. The conference had a definite program to work from, and a definite plan for dealing with it. The question of equal rights for women was not in that plan. When the Fifth Pan-American

Conference in Santiago de Chile in 1923 recommended on vote of Maximo Soto Hall, delegate from Guatemala, the inclusion in the agenda for the succeeding conference of a study of methods for obtaining equal rights before the law for the women of the twenty-one American countries, no one—probably not even Sr. Soto Hall himself—expected much."

Despite the expectations raised five years earlier in 1923, not one woman was included in the delegation of any country. Lee noted in her report that the "Sixth Conference [. . .] certainly did not dream of a feminine invasion. Women had never disturbed the Pan-American delegates by so much as a petition." The conference delegates argued that only they were allowed to speak on the floor and that the meeting's agenda had no room for discussion of a treaty on equal rights.

After a month of protests and active campaigning in Havana, the women were finally allowed a voice at the conference. They had successfully petitioned to gain the necessary "invitation" for an open hearing. For the first time women would officially speak at a plenary and public session. Lee and seven others—two women from the United States, four from Cuba, and one from the Dominican Republic— presented their case briefly and urgently. To hear their speeches, women thronged the galleries, staircases, and the conference floor of the University of Havana's great hall. Lee described the scene in her report: "Fifteen hundred women who had crowded into the Aula Magna of the university and had been standing, waiting, an articulate, swaying mass, for more than three hours, burst repeatedly into joyous applause which was echoed here and there from the places where the delegates listened with divided emotions but unified attention. Outside, thousands were crowding up the splendid flight of white stairs, while the radio amplifiers carried the speeches through the bright Cuban air."

Addressing the conference with brilliant poise, Lee spoke elegantly and intelligently; and like the NWP's lead speaker, Doris Stevens, she invoked the ideals of Pan-Americanism:

Many temples have been built to shelter Pan-Americanism. Some of them have been built with marble, some with words. [. . .] But here, today, you have before your eyes a concrete demonstration of that very thing: a Pan-Americanism that includes all, that excludes none, that makes not the slightest difference between one and another. The women of all the Americas have one need. Every enlightened woman of this hemisphere desires for her sister of another country, the same good which she craves for herself. The woman of no country of our Americas believes that equal rights for herself will in any way give her or her country an advantage over her sisters to the north or the south. She does not wish such advantage. She does not ask for one thing and pay with another; she is not carrying on a barter of power, of friendship, of advantage. She asks for herself and for every other woman in all of our countries, one thing, for the good of all—for the good of those countries which we women have helped upbuild and are helping uphold.

Furthering her idea of a "Pan America" where freedom and equality truly reign, for she was also the only person representing Puerto Rico in any way at the conference, she stated: "Our position as women, amongst you free citizens of Pan America, is like the position of my Puerto Rico in the community of American States. We have everything done for us and given us by sovereignty. We are treated with every consideration save the one great consideration of being regarded as responsible beings. We, like Puerto Rico, are dependents. We are anomalies before the law. We, the women of the Americas, ask for a treaty granting us equal rights before the law. We ask this not for one woman, not for one country, not for one race, but for the women of Pan America; for the women who are proving to you here today by their solidarity and mutual trust that Pan-Americanism is a fact."[26]

In an editorial that appeared on the afternoon following the women's speeches, Cuba's leading newspaper said that "we are glad the conference granted the women that hearing, else we should likely have seen something comparable to the storming of the Bastille!"[27]

The Equal Rights Treaty was not ratified. However, Lee and her group of feminists did gain an immediate response from the delegates of the conference, who unanimously voted to have the report on equal rights received and discussed in plenary session rather than in one committee. When that report was made, a resolution was passed declaring that an Inter-American Commission of Women be organized to prepare information to enable the next Pan-American Conference to study constructively the civil and political equality of women. The commission would initially consist of seven women designated by the Pan American Union, and the number would be increased by the commission itself until each of the twenty-one member nations gained representation in it. The first intergovernmental agency in the world created expressly to ensure recognition of the civil and political rights of women, the commission was destined to form an integral part of the Pan American Union and subsequently the Organization of American States.

The creation of the commission, of which Stevens served as first president, reflected the growing cooperation between the women of North and South America, a Pan-American sisterhood in which Lee would play a leading role in the years to come. In the *Nation*, she noted that "the enthusiasm and energy of the Cuban women was [an] unequivocal answer to all who had ever said (and how many they have been!) that the Latin woman does not want her rights; that the Latin woman will not speak in public; that the Latin woman is bound by customs which she cannot break." She concluded her report with a bold statement of her conviction: "The struggle for equal rights has become an inter-American movement. The women of no country will look upon the cause as won until it is won for all. Here at last is a unity of ideal and effort which establishes a real, a spontaneous, a spiritual commonwealth of Pan America."

During the summer of 1928 (as well as 1929), Lee took a leave from the University of Puerto Rico to work as director of public relations for the Inter-American Commission of Women in Washington. After prolonged consultations with jurists and feminists, Stevens had decided that the vexed subject of the nationality of women would be the first subject of research by the commission. Lee conducted juridical research for this project in addition to doing public relations work for the commission and helping run its office.

To help gain support for the commission, she wrote articles and gave lectures about it. In the October 1929 issue of the *Pan-American Magazine*, she published one such article, "The Inter-American Commission of Women: A New International Venture," in which she said: "There can no longer remain in the mind of anyone privileged to witness the swift development of this splendid feminist activity, any lingering doubt as to whether a Pan American movement can flourish in spite of barriers of race and language. The Inter-American Commission of Women is proving every day that such barriers are imaginary; like the wall in the fairy story which is there only so long as one believes it to be there, but which can be walked through and brushed aside by the ardent spirit with an invincible ideal."

In addition to doing articles and lectures in English, she did the same in Spanish, spreading the good news throughout the Americas.

WITH THE WORLD ON HER BACK

Lee's marriage with Muñoz had become increasingly strained ever since their return to Puerto Rico in 1926. Their lives were diverging as they pursued their different passions for public life and politics, as when he had left her for the island in 1923. The family's financial security did not last long. In the summer of 1927, for largely political reasons, he was forced out of his job at *La democracia* and went to live in New York without Lee and their children. He had told a colleague "the flame trees" were giving him "indigestion" and that he needed to spend some time in New York, where "the evening lights of Fifth Avenue, as agreeable as usual, are a marvelous tonic."[28] He stayed at the swanky Vanderbilt Hotel on the corner of Park Avenue and 34th Street. Initially he busied himself as the representative of the Economic Commission of the Legislature of Puerto Rico, with the purpose of persuading American businessmen to invest in the island's economic development.

Two months after Muñoz left he sent Lee a cable from New York. He was flat broke and needed her to send him some money; he had spent almost all of what little he had. At the time, Lee was essentially the main supporter of her household, on her annual salary of eighteen hundred dollars from the University of Puerto Rico. She responded to him with a letter that said:

> Your cable yesterday afternoon inspired me (you will forgive me?) with a wild desire to shriek with laughter. Doubtless you will realize why, reading the letter I had just mailed you before receiving the cable. I am so sorry you are in difficulties but I can do nothing. I can't even send you a cable saying "Impossible." I can appeal to no one. [. . .] You *must* learn to select, to control, to manage, Luis, if you are ever to have any comfort or pleasure in life—or any freedom. I know you have had a very difficult two months. So have I. The *Democracia* has not paid Mamá anything so far this month [. . .]. I not only cannot help you in any financial way, but I shall be utterly lost and undone if you cannot manage to help us *immediately*. Believe me, our need is desperate, or I should not beg for money— and continue to beg. [. . .] It is hard for me to write about anything but money because that is what fills my mind and keeps me awake nights. We cannot help you, Luis. I don't know how you can arrange to help us, but you must.[29]

Despite this tension in the fall of 1927, which eased only sporadically, Lee and Muñoz were soon together in Havana at the Pan-American Conference, where he was relegated to the role of an English-Spanish interpreter. But then she went back to Puerto Rico, and he to New York. For nearly three years he lived there on his own, earning some money from his writing and also enjoying himself, as when he bought a beat-up Ford and traveled across the country.

In January 1930, Lee published her "Rich Port" in Mencken's *American Mercury*. This confessional poem, which later appeared in several anthologies, records her own misery in terms of Puerto Rico's. The poem alludes to the devastating earthquake of 1918; its epicenter was located northwest of Aguadilla in the Mona Canyon (between Puerto Rico and the Dominican Republic). Accompanied by a tidal wave that was twenty feet high, the earthquake had a magnitude of nearly eight on the Richter scale and caused severe damage to numerous houses, factories, public buildings, bridges, and other structures. Here the devastation that Lee's marriage had suffered is likened to this natural disaster with its foreboding of doom:

> This desperately tilted plane of land, our island,
> Toppling from its gaunt sea-rooted pillar,
> Slanted ever more definitely toward the sea-floor,
> Toward that bottomless rift in the floor of Mona Passage,

Slipping,
   sliding,
      creeping,
         ever more surely
This doomed beloved rock edging inch by inch with the earthquakes
Toward implacable disaster,
Some day will lurch, will plunge, the long tension ended,
And the ceibas and the yellow fortress and the lizards and the market-place,
The wild beauty of mountain cliffs hung with blue morning-glories,
Immaculate cane-fields and the cool breath of coffee-groves,
Thatched hovels and trolley cars and Ponce de Leon's palace,
Flame-trees and tree-ferns and frail white orchises,
My love and your pride,
All, all will lie in crushed indeterminate wreckage for a thousand thousand years
In the crevasse beneath the floor of Mona Passage,
With aeons of sea creatures moving lightly through the heavy masses of water
Far above the shattered nameless shards
That in 1930 were you and I
      And flame-trees and Porto Rico.

When Muñoz returned from New York to Puerto Rico in early 1930, Lee was liv-
ing with their children and his mother, and he stayed at the Palace Hotel. They
would later live together in a certain fashion for a few years, however, before sep-
arating for good. It is hard to pinpoint exactly when, but he ultimately left her for
another woman, a political associate of his, named Inés Mendoza, with whom he
started a relationship around 1935. The daughter of an illiterate *jíbaro* (peasant), she
had become a schoolteacher, then joined Muñoz's peaceful revolution to free the
poor *jíbaros* from hunger. She worked closely with him in his grassroots campaign
and traveled with him all over the island (in 1938, he recalls in his memoirs, in the
"human and spiritual sense," his marriage with her began).

DOING FOR OTHERS AND FOR HERSELF

In June 1930, Lee took an extended leave of absence from the University of Puerto
Rico to work for the NWP in Washington. She lived at the NWP headquarters
(Alva Belmont House) with her two children, and she served for two years as
director of national activities, which involved writing publicity, arranging radio
broadcasts as well as national and state conferences, and giving lectures on the sub-
ject of women's rights, in particular their right to work. The Depression was slowly

beginning to affect working women and their jobs. Plants and offices were forced to fire hundreds of women employees, and many factories reinstituted old regulations prohibiting women from working at night.

Facing an economic calamity that could imperil the future progress of women's rights, the NWP launched a major nationwide campaign to protect women's employment. The party primarily campaigned in protest of laws and regulations that enabled bosses to fire women on the basis of marital status or job conditions, such as night jobs.

In accord with the NWP position, Lee argued all over the country against so-called protective legislation for women workers. Speaking about their right to work at night, she said: "The Woman's Party, as we should make clear, does not advocate night work. If night work is bad, it should be discontinued for both men and women. But it holds that night work is preferable to no work at all." She became widely known for her opposition to "any legislation on a sex basis" and her belief that all laws and regulations governing workers "should be based upon the nature of the work and not upon the sex of the worker."[30]

In 1931, in line with these convictions, she battled the action of the Cotton Textile Institute that had discontinued night work for women in cotton textile plants both in the North and the South. Her opposition had no immediate effect, but the policy of nondiscrimination against women workers, for which she argued using both the spoken and written word, later found its way into legislation in various states. (Discrimination against women in employment was not prohibited until the passage of the federal Civil Rights Act of 1964, the year before Lee's death.)

This ardent feminist activism, together with her other efforts on behalf of women's rights, in particular her work with the Inter-American Commission of Women, established her as one of the prominent feminists of her day, advocating for social reform throughout the Americas.

Lee's report titled "Equal Rights Approved by American Institute of International Law," which had originally appeared in November 1931 in the NWP's weekly journal, *Equal Rights,* was published that year as a book by the Inter-American Commission of Women. The news pertained to the party's latest advances in its continued crusade to have its Equal Rights Treaty adopted—now by the upcoming Eighth Pan-American Conference in Buenos Aires.

This publication included the text of the treaty. With her characteristic flair for rhetoric, she opened with these rousing words: "The dignity of woman was most dramatically recognized in action just taken by the American Institute of International Law, and the steady march of women toward equality was greatly accelerated by this distinguished body of men. In their unanimous recommendation of Doris Stevens for membership in the American Institute of International Law, jurists of this hemisphere bestowed upon this gallant and beloved Feminist the highest honor within their gift. [. . .] Miss Stevens is the first woman to be a member of this distinguished juridical body, membership in which is limited to five international publicists for each of the twenty-one American republics."

Stevens had also been selected to serve on the institute's special committee that was delegated to travel to Buenos Aires. This committee would render its services to the Pan-American Conference in the discussions about the proposed treaty, which the institute had just endorsed. Lee celebrated that "for the first time, a body of men has taken the wholly just and enlightened step of appointing a woman rapporteur of a committee on the rights of women." And about their endorsement of the treaty itself, she rejoiced in the fact that "never has Equal Rights been so quickened in the American hemisphere."

While in Washington Lee still found time to spend a term as associate editor of the *Carillon*, a quarterly magazine of poetry published there, and to contribute poems to *Poetry, American Mercury, Commonweal,* and *New Republic,* among other magazines.

The occasion of the first Pan American Day on April 14, 1931, inspired Lee to write "Pan American Day in the Park," an apparently unpublished work. It is a poem of protest as much as it is a poem calling for Pan-Americanism. The new holiday called Pan American Day was (and still is) observed throughout the Americas; the date was chosen to commemorate April 14, 1890, when the Pan American Union was established. It became an annual event celebrating the diverse cultures of the Americas and stressing inter-American goodwill. But in 1931, the first year of the holiday, U.S. intervention had been taking place in Nicaragua for four years, and a pure celebration of Pan-Americanism was at odds with the political reality. In a departure from her confessional love poetry, Lee's narrative verse protests the abandonment of the American ideal of liberty:

> Washington on a bronze horse called across the park,
> "Ho, Bolívar, are you listening?" and the Liberator heard,
> Lifted up a brazen sword and answered through the dark,
> "Listening, my comrade! What will be your word?"
>
> Lincoln in a marble chair propped his elbow on his knees,
> San Martín in a marble cloak attentively gave ear,
> Washington spoke boldly so that all of them might hear,
> And his speech flamed like a comet through the April trees:
>
> "Yorktown and Ayacucho were one victory," he said;
> "At Aconcagua and at Valley Forge we prayed one prayer;
> The eagle and the condor the same symbol overhead,
> Our conquering banners made a single rainbow in the air!

"Yet the twenty-one republics for whose liberty we died
I fear become forgetful of the oneness of their goal—
Each is proud and rich and mighty; but the greatness of the whole
Will come only when they dwell as sisters side by side."

"You may be right," Bolívar said, and the sternness of his thought
Made the sternness of the bronze a deeper shadow on his brow:
"I fear they grow apart," said Lincoln, "they seem sometimes strangers now."
Then a wailing cry of anguish to their startled ears was brought.

"It is Nicaragua weeping!" San Martín said, "In that cry
The stricken land, the valiant land, is keening for her dead!"
"Listen!" said Bolívar. Lincoln lifted up his head.
"Help comes! Hope comes!" said Washington. "See them hurry by!"

This poem expresses Lee's commitment to social justice that was at the heart of her work for the NWP—namely, equal rights. It defines the Pan-American ideal of freedom for all. Interestingly, the final line of the fourth stanza had originally depicted the nations of the Americas living "close in friendship side by side." Reflecting her feminist consciousness, her revision portrays them as sisters and thus creates the image of the American nations as family.

Returning to Puerto Rico late in the summer of 1932, she resumed her work for the university and resumed living with Muñoz as well. She continued to produce poems and essays in both English and Spanish and also translations of work by Latin American writers. Her "Ballad," which appeared in *Poetry* in the fall of that year, is reminiscent of her early love lyrics. It closes a sequence of five poems under the title "Carib Summer." This particular lyric reveals her return to a painful struggle with love and the madness of it:

She wandered singing down the street
    Nor looked at us at all;
"Love," she sang, "is warm as frost
    Kindling the hill in fall!"

"And love," she sang, "oh, love" she sang,
    "Is kind as nettles be;
Smooth thistles make its bed, its roof
    The shady cactus tree."

She sang the silliest mad song
    Of any woman born:

"Oh, love is sweet as juniper,
And gentle as a thorn!"

Only poetry offered her the language of indirection that she needed to validate her personal reality and to speak openly of the disaster her marriage had become, like her former "tale of old romance." The month after the October publication of her "Carib Summer," Muñoz was elected to Puerto Rico's Senate. The wife of a prominent public figure, Lee was known throughout the Americas by her married name, Señora Muna Lee de Muñoz Marín, and also as Mrs. Luis Muñoz Marín. But she always signed her own name to her poetry publications and in this way further affirmed her own identity.

Her "Deliverance," published in the *American Mercury* in the spring of the following year, articulates an acceptance of her being on her own again and an affirmation of the silver in the dark cloud of her life, namely, independence. The poem's very style expresses her independence as much as it shows the influence of contemporary trends:

I am my own now, never need there be telling
Of the thought that lures and lingers and brightens the mind's dark crevice;
Nevermore the difficult choosing of words to make words plainer;
I am my own now, my silence a proud possession;
From the crags and crannies of silence never need there be dispossession.
If the awful apocalyptic vision flare and thunder about me,
Only within myself need I seek for a clue and a meaning;
I may pick windflowers in the fields, showing none how earth has stained purple
The underleaf close to the ground; I may walk in the rain and the dark.
I am my own, and no other can stand between me and the mountains:
Beauty savored slowly in quiet replaces the haste and the voices.

Romantic love—"the thought that lures and lingers and brightens the mind's dark crevice"—would no longer shape her life. She had become more self-reliant since writing her early lyric, "I Who Had Sought God" (later retitled "The Seeker"). Then she was turning "blindly" to God with "a weary throng of [existential] questions" in her soul, "listening for heaven to thunder forth" her name. Now, as she says in "Deliverance": "If the awful apocalyptic vision flare and thunder about me, / Only within myself need I seek for a clue and a meaning."

Still, she struggled with the loneliness that her failed marriage had imposed upon her. Her "Alcatraz," published in *Poetry* in 1934, echoes the sentiment of the group of lyrics in *Sea-Change* called "Imprisoned," and depicts this imposed solitude and her implicit struggle to endure her husband's abandonment of her, like the abandonment of her youth in the Southwest, which had left her feeling cut off from life:

> Noon after noon the seabird seeks this rock,
> He who has freedom of all sky, all shore,
> Noon after noon he comes from far clouds flying
> To perch hereon, as all the noons before.
> This crusted boulder, this casual piece of granite,
> Is the seabird's star in a universe of cloud,
> His plot of earth, his verity, his comfort,
> The one fixed point in fluctuant tides allowed.
> Not in wide space his joy nor far horizons,
> This wildest, freest thing who in unknown
> Unbounded oceans of air, oceans of water,
> Has found but this harsh certainty of stone.
> Launched at the ether from daybreak unto daybreak,
> Midway of dawn and dusk his wings decline
> For renewal of endurance, renewal of rapture,
> To this rock which is his certainty, and mine.

The actual "Alcatraz" in San Francisco Bay had just that year been converted from a military prison into a federal prison, which was touted as virtually escape proof. Lee's lonely private life with its "harsh certainty of stone" marital reality felt that way to her. Like any prisoner, she envied the freedom of birds. But by taking flight with words in the composition of poetry, she found for herself "renewal of endurance" and "rapture" to help sustain her spirit.

At the same time, while forced to be so self-reliant, Lee had found a good measure of love in her relationship with her children, as shown in the opening poem of her "Carib Summer." Titled "Garden Episode," this poem celebrates her paternal grandmother and her daughter, Munita, then twelve years old:

> My grandmother would never have recognized her great-grandchild,
> Not the dark hair nor the shining dark eyes, nor the dark-bright flowing of her alien
>   speech.

The poem elaborates the differences and similarities that Lee could see in the line of women in her family, culminating with her Latin daughter, in whom she recognized her Anglo-Saxon grandmother:

> Seeing bronzed legs and tossed dark hair stop short before a bough of pink laurel.
>   Dawn-flushed, lighter than spray,

Seeing dark eyes gaze on the blossom one long wordless moment
And slim hand lifted in a gesture reticent and swift
To pluck a single narrow gray-green leaf,
    Seeing my child leaving the tossing foam of petal on its airy twig,
    Leaving it, loving it with a backward glance, but leaving it [. . .]

It was Lee's grandmother who had instilled in her as a child an abiding love of flowers, which later would not merely decorate her poetry but also form an important element of its character. In celebrating her daughter of color with "the sudden flaming in her cheek and brow" and seeing in her a distinctive trait of this grandmother, Lee also celebrates the ethnic diversity and fusion of Latin- and Anglo-American cultures that she believed was the hope for the future of the Americas.

By 1935, as seen in her "Lyric to the Sun," which appeared in *Commonweal*, Lee could write more openly about her estrangement from Muñoz. She could say it in public. But more than that, she had moved beyond her resentment of his abandonment of her and could celebrate life:

Nightlong I dreamed of one estranged,
And in my dream was nothing changed;
And then dawn came and I awoke
And into fragments the frail dream broke.

Thinking of him, like a bell is tolled
Something within me hard and cold;
Something within me stony and tall
Rises against him like a wall.
From a burled rancor deep in my heart
An hundred roots and branches start;
Resentment like a flag unfurled
Will quit me never in the waking world.
Far back, far back, in a dream we ranged,
But I wake to exult that the world is changed,
Is vivid and salt because we are estranged.

Not only did Lee write serious poetry during these years, she also composed light-hearted verse that she published in newspapers and popular magazines. On December 31, 1935, in the famous "The Conning Tower" column in the *New York Herald Tribune*, columnist Franklin P. Adams wrote whimsically: "We shall never be satisfied until we see a poem about Mauna Loa by Muna Lee." (Located in Hawaii, Mauna Loa, the Earth's largest volcano, had just erupted again for the ninth time since 1900.) Two months later, Lee responded with these lines, which appeared in "The Conning Tower" under the title "On Not Writing about Mauna Loa":

> Shall Muna Lee set on Mauna Loa
> Foot shod or metric? She answers *Noa!*
> (All her life, those who would tisa
> Have called her "Mauna Loa" or "Mona Lisa.")
> If thoughts of Hawaii drive you haggard,
> The poet for you is Genevieve Taggard.
> But Muna Lee, tell them as sico,
> Hymns *not* Hawaii, but Puerto Rico![31]

Among her diverse activities as a writer during the 1930s, Lee also branched out into murder mysteries—for fun and profit. Between 1934 and 1938, under the pen name of Newton Gayle (her maternal grandmother's maiden name), she coauthored five mystery novels with Maurice Guinness, an Englishman and Shell Oil executive stationed in the Caribbean, who lived in San Juan: *Death Follows a Formula* (1935), *The Sentry Box Murder* (1935), *Death in the Glass* (1937), *Murder at 28:10* (1936), and *Sinister Crag* (1938). A friend of Lee's, Guinness was married to the daughter of Dr. Bailey K. Ashford, whom Lee had celebrated in her 1928 essay, "Conquistador for Science," published in the *North American Review*.[32]

Their novels feature a wry British sleuth who solves crimes in Britain, the United States, and Puerto Rico, while occasionally referencing broader political themes. No less a publisher than Scribner's issued them; they received decent reviews and were translated into Spanish and Italian. Although they lack the psychological torture required to satisfy more recent taste, they are still good reading—especially *Murder at 28:10* for its ravaging hurricane in San Juan. About this book, which involves the murder of a Roosevelt New Dealer bent on Puerto Rican reform, the *New Statesman and Nation* said: "Mr. Newton Gayle has not only hit on a perfect novelty in the way of a setting for a detective story, but he has risen to the occasion and writes better than he ever wrote before; he even documents his hurricane throughout with authentic weather charts supplied by the U.S. Weather Bureau so that the reader can see from hour to hour what is coming his way."[33]

Of interest is the occasional use of bilingual dialogue, which confronts readers with Spanish not only for the sake of literary verisimilitude but also for the Pan-American challenge of it. Beyond that, Lee's contribution of vivid descriptions to the narrative is readily apparent, as seen in this passage about the impending hurricane:

> The waves were breaking now in turbulent mountains that rained occasional
> sleety spray all about us. Streaks of dull sulphurous flame stained the horizon's

gray bank. The sultry air was charged with tension more psychological than electrical. One felt a dull unbelieving wonder at the realization that beyond the sullen horizon the wild whirling dervish of storm was headed toward us. Our palmy green island, prone in its path, had no escape and no stay.

Between the brief squalls the air was heavy, inert. Velvety large-petalled mauve flowers on an exuberant trellised vine barely stirred in the uncertain whiffs of breeze that came shoreward. A starry white cloud of jessamine beside the door and delicate rosy-lilac clusters twining with it, crisp and dainty, made incongruous patterns of April against the menacing August sky.

"Dick!" breathed Cay, "take a good look at the garden before we go in. We may never see it so beautiful again!"

Then unexpectedly, with a little crooning sound, she snatched up a pair of shears from the garden-bench and sprang toward her cherished vines. Ruthlessly, even as Patria and I exclaimed together in protest, she slashed through the thick twining stems and tore down springing masses of fragile flowering branches. Not one did she leave. And that act of vandalism accomplished, she turned toward us and said,

"Help me take in my flowers. At least, the wind shan't twist them up by their roots!"[34]

The distinctive cadences of Lee's prose, together with her characteristic use of flower images to signify the goodness of nature, reveal her poetic voice. Guinness had nothing like it. Earlier in her career as a writer, during the mid-1920s, she had attempted to write an autobiographical novel; it was to be called *Frontier*—"the frontier of life, of course," she said, "as well as the other thing," namely, her life in Oklahoma—but it never came to fruition.[35] She was essentially a poet, not a novelist.

During the 1930s Lee's professional activities were, as always, wide-ranging. In 1930 she started serving as a permanent member of the Council of the Poetry Society of America. From 1933 to 1939 she was literary and foreign news editor of *La democracia*. From 1932 she was a contributing editor to *Books Abroad*, the worldly journal from Norman, Oklahoma, as well as contributing editor to *Equal Rights*, the weekly (until 1934), then semimonthly, magazine published by the NWP. In 1937 she edited *Art in Review*, a special retrospective issue of the *University of Puerto Rico Bulletin* published in December of that year that celebrated a decade of artistic development in Puerto Rico.

In August 1939, on the campus of the University of Puerto Rico, Lee addressed the biennial Congress of the World Federation of Education Associations at the unveiling of the bronze plaque commemorating the centenary of Eugenio María de Hostos, the Puerto Rican writer, patriot, and educational reformer (founder of the modern educational systems in Chile, the Dominican Republic, and Venezuela). The plaque for Hostos's statue on the campus had been authorized by the Eighth Pan-American Conference. At the ceremony by the statue where the Congress delegates were gathered, Lee delivered an address that focused on the international significance of Hostos as an educator. It was an elegant and erudite speech that she began with charm and humor in a retrospective look at the world in 1839, the year of Hostos's birth: "In 1839 in the United States, Van Buren was in the last year of his unpopular presidency and the turbulent political campaign of 1840 was brewing; so that it is highly improbable that it occurred to anyone that the really significant event of that year in the States was the first application of the screw propeller to an ocean steamer."

After reviewing Hostos's achievements and legacy, she ended on a stirring note showing her capacity for rhetorical brilliance: "In view of this tremendously productive and inspiring life, it is not too much to say of Eugenio María de Hostos, as he himself said of Hamlet, in his famous essay, that he was 'a moment of the human spirit'; not a moment of gloom and vacillation, but a moment of resolution and courage not to be extinguished even by the hazard of birth in an impoverished sea-girt Caribbean colony, in that harassed and threatening year 1839."[36]

Lee's ability to shine at such public appearances and performances had grown over the years through her experience in a range of different contexts.

The 1930s saw her rise to prominence throughout the Americas for her diverse literary and political work. She had appeared in every edition of *Who's Who in America* since 1928. She appeared in the first (1933–34) and second (1936–37) editions of *Quien es quien en Puerto Rico* (Who's Who in Puerto Rico). The 1939–40 edition of the biographical dictionary *American Women* (the official who's who of the women of the nation) included the basic information about her, along with a subtle revelation of her personality seen in the "hobby" category, where she entered just one thing: "islands." It is, moreover, noteworthy that the 1940 Federal Writers' Project publication, *Puerto Rico: A Guide to the Island of Boriquén*, listed her among the important "contemporary Puerto Rican writers" in its chapter on the island's cultural life, describing her as "a continental American living in Puerto Rico" who had "gained her high reputation as a poet on the mainland."

In April 1940 *Holland's, the Magazine of the South* published a glowing feature about her titled "Muna Lee: Poet and Feminist," written by Mary Reid. Lee was at the time an active member of the Ibero-American Institute of the University of Puerto Rico and of the governing council of the World Woman's Party founded by Alice Paul. This newly organized international feminist venture was made urgent by the precarious position of women around the world; the party was dedicated to preserving and extending equality for women and combating attempts in international treaties to take away their rights to employment, among other injustices.

In *Holland's*, in response to the question about how she started writing poetry, Lee said: "My real incentive to write poetry was inherited from my mother, who published verse occasionally in her girlhood and who had and has a poised and sensitive appreciation of beauty in all its manifestations; from my father, who was and is gifted with sympathy and discernment; from my grandmother, who loved flowers and to whom flowers responded as to no one else I've ever known. But whatever poetic gift I have has also been fostered by every favoring environment: the beautiful simplicity, dignity, and pride of Mississippi; the thrilling sweep and color of the Indian Territory prairie; the heartening friendliness of great cities, New York, Washington, Paris, Madrid; the remoteness and completeness and intensity on this tropic island [Puerto Rico] that has been a rich port to me."

Not mentioned was her lifelong and fierce inner need to gain, through the act of creation, a sense of order in her life of emotional extremes and also to speak in public what only poetry allows, the truth and beauty of things that she forever sought and needed to articulate for her personal well-being.

WORKING FOR PAN-AMERICAN UNION

In the fall of 1941 Lee began a new phase in her career that would span the rest of her life. When she was offered a position as a cultural affairs specialist in the State Department, she moved to Washington, D.C., with her two children and her seventy-one-year-old mother who had joined her household (she and Muñoz would later be "formally" divorced). Her job was to confer daily with ambassadors and ministers of Latin American countries, arranging for exchange of literature, art, and films, and she was instrumental in persuading artists and writers (Faulkner among them) to go abroad as goodwill ambassadors for the United States. Indeed, she would become a valued counselor at all official levels in the State Department on matters related to Latin America.

In a news article about Lee headlined "Pan-American Literary Ties Urged on U.S.," which appeared in the *New York Herald Tribune* on November 30, 1941, she stressed the goodwill value of translation, saying that there was "no better way to develop friendship between the United States and Latin America than to translate and publish the literature of each region for the other." She briefly discussed her current work as a poetry translator and added, "To the best of my belief, Latin-American poets are equal to any in the world." The article went on to describe her recent arrival in Washington and her position in the State Department, ostensibly just for a year's sabbatical leave.

Lee's government work was initially part of the broadening of Roosevelt's Good Neighbor Policy during the late 1930s in response to the gathering of war clouds in Europe and the Far East. Washington then stepped up its program of cultural exchange to help ensure the hemispheric solidarity of the Americas.

In addition to her new duties and responsibilities at the State Department, Lee was very much involved with New Directions's forthcoming publication of the bilingual *Anthology of Contemporary Latin-American Poetry.* The book's editor, Dudley Fitts, had invited her to contribute translations just before she left San Juan for Washington. The 667-page anthology was a landmark publication. Nothing as comprehensive had appeared in the so-called modern era, and regrettably, nothing like it would appear again for nearly three decades—nothing that could give the English-language audience a decent view of the vast range of poetic genius in South America.

The invitation to contribute to this anthology appealed to Lee not only because it would help further the Pan-American cultural relations to which she was dedicated but also because she could engage herself with poetry and pursue that passionate need of hers. The group of sixteen translators assembled for the book included John Peale Bishop, Angel Flores, Langston Hughes, H. R. Hays, Robert Fitzgerald, Rolfe Humphries, Lloyd Mallan, and Fitts himself.

In September 1941 Fitts had asked Lee for help in a letter that became part of a lively yearlong correspondence between the two about this book project.[37] He was "hard pressed for translators," to which she replied: "Why should you be? I'm here, and translating Spanish for my own pleasure has been my avocation for a long time." This was happy music to his ears. He valued her translations more than those produced by most of the other translators working for him; he "had to rewrite at least two thirds of all the material" they sent him.

Fitts wanted translations that had a "maximum of literal fidelity"—the translations could also be poems in their own right, but that was of secondary importance to him. In Lee he found a model translator whose renderings were both literal and poetic. "I can't tell you," he wrote to her in early October, "how strange and how refreshing it was to read your pieces and find that only by hairsplitting could I make any objections at all. And for that reason I want very much to send you some more things." She responded: "By all means send me more things—send me whatever you like. *I* like translating."

Lee worked on making translations for him whenever she could find the time. By the end of October, she sent him a group of poems that, he said, "couldn't have been better planned for this anthology!" These poems included specific translations he requested as well as other translations she offered on her own (for example, César Vallejo's "Dregs"). He told her: "Every one is right bang in the period. You should be getting out this book, not I—and yet I could hardly wish that you were, for it is mostly an uninterrupted and highly ungrateful headache."

In mid-November, just as Lee was settling into her new life in Washington, she wrote to Fitts: "Naturally, work at the State Department will not interfere with my translating. The thing is—it just occurs to me—that someday this anthology of yours will be finished. And then what shall I do with the spare time that I never knew I had until it irrupted on my horizon?" She also contributed to the writing of the biographical notes about the poets represented in the anthology. The book was finally done by the summer of 1942 and was published in the fall of that year.

Lee contributed some thirty-seven different translations representing twenty-two poets from all over Latin America. Some of her work had been done previously, but she made many of her translations especially for this book project. Among the poets to whom she gave an English-speaking voice were Chile's Gabriela Mistral, Peru's César Vallejo, Argentina's Rafael Alberto Arrieta, Cuba's Eugenio Florit, Uruguay's Ildefonso Pereda Valdés, Mexico's Jaime Torres Bodet, Venezuela's Antonio Spinetti Dini, Guatemala's Rafael Arévalo Martínez, Honduras's Constantino Suasnavar, Costa Rica's Asdrúbal Villalobos, Ecuador's Jorge Carrera Andrade, and Puerto Rico's Luis Muñoz Marín.

Lee's translation of Muñoz's "Pamphlet" and "Proletarians," written in his youth, offered readers the poetic background of his current political work. In her translation of Vallejo's "Dregs," she re-created his complex images that sometimes work on two or even three levels, and she showed the poetic power of the Peruvian, whose profoundly humanitarian voice was little known at the time to English-language readers:

> This afternoon it is raining as never before, and I,
> my heart, have no desire to live.
>
> This afternoon is sweet. Why shouldn't it be?
> It is dressed in grace and sorrow; dressed like a woman.
>
> It is raining this afternoon in Lima. And I remember
> the cruel caverns of my ingratitude;
> my block of ice crushing her poppy,
> stronger than her "Don't be like this!"
>
> My violent black flowers; and the barbarous
> and enormous stoning; and the glacial interval.
> And the silence of her dignity will mark
> in burning oils the final period.
>
> And so this afternoon, as never before, I go
> with this owl, with this heart [. . .]

Her rendering of Mistral's "The Little Girl That Lost a Finger" offered the very different voice of the woman who in 1945 would become Latin America's first Nobel Laureate in Literature "for her lyric poetry which, inspired by powerful emotions, has made her name a symbol of the idealistic aspirations of the entire Latin American world":

> And a clam caught my little finger,
> and the clam fell into the sand,
> and the sand was swallowed by the sea,
> and the whaler caught it in the sea,
> and the whaler arrived at Gibraltar,
> and in Gibraltar the fishermen sing:
> "News of the earth we drag up from the sea,
> news of a little girl's finger:
> let her who lost it come get it!"
>
> Give me a boat to go fetch it,
> and for the boat give me a captain,
> for the captain give me wages,
> and for his wages let him ask for the city:
> Marseilles with towers and squares and boats,
> in all the wide world the finest city,
> which won't be lovely with a little girl
> that the sea robbed of her finger,
> and that the whalers chant for like town criers,
> and that they're waiting for on Gibraltar . . .

Most impressive were Lee's nine translations of poems by Carrera Andrade, who was (and still is) considered not only the premier poet of Ecuador, but one of the foremost Spanish-language poets of the century. Her renderings of his work formed the body of the anthology's opening section and included his "Sierra":

> Corn hangs from the rafters
> by its canary wings.
>
> Little guinea-pigs
> bewilder the illiterate silence
> with sparrow twitter and dove coo.
>
> There is a mute race through the hut
> when the wind pushes against the door.

The angry mountain
raises its dark umbrella of cloud
lightning-ribbed.

Francisco, Martín, Juan
working in the farm on the hill
must have been caught by the storm.

A downpour of birds
falls chirping on the sown fields.

The poetic success of her many different translations stems from the rare combination of her near-native fluency in Spanish, her intimacy with Latin America and its literature, her critical astuteness, her knowledge of contemporary North American poetry, and her creative skills as a poet in English.

Among the grateful readers of her Carrera Andrade in particular was William Carlos Williams. She had sent him a group of her translations in July 1942, before the anthology's publication, and he responded enthusiastically with the following note: "Let me tell you how much pleasure you gave me by your translations of the work of our Ecuadorean poet [. . .]. I don't know when I have had so clear a pleasure, so unaffected by the torments of mind which are today our daily bread. The images are as you say so extraordinarily clear, so related to the primitive that I think I am seeing as an aborigine saw and sharing that lost view of the world. It's a sad pleasure but a great one." Williams concluded with these words of respect for Lee's work: "Thank you for introducing me to Andrade. We all need to know each other better, we need it badly. We need it more than anything else in the world."[38]

The subsequent edition of the anthology, published in 1947, would include the addition of a single poem—"Song to the Glory of the Sky of America" (1942)—by Uruguayan poet-physician Emilio Oribe, translated by Lee with lyric brilliance, that became the book's final word and called for Pan-American harmony: "A poem from grey barrens tearing free / Where the North Pole hypnotizes the Pole Star, / Rainbow-like above the crystal of twenty countries arches far, / Then again plunges strong / Amid icebergs of the South into the sea."

TRANSLATING ECUADOR'S PREMIER POET

The translations of Carrera Andrade that Lee contributed to the New Directions anthology were part of another book project on which she was working at the time. She was translating his *País secreto* (Secret Country), a book of poems originally published in 1940. A diplomat as well as a writer, he had started serving as the Consul General of Ecuador that year in San Francisco, and Stanford University Press had expressed an interest in publishing her translation of this book. The Office of Pan-American Relations of Stanford's Hoover Library on War, Revolution and Peace (now Hoover Institution) supported this publication initiative.

Lee and Carrera Andrade started corresponding soon after his arrival in San Francisco, while she was still living in Puerto Rico. It was an exchange of letters filled with mutual admiration and respect. He thought her translations of his poetry "unsurpassable" (*insuperables*) and encouraged her to translate his work. They often discussed the ideas behind his images, in order to clarify them for her translations. Concerning any confusion caused by what he called his "poor images" (*pobres imágenes*), he told her that he trusted in "the brilliant insight of Muna Lee to make them beautiful" (*la penetración luminosa de Muna Lee para su embellecimiento*) in English.[39]

In the November 1942 issue of *Poetry*, Lee published a review, "An Ecuadoran Observes His World," of his *Registro del mundo* (Record of the World), a new anthology of his poetry written between 1922 and 1939. Despite his great literary stature, no collection of his poems was yet available in English translation; all that had appeared in book form so far was a slim volume presenting a single long poem, "Canto al puente de Oakland," which Stanford's Hoover Library published in 1941 in a bilingual edition titled *To the Bay Bridge*, translated by Eleanor Turnbull.

For Carrera Andrade, poetry was the exaltation of human hope. By experimenting with poetic form, he sought the most effective means of conveying the stormy experience of poetic inspiration. His work is characterized by objective yet emotional descriptions of physical objects, simple vocabulary, and brilliant metaphorical images; and he often treats social themes. In her review, Lee says: "All his poetry has its own accent, its own freshness; and most of its images—it blooms profusely with images—are set down with the shrewdness and the sagacity of a peasant or a child."

Elaborating on his individual style, she adds: "For the past ten years [. . . he] has been what Latin American critics love to denote a *poeta de vanguardia* [vanguard poet], though in him successful experimentation with new rhythms has never meant a break with the traditional rhyme and assonance which he handles so deftly and to which he returns so often. Sometimes intricately patterned, sometimes simple as folksong, his poems are usually brief, terse, imagistic—always with a lovely play of echoes for the eye as well as for the ear—and they frequently show a most un-Latin delight in scents and sounds and textures of the countryside. Essentially vigorous, vivacious, and authentic, they not only reveal but impart a freshened vision of the world."

Lee offers as examples of his work her translations of two poems that would be included in *Secret Country*, "Nameless District" and "Biography for Use of the Birds," which appear in the anthology (they were not included in *País secreto* but were added to the book in English as a consequence of her telling him: "I love these poems so much that it is hard to bear their omission!"). About "Nameless District," she says that it shows Carrera Andrade at his best as a "single-hearted regional poet":

> In my district there are groups of houses and cattle,
> sacks of cloud that pour forth silver kernels of sleet,
> a sky that suddenly opens and closes its showcases,
> pumpkins heavy with dream that drowse by the roadside,
> a torrent emerging from a counterfeiter's cave,
> morning vegetables traveling to town on muleback,
> all the insects escaped from the multiplication table,
> and air that at every hour fondles the fruit.
> In my district the flowers offer up in their tiny open hands
> or in their little close-shut fists,
> the essence of earth's silence [. . .]

Around the time of the publication of this review, Carrera Andrade asked John Peale Bishop to write an introduction to Lee's translation of his book. In a letter to fellow patrician poet Allen Tate, Bishop mentioned this project and said he thought that she "was one of the best translators we discovered for the Fitts anthology."[40] He was working as publications director in the New York office of the Council of National Defense, in the section dedicated to inter-American cultural affairs, which had supported the New Directions publication.

Lee was very pleased about Bishop's offer to contribute the introduction to *Secret Country*. She told him in a letter written in January 1943 that it gave her "deep satisfaction to know" he was going to write it: "I believe with you that his [Carrera Andrade's] problems are the problems of us all. I believe also that no one comprehends those problems better than you. It will add a fresh delight to the always quickening attention with which I re-read even the most familiar of his poems to have this interpretation of his work as companion in the reading." About her work, she explained, "I think I have said in English in every case what he has said in Spanish, and I believe that even in the obscurest cases I have glimpsed his original meaning."[41] A few years later, *Secret Country* was published by Macmillan, the publisher of her *Sea-Change*.

During this period, still speaking out for the betterment of women throughout the Americas, Lee addressed the 1943 Pan American Day Conference on the Contribution of Women to Hemisphere Solidarity. This gathering was sponsored jointly by the *New York Times*, National Council of Women, and Pan American Women's Association and was held at the New York Times Hall in New York. She talked about the war-charged significance of the Caribbean countries and the current role of women in the Caribbean, "where again the Greater and the Lesser Antilles, the Leeward and the Westward Isles, are outposts, sentries and bastions of the Americas."

Lee argued that "women in the Caribbean area are, politically and educationally speaking, among the most progressive in our hemisphere." And she maintained: "Through the difficult days of colonization when they contributed as fully as their husbands, sons and brothers to the development of the New World; through the heroic days of the Era of Independence when they suffered and often died for the freedom they cherished; in the wake of pirate raids and of hurricanes; in times of prosperity and through long periods of distress; the women of the Caribbean have proved time and time again their patriotism, courage and devotion."

Lee cited numerous historical facts to support her claims and concluded her address with a vision of Caribbean women contributing much to the war effort and actively engaged in social action in defense of the Americas: "The future and continuing contributions of the Caribbean woman will include many [social and war-related] services, I believe, both within each country and beyond its borders wherever the need and desire for cooperation exist. A citizen of the hemisphere, she knows that what is basic in our lands is not the seas or the rivers or the mountains that seem to separate us, but the conviction of equality and will to freedom, our common democratic faith and heritage, that hold us together."

Lee's remarks appeared five days later, on April 19, 1943, in the *Puerto Rico World Journal*, the San Juan daily English-language newspaper that published a regular column—"'M. L.' in Washington"—that she contributed for a brief period during the early 1940s.

DOING THE AMERICAN STORY

In 1943, Lee proposed a creative Pan-American project to poet Archibald MacLeish, then serving in Washington as the Librarian of Congress. She wanted to collaborate with him on writing a series of programs for NBC radio's new Inter-American University of the Air; the NBC Inter-American University of the Air was the first endeavor in network history in the United States to provide instruction in a variety of subjects, correlated with existing courses in universities and colleges throughout the nation. MacLeish had developed over the years a strong interest in Latin America.

In his 1939 "Remarks on the Occasion of the Dedication of the Hispanic Room in the Library of Congress," he made the following comment while making reference to the importance of the Spanish chronicler Bernal Díaz del Castillo: "Some twelve years ago in a Paris library I came upon a copy of Bernal Díaz's *True History of the Conquest of New Spain*. There, in that still living, still human, still sharply breathing and believable history of Mexico, it seemed to me that I understood for the first time the central American experience—the experience which is American because it can be nothing else—the experience of all those who, of whatever tongue, are truly American—the experience of the journey westward from the sea into the unknown and dangerous country beyond which lies the rich and lovely city for which men hope."[42]

MacLeish's vision of America was very much in sync with Lee's. She too had come to understand the Pan-American implications of the "American" experience. Thus he was receptive when she came to him with the idea for doing what became *American Story,* a series of ten scripts broadcast on NBC radio in February, March, and April 1944. Its underlying theme was that of the early discoveries along all the American coasts.

Lee said the series aimed "to give the peoples of all the American republics a sense of the community of the American experience by introducing them through the broadcasts to the fundamental and authentic expressions which make up the American record as history and as literature." She explained:

> The initial series dealt with the discoverers, the men of the several European countries who made the first landfalls in the New World, and with the discovered, those who, unknowing and unknown, awaited the coming of the westward ships. It included the accounts of the new lands, and of the animals and birds and trees and flowers and aborigines as they appeared to the voyagers in dazzling newness. Firsthand accounts of the actual settlement of the land, from the St. Lawrence to the River Plate, and of the nature of the settlers, as they seemed to themselves and to their companions, shaped separate broadcasts; as did contemporary accounts of life in the settlements; the relation between the New World and the Old, their mutual impact; and the chronicle in all our lands and languages of the undefined but ever advancing frontier against strangeness. The later colonial experience; the spontaneous and continent-wide impulse toward independence; and the wars of freedom were also evoked in the words of those who made the story: the words sometimes of leaders, but more often of the American—whether by the Mississippi, the Rio Grande, or the Amazon—who was part of the persistent, courageous anonymous horde that pierced the forests, and crossed the plains, and voyaged the perilous rivers, and fought the battles, and contributed to the fragmentary but perfectly coherent record a letter or a passage in a diary or a snatch of song, or a desperate message out of an hour of utmost need.

Expressing in poetic language the spirit of Pan-Americanism she shared with MacLeish, she said the *American Story* broadcasts were "based on the belief that there is in all our lands and all our natures, underneath the differences and variations, a core that is essentially American and identical; that the experience of being born on the free soil of America and growing into the free American air gives a shape to the American mind as distinctive as the shape of the live-oak leaf, and as unlike the European oak's."[43]

Lee maintained that whether the discoveries along the American coasts were made by the Spanish and Portuguese or by the English and Dutch and Scandinavians, the pattern was similar, and the struggles with the native peoples in the interior came about in much the same way. She did all the research for the broadcasts, and MacLeish stitched the material together. In the first script he said the purpose of the broadcasts was "to bring together from the ancient chronicles, the narratives, the letters, from the pages written by those who saw with their own eyes and were part of it, the American record—the record common to all of us who are American, of whatever American country and whatever tongue—the record of the American experience common to us all."[44]

In addition to research, Lee's contribution included making translations of all documentary texts in Spanish, Portuguese, or French that were not available in English. She also wrote the handbook that accompanied the series, recounting the stories of diverse figures in the European discovery of America; this handbook, *American Story: Historical Broadcast Series of the NBC Inter-American University of the Air*, was published by Columbia University Press in 1944. That same year, MacLeish published the scripts in a collection titled *The American Story; Ten Broadcasts*, which he dedicated to her:

To

MUNA LEE

A POET OF THE AMERICAS

Indeed, he credited her with the success of the series, praising her as "a poet [. . .] a sound scholar, a mistress of tongues, and a profound believer in a cause."[45] And he told her in a letter: "Thanks to you—not to me at all, but to you—*The American Story* has really begun to do the work you and I wanted it to do."[46]

With her distinguished credentials as an envoy of the Americas, Lee was widely sought after as a speaker. Her talks addressed different aspects of inter-American relations. In May 1944 she gave one such talk in Columbus, Ohio, as guest speaker at the annual dinner of the local chapter of Theta Sigma Phi, the honorary journalism sorority (now Association for Women in Communications). The title of her talk was "A North American Looks South." She started by saying that her early education had led her to believe "American history was a phrase exclusively descriptive of the United States. Fortunately, though," she added, "there are many roads leading from such a morass of ignorance as all that, and the first one that opened to me was through language." The written and the spoken word, she stressed, offered a direct way to understand the other American nations. She talked about books as "windows," and recommended Virginia Prewett's *The Americas and Tomorrow*, Blair Niles's *Passengers to Mexico*, and the soon-to-be published *American Story*. Citing various examples of similarities between the Americas in geography, history, and art, through the use of both North and South American literature, Lee concluded her talk with the remark, "When I look south through whatever window, I see what I believe any citizen of any of the southern republics sees when he looks north: America." She then read several of her poems with a Caribbean setting and three of her translations of poems by Carrera Andrade.[47]

Also in 1944 Lee published *Pioneers of Puerto Rico*, a children's book for which MacLeish wrote the introduction. This work sketches the history of Puerto Rico from colonial times to the poverty-ridden present of Muñoz Marín's efforts to readjust the island's economy. The book was part of the publisher's "New World Neighbors" series and was designed to give children of elementary school age, in storybook fashion, a panoramic view of the history and spirit of Puerto Rico. That same year, her translation of an essay on the challenges of Pan-Americanism, written by the celebrated Venezuelan writer and diplomat, Mariano Picón Salas, was published by the Pan American Union's Division of Intellectual Cooperation as a book titled *On Being Good Neighbors*.

In August 1945 Puerto Rico's major newspaper, *El mundo*, published a glowing appreciation of Lee's *Pioneers of Puerto Rico* as well as her life and other literary work. It was, on the whole, a very positive and flattering editorial about her. But a remark about her relationship with Puerto Rico, now that she was living in Washington, D.C., moved her to write a letter to the editor to correct what she acknowledged was a detail that might appear insignificant, but was, nevertheless, of utmost importance to her:

Yo no pertenezco, como indica el editorial, al grupo de personas quienes, luego de haber convivido con los puertorriqeños un tiempo, han abandonado su suelo. Muy al contrario, soy una para quien durante más de cuarto de siglo Puerto Rico ha sido, y sigue siendo, tierra y hogar. Mis dos hijos y mi esposo, mi querida mamá doña Amalia Marín de Muñoz Rivera, mi nuera, mis tíos políticos, y las amistades de más de media vida, son lazos entrañables. Por esta razón, a pesar de seguir fuera de la Isla durante la época de crisis mundial, mientras el Gobierno Federal puede hacer algún uso dentro de su gran tarea del poco que yo puedo aportarle, no he dejado de tener tanto mi residencia como mis afectos más profundos radicados perdurablemente en Puerto Rico.[48]

[I don't belong, as the editorial states, to the group of people who, after having lived together with Puerto Ricans for a while, have abandoned their soil. Much to the contrary, I am someone for whom during more than a quarter century

Puerto Rico has been, and continues being, hearth and home. My two children and my husband, my dear mother Doña Amalia Marín de Muñoz Rivera, my daughter-in-law, my uncles and aunts by marriage, and the friendships of more than half a life, are intimate ties. For this reason, despite still being away from the Island during the period of world crisis, while the Federal Government could make some use in its great task of the little that I can contribute to it, I haven't stopped keeping my residence as well as my deepest affections located forever in Puerto Rico.] (Tr. JC)

Lee had long ago become Puerto Rican in her heart. She felt this way for the rest of her life, even more so with the births of her grandchildren. The island remained always at the center of her life.

Adding yet another facet to her multifaceted career, in 1945 Lee started to serve a four-year term as president of the Washington, D.C.–based Society of Woman Geographers. She was a founding member, and had served on its executive council in the years just prior to her presidency. Established in 1925 by four exceptionally accomplished women in New York (Marguerite Harrison, Blair Niles, Gertrude Shelby, and Gertrude Emerson Sen)—all recognized explorers—the society was created to bring together women, like Lee, who shared ambitions and interests in unusual world exploration and achievements. No women's organization then existed for the sharing of worldwide experiences, the exchange of knowledge derived from field work, and the encouragement of women pursuing geographical exploration and research.

The Society of Woman Geographers filled this need. Its name was intended to mean "geographer" in the broadest sense to include such allied disciplines as anthropology, geology, biology, archaeology, oceanography, and ecology. Specialized aspects of the arts rounded out the broad spectrum of worldwide interests and professional activities of the society's members. The membership included (as it still does) women "explorers at heart" whose work involved extensive travel in the investigations of little-known or unique places, peoples, or things in the world. Lee's long involvement with this organization stemmed from her diverse interests in the Americas, natural history, feminism, and the arts.

When *Secret Country* finally appeared in 1946, critics responded favorably and excitedly to it. This publication, which included a poetic, critically astute introduction by Bishop, was the first major translation of Carrera Andrade's poetry (not until 1972 would another be published, belatedly, in the United States). M. L. Rosenthal praised it highly in the *New York Herald Tribune*, saying "Jorge Carrera Andrade is a poet for Americans to love and study. . . . [H]e thinks in images, and surely he must always have at hand a thousand simple, beautiful appropriate images for every experience known to man." Rosenthal stressed that with "an imagination so muscular and finely trained that it can handle any grouping of sense-effects and ideas without straining," the Ecuadorian poet "puts to shame much of our North American groaning after impossible images to symbolize inadequate experience."[49]

In the *New York Times*, Babette Deutsch also reviewed the book in glowing terms: "The poems are not political or programmatic, but they are, what is more important, profoundly humane. And whether they speak of strange landscapes or intimate interiors, of 'The Life of the Cricket' or in 'Defense of Sunday,' of the miracles of physical love or of the metaphysics of solitude, they speak with an immediacy and an inwardness that can be paralleled only in the work of such men as Rilke, Lorca and Pasternak. With these three so various poets Señor Carrera Andrade shares an acute insight into things that makes his poems, even at second hand, an unlooked-for treasure."[50]

About Lee's translations, Deutsch said that "the poet himself was correct in describing them as 'exceptionally good and very beautiful.'" The *Yale Review* said that "even where she has departed slightly from the actual words used she has rendered the text with fidelity and poetry."[51]

Praising her work in a letter to her, MacLeish said: "Knowing how pitifully inadequate my grasp—the word 'command' won't come—of Spanish is, you will know that I can speak of them only as poems in themselves. Speaking of them so, there is no question whatever of their authenticity. If your poet is as good as you make him he is more than remarkable. He is what one has always hoped to find." More praise of *Secret Country* came later from another poet friend, Carl Sandburg, whom she had first met years ago in the offices of *Poetry* in Chicago. "Dear Muna," he wrote, "Tell Andrade I have read him in Spanish once & your translations six times & that as writers I feel we are brothers"—he was his "brother in the poetry quest a little more than any other in this hemisphere."[52]

Lee's artistry as a translator can be seen in her translation of Carrera Andrade's "Biography for the Use of the Birds," in which, as she had said in her review of his *Registro del mundo*, he voices "that sense [. . .] of being carried too fast and too far by the shifting currents of the world":[53]

> I was born in the century of the death of the rose
> when the motor had already driven out the angels.
> Quito watched the last stagecoach roll,
> and at its passing the trees ran by in good order,
> and the hedges and houses of the new parishes,
> on the threshold of the country
> where slow cows were ruminating the silence
> and the wind spurred its swift horses.

My mother, clothed in the setting sun,
put away her youth in a deep guitar,
and only on certain evenings would she show it to her children,
sheathed in music, light, and words.
I loved the hydrography of the rain,
the yellow fleas on the apple tree,
and the toads that would sound from time to time
their thick wooden bells.

. . . .

The valley was there with its farms
where dawn touched off its trickle of roosters,
and westward was the land where the sugarcane
waved its peaceful banner, and the cacao
held close in a coffer its secret fortune,
and the pineapple girded on her fragrant cuirass,
the nude banana her silken tunic.

It has all passed in successive waves,
as the vain foam-figures pass.
The years go without haste entangling their lichens,
and memory is scarcely a water-lily
that lifts between two waters
its drowned face.
The guitar is only a coffin for songs,
and the head-wounded cock laments.
All the angels of the earth have emigrated,
even the dark angel of the cacao tree.

This particular version shows the polishing work she would do in the process of
making a translation, in her effort to re-create the poetic quality of the original
Spanish. The rendering she had presented in her review was rougher, its language
not yet fully naturalized in English, as seen in the poem's opening lines:

I was born in the century when the rose became defunct,
when the motor had frightened off the angels.
Quito saw the last diligence roll by
and after it all orderly ran the trees,
the fences, and the houses in new developments
where the lazy cows ruminated the silence
and the wind spurred its swift horses [. . .]

Very much a process writer in general, Lee knew only too well that faithful and poetic translations require time to make, in particular when working with the deceptively simple, yet complex, language of poets like Carrera Andrade. She understood that the act of translation is at once critical and creative. Although she could not replicate the music of his Spanish, she also understood that for a translation to have literary value, it has to be composed as if a poem written in English with verbal music of its own, true to the "sound" of the original. To her, translation meant "continual experiment, continual attempt," as she explained to Bishop in her correspondence with him. "It is all nonsense to say that the way of the translator is hard," she added. "[I]t is difficult sometimes, as mountain climbing often is, but it has the same delights and rewards."[54]

Lee's demanding job at the State Department kept her busy both in and out of the office. Public speaking, as always, was part of it, as shown by the notice of her lectures in the April 1946 issue of the *Americas*, a then new quarterly review of inter-American cultural history (to which she contributed numerous book reviews over the years):

Miss Muna Lee, of the American Republics Area Division of the Department of State, has just completed an extensive series of lectures on various Latin-American subjects. Her lectures included: "What Do the Other American Republics Expect of the United States," at the Sunday Evening Forum, Essex, Conn.; "Cultural Relations Between Puerto Rico and the U.S.," at the World Fellowship Committee meeting, Washington, D.C.; "Puerto Rico: An Example of Cooperation," at the Zonta Club, Washington, D.C.; "What Do the Other American Republics Expect of the United States," at the Kiwanis Club, Cumberland, Md.; "Women in the Other American Republics," at the Business and Professional Women's Club, Alexandria, Va.; "Cultural Cooperation Between the Americas," at Ginter Park Women's Club, Richmond, Va.; "Vocational Opportunities for Women in Latin America," at the Altrusa Club, Atlantic City, N. J.; Miss Lee has also given three lectures at an institute on Latin American affairs held at the State Teachers College, Farmville, Va.

She spoke effectively and engagingly on each occasion, as indicated by the letters of gratitude she received. "Miss Lee was delightful" and "the best program we have had" were typical of the comments made by her audiences, which these letters relayed to her.[55]

Although known in public as Miss Muna Lee, she and Muñoz were still legally married, but that was soon to change. On November 15, 1946, after more than a decade of estrangement and separation, they finally were divorced legally. The following day he married Mendoza, with whom he had been living and with whom he had already fathered two children. His marriage to her was to have bitter implications for Lee. Soon to be Puerto Rico's First Lady, Mendoza made mention of Lee's name taboo in Puerto Rico (it still is); motivated by both jealousy and political image-consciousness, she did not want the public image of her husband—as well as her own image—sullied in any way. In 1948, he became Puerto Rico's first elected governor, serving four terms for a total of sixteen years and establishing his place in history as the "father of the Commonwealth of Puerto Rico." Attention paid to his relationship with his first wife could be painfully embarrassing for both him and Mendoza. After all, Catholicism, the dominant faith in Puerto Rico, frowned heavily on divorce, with the attitude that an absolute divorce can never occur, at least not after a marriage has been consummated.

Even though Lee's marriage to Muñoz had dissolved long before their actual divorce—a fact she had come to accept—and the emotional pain she had endured was no longer a living reality of hers, the legal process and event struck a sad chord in her heart, in which love, for the second time, had been "like a hangman." Now, at the age of fifty-one, she was in every way Miss Muna Lee again.

Three days after the divorce proceedings were completed, Lee sent a letter to her daughter, Munita, in which she explained: "I really mind less than I had expected. In a sense it is a relief, as anything definite and above all definitive must be, in comparison with incompletion, tenuousness and uncertainty." Lee did not want her daughter to feel "too badly" that her marriage to her father had been terminated legally. Moreover, in keeping with the loving person she was, she told her: "And don't stop being friends with your father. He wants your love, and needs it, and he has always loved you dearly."[56]

The following year, Lee published *The Cultural Approach: Another Way in International Relations*, coauthored with Ruth Emily McMurry, who also had long experience in the field of cultural relations. MacLeish wrote the cogent introduction. This publication was the last book of Lee's own writing that she published in her lifetime (the book was later reprinted by Kennikat Press in 1972). It documents the efforts of various nations to promote cultural and intellectual exchange. Like McMurry, she had long been concerned with familiarizing cultural output across national borders, believing that only through knowledge of one another can diverse peoples manage amicable relations.

In *The Cultural Approach*, Lee and McMurry provide a summary of the official information about bilateral long-range programs of cultural relations as carried on since 1900 by some ten countries: France, Germany, Japan, the Soviet Union, Great Britain, four republics of Latin America, and the United States. Writing in the aftermath of the Second World War, the authors conclude: "We may say that the peoples throughout the world seem agreed upon the importance of mobilizing those forces which give promise of building trust and confidence among nations. In a world torn by diverse and conflicting political and social philosophies, it is difficult to find middle ground. Admittedly government programs of cultural relations abroad have been used as instruments of aggression. Such programs are dangerous to the freedom-loving peoples of the world, unless they are understood and unless adequate measures are taken to offset them. On the other hand, they have been used by some countries as measures for creating a better atmosphere of mutually beneficial cooperation among nations."[57] The book's broader significance at the time of its original publication was its implication that the entire problem of the conduct of foreign affairs urgently required reexamination.

The years immediately after the war would see the demise of the old Pan-American movement and the rise of the United States as a postwar leader and protagonist of the Cold War. Lee's work with the State Department continued, and while culture had become significant to U.S. foreign policy, she was never complicit in the covert propaganda wars to be waged in the 1950s and 1960s. She never willingly involved herself with programs of cultural relations used as "instruments of aggression." While open-eyed, she was always noble and sincere, remaining true to her humanistic Pan-Americanism throughout the coming years.

In April 1947 Lee made a return trip to Mississippi to speak at Blue Mountain College for the revival of its Southern Literary Festival, which had been suspended during the war. Five years before, she had made her first return trip—after a "lifetime of absence"—to speak at Hinds Community College in her hometown of Raymond. At Blue Mountain she gave a talk on writing titled "Poetry Every Day," in which she professed: "There is nothing to be afraid of in the name of poetry, though it is in all languages and in all ages a name for wisdom and beauty. Whether we know it or not, poetry is a part of the everyday life of us all. It is about us, and inside us, all the time. More often than not, we do not recognize it. Even when it is most present, we may not realize that what we are seeing or hearing or even saying is poetry. But we can learn to recognize and realize it: and to the extent to which we do so, we ourselves become poets."

Lee was introduced to the Blue Mountain audience as a "poet, translator and international leader for equal rights for women." Although she had only lived in Mississippi during the first seven years of her life, and then spent a couple more years there during her college years, she was considered an important southern writer; early Mississippi collections such as Ernestine Deavours's *The Mississippi Poets* (1922) and Alice James's *Mississippi Verse* (1934) include her as a prominent poet. (She was also considered an Oklahoma poet: her biography appears in the 1939 *Handbook of Oklahoma Writers*, and her verse in *The Oklahoma Anthology for 1929*, among other regional collections.)

Two years later, in 1949, Lee published another major translation, *A History of Spain* written by the distinguished Spanish historian Rafael Altamira. This seven-hundred-page book—the last book, in fact, that she would publish in her lifetime—provides a history of Spain written for the general reader, covering prehistoric times to the 1940s, and reveals reciprocal influences of the outside world, including the voyages of discovery and colonization in the Americas. Although primarily a cultural history, it discusses political events and personalities. The *Nation* said it was "one of the best" guides to the Spanish story available in English. For Lee, the experience of translating this history allowed her to further explore for herself a history to which she felt connected.

GETTING FAULKNER TO TRAVEL

In November 1949, soon after the announcement that Faulkner had won the Nobel Prize in Literature, Lee played a major role in getting him to go to Stockholm to receive the prize in person. He had refused to make the trip. It was an unwelcome imposition on him at the time; he was more interested in staying in Mississippi to go on his annual hunting trip with his buddies. Considerable disappointment was expressed by leading Swedes. In the face of international embarrassment over his refusal to go, State Department officials were much concerned but at a loss about what to do.

According to Faulkner's biographer, Joseph Blotner, the American embassy in Sweden turned for advice to one of its former officers, Morrill Cody, a career man then in Paris. He advised Eric Bellquist, first secretary and public affairs officer, to contact Lee. Cody mistakenly thought that Faulkner and Lee knew each other because of their connections in Mississippi, but she nevertheless proved to be the right choice. Lee turned to one of the most distinguished female members of the bar in the South, Lucy Somerville, who suggested that she try Faulkner's early mentor and fellow townsman, Phil Stone, whom Lee knew from her student days at Ole Miss; she also suggested her cousin, Ella Somerville, who lived in Faulkner's town of Oxford.

With the Nobel ceremony just weeks away, Lee called Ella Somerville who advised her not to try to work through Stone, because she felt that he and Faulkner were on the outs. Faulkner's friend Colonel Hugh Evans was recommended instead. He might be able to act as an intermediary for Stockholm and Washington. At the time of Lee's call to him, he was out duck hunting, but when he finally returned her call, he agreed to help; he would try to persuade Faulkner to go.

Lee had made major progress. A week later, after Faulkner returned from his hunting trip, Evans explained to him that he had talked with Lee, and that she had stressed how much the government wanted him to make the Stockholm trip. As time seemed to speed up and tensions heightened, Lee's efforts, together with those of Faulkner's immediate family (who could not do it alone), finally convinced the man that he had to go to Sweden to accept the prize.

Lee's relationship with Faulkner grew from this point. They later talked by telephone and corresponded with each other about his going on goodwill missions abroad. In 1954 and 1961 (the year before his death), she persuaded him to make two trips to South America—Brazil and Venezuela, respectively—to help further Pan-American cultural relations. She also got him to go to Denver in 1959 to serve as "consultant" at the Seventh National Conference of the U.S. National Commission for UNESCO (the conference's formal title was Cultures of the Americas: Achievements in Education, Science, and the Arts), of which she was program coordinator.

Lee had tapped Faulkner's very real and deep patriotic impulses. More than that, she had his respect not simply as a government official, but as a fellow artist and Mississippian. Blotner points out that if such appeals to Faulkner to serve as a goodwill ambassador had come from anyone other than her, he probably would have refused.

When, in April 1961, Faulkner traveled to Venezuela, the formal occasion of his two-week visit was the year-long celebration of the sesquicentennial of Venezuelan independence. He took part in several special programs and also received the Order of Andrés Bello, the country's highest civilian award. In order to read his acceptance speech in the native language of his presenters, and thereby make the ultimate goodwill gesture, he arranged to have what he had written in English translated into Spanish; it is speculated that his interpreter in Venezuela was the translator. After Faulkner gave his speech, he took from the buttonhole the prized rosette of the Legion of Honor (the premier French order and decoration) and replaced it with that of the Order of Andrés Bello. The great success of his Venezuelan visit pleased Lee, who was responsible for it, as much as it pleased the State Department.

She later made an English translation of the Spanish rendering, which had been published in the Caracas newspaper *El universal* the day after the ceremony. For more than three decades, until the original single-page holograph draft was found, scholars thought that Faulkner's original English version had been lost. They relied on Lee's "second-hand" translation. In his Faulkner biography, Blotner presents a lengthy excerpt from it in his account of the award ceremony without identifying its origin, as if Faulkner's own words; her translation, with proper attribution, appears in *A Faulkner Miscellany*.

In 1950, the year after her initial involvement with Faulkner, Lee received a commendable service award from the State Department "for exceptional contributions in the field of Latin American culture during the last twenty-five years and for the fostering of friendly relations with the Latin American republics through her literary achievements," and in 1951 she was promoted to cultural coordinator in the

Office of Public Affairs of the Bureau of Inter-American Affairs. She served as chief of the South American Affairs Section. Much sought after as an adviser, in the remaining fifteen years of her life she appeared as a United States delegate at many conferences around the world.

Her political activity on behalf of women's rights had become limited as a consequence of her other commitments. In a revealing letter she sent in 1954 to Amelia Walker, the national chair of the NWP, Lee makes clear her undying support for the party and its feminist mission, namely, its proposed equal rights amendment to the Constitution:

> My mother's prolonged and serious illness, together with heavy office duties, keeps me perpetually behindhand in my reading. So it is that I have only just found, with astonishment, gratitude, and regret, that the October 1954 copy of *Equal Rights* lists my name as that of a member of the National Council of the National Woman's Party. The astonishment was at the unexpectedness of finding myself there, since the listing came as a complete surprise; the gratitude of course is for having been made the recipient of so great and undeserved an honor (I am well aware how great an honor it is to be a Council Member of the National Woman's Party, and no less aware how far I am from meriting this honor); and the regret—very sincere and very deep—is because I cannot serve. The fact that the National Woman's Party is dedicated to working for Congressional action—for the enactment of specific legislation—makes it incompatible with my present duties to hold office in the Party or be a member of its Council. Therefore, with every sense of having to forego the high privilege of close working association with a noble and distinguished group of women, many of whom I have known and loved for years and all of whom I admire, I must request that you remove my name from the list of members of the National Council.[58]

Lee's statement that she was "far from meriting this honor" was typical of her modesty. Her ability to help lead the NWP had been made clear long ago. Although she was not able to formally join the NWP's leadership, her sympathy with the party remained strong. Her official duties that prevented her from working with the NWP would, nonetheless, allow her to contribute to the cause of women by serving the State Department as, for instance, an adviser on the United States Delegation to the Eleventh General Assembly of the Inter-American Commission of Women held in June 1956 in the Dominican Republic.

Lee's work as a literary critic continued. Since the early 1920s, she was often invited to review newly published books. In reviewing Stanley Williams's landmark 1955 publication *The Spanish Background of American Literature* for *Américas* she pointed out how misleading it is "to limit 'American' to the 'United States' and to employ

'background of' where 'contributions to' or even 'currents in' would seem preferable."
Nonetheless, she welcomed this two-volume critical work that addresses the history
of Spanish culture in the Americas and the Pan-American literary tradition, since
none as comprehensive had yet appeared in English. It is still considered an essen-
tial text for anyone who wishes to undertake a comparative study of literary relations
between the United States and Spanish America. She acknowledged that "not
everything could be included from so ample a field, of course; not even in a listing."

Still, she lamented the absence of "at least mention of the fact that Robert
Frost's first poem—from his own account, it would seem his first consciously cre-
ative impulse toward poetry—was inspired by the story of Cortés." She also cited
other important omissions, such as acknowledgment of "the recurrent reflections in
Williams Carlos Williams' poetry and prose of his mother's vivid lifelong recollec-
tions of her Puerto Rican girlhood [. . . and] the haunting, brilliant, evanescent His-
panic names and illusions that flit like hummingbirds through Emily Dickinson's
poetry (not singing there, but shining)."

The final omission she pointed out reveals her personal feelings as much as her
critical judgment: "And one wonders why Luis Muñoz Marín is mentioned in pass-
ing because of a book review rather than for his own varied writings in Spanish and
in English and for the bilingual literary magazine *La Revista de Indias*, which he edited
in New York as a young man."[59] She always cared for him and respected his achieve-
ments, and despite their personal history, she always took the high road in public
where he was concerned. In reality, as her friend MacLeish recalled: "She never
ceased nor desisted to be very much in love with him and the fact that he shunted
her off and married again didn't make any difference to her feelings. She was simply
devoted to him."[60]

By this time, Lee was no longer actively publishing her poetry in magazines,
though she was still writing verse and still highly regarded as a poet for her earlier
publications. In 1960, in recognition of her importance, the Library of Congress
invited her to give a recorded reading of her work for its Archive of Recorded
Poetry and Literature, and in April this recording was made.

Speaking with a strong voice graced by the southern accent that she never lost,
she introduced herself and her work: "These first poems, from which I am reading,
have all been published in magazines over the years—*The New Yorker, The American
Mercury* (when H. L. Mencken edited it), *Poetry: A Magazine of Verse, The Commonweal,*
and many others—but have not been collected in book form. Afterwards, I shall
read some from my one volume of verse, which has been for a number of years out
of print. Most of the poems [. . .] have a tropical setting. They reflect the environ-
ment of Puerto Rico, which has been my home for a number of years."

The very list of the poems' titles reveals the range of geography and personal
experience that shaped her life: "Rich Port"—"Legend"—"Of Writing Verse"—

"After Reading in the Spanish Mystics"—"Hacienda"—"Dies Irae"—"Moonrise"—
"On Going Ashore"—"Cottager"—"Dialogue"—"Device"—"Old Story"—"Aca-
cia"—"Christmas Eve"—"Night of San Juan"—"Atavian"—"Carib Fantasy"—
"Caribbean Marsh"—"Encounter"—"Visitant"—"Deliverance"—"Champion"—
"Doom"—"Carib Garden"—"Stalactite"—"West Indian Plaque"—"Caribbean
Noon"—"Summertime Notation in a Troubled World"—"Apology for All That
Blooms in Time of Crisis"—"Housewife"—"Fruit Tree"—"The Carnival"—"The
Drugstore"—"The Duelists"—"Roebuck Men"—"The Revival"—"The Blacksmith's
Wife"—"Prairie Sky"—"August"—"Apology"—From *Sea-Change:* "The Thought of
You"—"The Stars Are Colored Blossoms"—"My Dreams of You Are Somber in the
Twilight"—"The Little White Flower"—"The Blackbirds Fly Before the Cold"—
"Melilot"—"Song (What Is Love Like?)"—"As Helen Once"—"Lips You Were Not
Anhungered For"—"Survival"—"Dirge"—"April Wind"—"I Remember You Because
of a Grassy Hill"—"I Have Had Enough of Glamour"—"A Woman's Song"—
"Choice"—"Harvest"—"Gifts"—"Imprisoned"—"You Who Hear Only the Words"—
"Release"—"The Confidante"—"Spring"—"November"—"The Host"—"Out of
My Turbulent Days"—"Yellow Leaves"—"Apple Boughs"—"Foreword"—"Sonnets
(I–XII)"—"Song in the Hills"—"Mid-Western"—"Tropic Rain"—"A Song of Dreams
Come True"—"Pomarrosal"—"The Flame-Trees"—"Barrier"—"Morning in the
Woods"—"The Seeker."

By ending her reading with "The Seeker," the closing poem of *Sea-Change* in
which she affirmed her youthful quest for continued development as a woman and
poet, she reaffirmed its vision of earthly truth and beauty and her unceasing com-
mitment to them.[61]

Also in April 1960, Lee traveled to Tufts University to be the guest speaker in
its series called the Steinman Poetry Lectures. On the thirteenth of the month, the
eve of Pan American Day, she gave her lecture titled "Two Seventeenth-Century
Women: Mistress Anne Bradstreet and Sor Juana Inés de la Cruz."[62] She had given
this lecture before; it was a favorite of hers, bringing together her passions for
poetry, feminism, and Pan America. The first time she presented it was at the Pan
American Union in Washington, D.C., in April 1954, when she addressed the
Biennial Convention of the National League of American Pen-Women; the title of
that version was "Two Seventeenth-Century Pen-Women: Anne Bradstreet of Mas-
sachusetts and Sor Juana Inés de la Cruz of Mexico."

She made it clear in her opening remarks that "in comparing their personalities
and their lives," she was "not implying, nor could any serious critic imply, any equal-
ity of their genius." Sor Juana was "the greatest woman poet whom the whole of
America has produced," and despite her literary achievements, Anne Bradstreet was
simply not a great poet. New to Lee's lecture was the following passage about the
two poets:

Many books in several languages have been written about Sor Juana. Every aspect of her poetry and her prose has been analyzed; every recorded act and word of hers has been scrutinized from the viewpoints of art, theology, and psychology. About Anne Bradstreet relatively little has been said. Some eighteen years since Archibald MacLeish rediscovered her as a valid poet, and so reported in the course of a public address. Four years ago a much younger poet, John Berryman, published a strange and compelling poem entitled "Homage to Mistress Bradstreet" which has been termed "a sort of miniature 'Waste Land,'" and which Conrad Aiken has characterized as "one of the finest poems ever written by an American, a classic right on our doorstep."

Though a memorable tribute from a well-known poet to one too little known, Mr. MacLeish's reference to Anne Bradstreet was brief and in passing; Mr. Berryman's poem—fifty-seven eight-line stanzas—portrays her not so much as a poet as an impassioned, imaginative woman in an environment of rigid controls. That also was Sor Juana's situation, of course. In each instance, the most illuminating, the most important, and by far the most interesting fact is that both impassioned, imaginative, controlled women were poets.

To conclude her lecture, Lee read a few of her translations of Sor Juana's sonnets. Among them was the following stinger, which, in view of her own travails with love during her youth, gave her a well-matched persona, and to which she gave a natural lyric voice:

> Silvio, I abhor you and still condemn
> Your being in such wise present to my sense;
> Iron to the wounded scorpion is offense,
> And mud to whom its slime disdains the hem.
>
> You are like a poison wherein death-throes wait
> For whosoever pours it forth by chance;
> You are, in brief, so false and foul of stance
> That you are not even good to hate.
>
> I give your sorry presence place again
> In memory, though memory would say nay,
> Forcing myself to bear deservéd pain;
> For when I recall how once my heart approved you,
> Not only you I come to loathe straightway
> But myself also, for what time I loved you.

This translation had been made nearly four decades earlier during the period of Lee's excited discovery of Sor Juana, about whom she published her perceptive article, "A Charming Mexican Lady," in the *American Mercury* in 1925. She told Mencken then that Sor Juana was "the first feminist in this hemisphere."[63] Her poetic renderings of Sor Juana in English expressed beautifully the Mexican's dramatic use of paradox and positive contradiction. At the age of sixty-five, Lee still had the intellectual vitality of her youth that enabled her to portray in vivid terms these two sisters of poetry—each of whom, as she emphasized in her lecture, had been hailed in her own day as the "Tenth Muse" of America.

In March 1962, in recognition of her career achievements as a Pan-Americanist, Lee was elected to the Inter-American Academy of the University of Florida, as one of the fifty living leaders in the hemisphere who had done the most to improve and advance inter-American understanding and cultural cooperation.

The following year, the executive director of the Bureau of Inter-American Affairs nominated her for the State Department's Distinguished Service Award. In his impassioned letter to the honor awards committee, he said: "Although widely honored by United States and Latin American scholars, political figures, organizations and institutions, among whom she has become revered as a wise counselor and sure guide to inter-cultural understanding, Miss Lee has received no significant recognition of her work and contribution from the Department of State, for which she has worked with single-minded devotion since December, 1941. [. . .] In her years with the Department, Miss Lee has placed at the service of her country unstintingly the personal prestige she had previously accumulated throughout the hemisphere as poet, educator, champion of women's rights, critic, cultural interpreter and defender of democratic processes."

He concluded with the statement: "Bestowal of a 'Distinguished Service Award' on Miss Lee would have favorable repercussions throughout academic, intellectual and cultural circles in the United States and throughout the hemisphere, taking her out of the category of a prophet without honor in her own country. It would also appropriately crown her long career of service, which has only two more years to run before mandatory retirement."[64]

Despite the strong support Lee had for this special recognition, it was not bestowed on her, at least not officially. The nomination itself, of course, meant much to her. But at this point, at the age of sixty-eight, she had already received several high honors for her work: the Commendable Service Award of the State Department (1950), Medal of the Fundación Internacional Eloy Alfaro of Ecuador (1954), Star of the Fundación Internacional José Gabriel Duque of the Dominican Republic (1954), Public Citation of the National Federation of Business and Professional Women (1961), and Meritorious Award of the General Federation of Women's Clubs for "commendable service as a public servant" (1962), in addition to her recent election to the Inter-American Academy.

Toward the end of her busy career with the State Department, working tirelessly as always for Pan-American union, she started to translate a collection of essays—most on literary figures—by Puerto Rican writer and critic José Agustín Balseiro, which the University of Miami Press published in 1969, after her death. The press had received a Rockefeller Foundation grant for the translation, but this was a project Lee never finished herself. Her daughter, Muna Muñoz Lee, who had become a professional Spanish-English translator, would make the translation in her mother's place.[65]

Balseiro's essay explicitly on inter-American relations gave the book its title, *The Americas Look at Each Other.* Having set himself the goal of interpreting the spirit of Latin- and Anglo-American cultures to the other, he had become a cultural ambassador in the United States, where he lived for most of his adult life. His writings on the arts and the role of the artist as a conduit between those cultures earned him praise throughout the world, especially within the Spanish-speaking countries. Among the many favorable critical responses to the book, the review in *Library Journal* made note that "the title essay should be required reading for anyone involved in Latin-American policy making."[66]

Balseiro argued that the sooner we approach our neighbors by the disinterested paths of art, literature, scholarship, and open-hearted friendship, the sooner we will demolish the prejudices that hamper the constructive development of human nature. Lee was of the same mind; she had long embraced the same ideal. Although she never finished her final undertaking as a translator of Balseiro's work, it was intended to be—like most of her translation ventures—another expression of her lifelong dream for the Americas, another labor of love for her "commonwealth of Pan America."

IN THE END

Lee's spirit and energy sustained her until the end of her life. She was constantly in flight, appearing as a delegate at conferences all over the world. When she retired from the State Department in February 1965, she still had ambitious plans. At her retirement ceremony she said: "I expect to be just as active in inter-American affairs as I was previously. Now I will have more opportunity and time to devote to my special interests—hemisphere relations—from a personal angle."[67] She also planned to use her new leisure to pursue literary projects, especially poetry: "You must have leisure to write poetry; time to dream and to think," she said. With her characteristic vigor, she looked forward to returning to Puerto Rico, her legal residence for the past forty-odd years and where her two children and seven grandchildren lived. She owned a beautiful home there, in Old San Juan, overlooking the bay.

One of the oldest houses in Puerto Rico, Lee's home—located at 2 Calle del Sol—had originally been the residence of conquistador-colonizer Juan Ponce de

León, the first Spanish governor of the island, then called Borinquén. With retirement in mind, Lee purchased it in 1958 and oversaw its restoration, which brought back the beauty of its centuries-old colonial architecture. She had made it a sanctuary of her own, filling it with her collection of books and paintings and memorabilia from her travels of the world. Among her antique furniture, mostly Spanish in style, was a maple folding-top desk from the old schoolhouse of Raymond, Mississippi.

But just two weeks after her return to Puerto Rico, Lee was admitted to the Mimiya Clinic in San Juan: the recently diagnosed cancer in her lungs (secondary to breast cancer treated in the late 1950s) was taking its toll. Without ever leaving the hospital, she died peacefully—on April 3, 1965—surrounded by the "flame-trees and tree-ferns and frail white orchises" that she had celebrated in her poem "Rich Port." In keeping with her wishes for a prompt burial, a funeral service (closed casket at her request) was held for her that day in the afternoon, and she was buried in the old cemetery by the sea not far from her home.[68]

The next day her obituary appeared in the *New York Times*, which acknowledged her achievements as a "poet, author, translator and lecturer" whose "works were published throughout North and South America"; her activism as an "enthusiastic advocate" of women's rights and "exporter" of this cause; and her public service as the "cultural coordinator in the Office of Public Affairs of the State Department's Bureau of Inter-American Affairs." Hers was the lead obituary in the *Washington Post*: "Muna Lee, 70; Poet, U.S. Cultural Official." The article highlighted her career in the State Department, her contribution to Puerto Rico's political progress, her poetry and other literary work, and her political activity with the NWP.

Also on April 4, the *New York Herald Tribune* published the most intimate and informed obituary, which was written by one of Lee's friends who worked for the newspaper. It was that day's lead obituary, but unlike the obituaries in the *Post* and *Times*, it provided a vivid picture of Lee as a poet, opening with an account of her literary beginnings:

> Muna Lee's first published work was exactly three lines in the old *Smart Set* magazine in 1914 [sic]. She thought she had written a poem, but to her amazement the late Edward J. O'Brien double-starred it in his *Best Short Stories of 1915*.
>
> The lines that launched a writing career and either confused or bemused the great student of the American short story were:

> THE VIGIL
> By Muna Lee

> His gaze a strained attention, he stood in the door of the mad-house.
> "How are you today, Charley?" asked the doctor:
> And he said, "I shall know her when she comes."

Miss Lee proved, however, that she was a poet in the same year the anthology containing her three lines was published. She was awarded the Lyric Prize by *Poetry* magazine.

The rest of this article reviewed Lee's life and multifaceted career, with emphasis on her work for the NWP during the early years of the Depression when she championed the policy of nondiscrimination against women workers.

Two days after her death, the executive secretary of the Inter-American Commission of Women, Esther de Calvo, sent a condolence letter to Secretary of State Dean Rusk, in which she told him:

> On behalf of the Inter-American Commission of Women, and in a most personal way, I wish to express to you, Sir, our profound sorrow at the death of Miss Muna Lee, who was for so many years a beloved and dedicated figure in the service of the Government of the United States. Her passing is motive of especial regret to the Inter-American Commission of Women, of which she was a founding member and which, for thirty-seven years, was beneficiary of her wise and sympathetic counsel. After her recent retirement [. . .] her continuance in the position of Alternate Delegate of the United States was a particular privilege and source of strength for the Commission. Her loss is, therefore, all the more keenly felt.
>
> Miss Lee elicited not only the devotion of her friends and colleagues throughout the United States but the unanimous regard and affection of her multitude of friends and co-workers in Latin America.[69]

Soon after she passed away, her close friend and colleague, poet Ernest Kroll, a Japanese affairs specialist in the State Department during her tenure there, wrote a eulogy titled "Muna Lee (1895–1965)," which celebrates her remarkable vitality:

> The last we saw of you, you tossed your head
> Like F.D.R. while reading verse that stirred
> A murmuring of friends, who said good-bye
> And sent you off to your Caribbean
> Elysium, the crossbeamed house that once
> Roofed over the youth-struck Ponce de León.
> And then we heard you had seen the raven
> Hover over your life with downward eyes,
> Keeping the secret even as we thought
> You winged for good to step from cloudless skies;
> And, realizing you had changed direction
> Quite in mid-air, slipping an earthly haven to

Dare your spirit slip right into heaven,
We thought how *like* you to save this last surprise.[70]

Muna Lee's enduring contributions to American literature and society have sadly been forgotten, obscured by the dust cloud made by the generations of writers and social activists who followed in her footsteps. Her belief in a common New World character has been eclipsed by increasing criticism of its assumptions. Her glory days were of another time (like the taste for her love songs), but not so distant from the turn of the present century. She left us a compelling body of widely varied writing replete with lyricism, brilliance, and progressive ideas. Moreover, she expanded the bounds of our own national literature, as part of her legacy, by rendering in English the voices of more than sixty different poets from Latin America, many of whom had not been known in the North until she gave them to us. In order for us to fully appreciate our literary and social traditions, especially with regard to poetry and women's rights, we must come to terms with what she—and other forgotten leaders like her—did to advance them; for she was one of the great Pan-American pioneers, who dedicated her life to finding our common ground with our sister republics and bringing the diverse peoples of the Americas together, through literature, social change, and cultural relations.

Ultimately, the extraordinary Muna Lee was not Mississippian, Oklahoman, or Puerto Rican, not simply North or South American, Latin- or Anglo-American, but uniquely American in the original sense of the word, which implies the Pan-Americanism that defined her.

NOTES

1. Muna Lee, "Contemporary Spanish-American Poetry," *North American Review* 219 (May 1924): 698.
2. As quoted in Elaine Hughes, "Lee, Muna: 1895–1965," *Lives of Mississippi Authors, 1817–1967,* edited by James B. Lloyd (Jackson: University Press of Mississippi, 1981), 293.
3. As quoted in Mary Hays Marable and Elaine Boylan, "Muna Lee (Mrs. Luis Muñoz Marín)," *Handbook of Oklahoma Writers* (Norman: University of Oklahoma Press, 1939), 67.
4. As quoted in Marable and Boylan, "Muna Lee," 67.
5. Ibid., 67–68.
6. David E. Guyton, "Potluck with the Poets," *Four Talks on Writing; Delivered at the Southern Literary Festival* (Blue Mountain, Miss.: privately printed, 1947), 5.
7. Guyton, "Biographical Sketch," *Four Talks on Writing,* 13.

8. Born in Ardmore, Oklahoma, John Peebles McClure (1893–1956) entered the University of Oklahoma in 1911 and received his AB in 1915. He had spent the year 1913–14 abroad, studying in Paris. After his graduation, he worked as assistant librarian at the University of Oklahoma for three years. In 1918 he got married and then was drafted into the army. During that year, Knopf published a collection of his verse, *Airs and Ballads,* as well as a collection of drinking songs, *The Stag's Hornbook,* which he edited (an expanded edition of this volume, which he coedited with William Rose Benét, and to which war poems were added, appeared in 1943). He served in the 304th Cavalry in the First World War. After his discharge, he and his wife settled in New Orleans, where they operated a bookstore for six years.

   H. L. Mencken thought very highly of McClure; in 1919 Mencken said he was the finest "lyric poet the United States has produced in fifty years" ("Letter to Fielding H. Garrison," *The New Mencken Letters,* edited by Carl Bode [New York: Dial Press, 1977], 102). He was, for a short while, associate editor of the *Southerner: A Magazine of the New South* (four issues published in New Orleans between December 1919 and May 1920). In 1921 he joined the staff of the New Orleans *Times Picayune,* for which he worked until his retirement, first as copyreader, then editor of the Sunday book page, city editor, and finally head copyreader. From 1921 to 1926, he was associate editor of the *Double Dealer,* a literary magazine to which Lee contributed one poem and two book reviews. Between 1914 and 1923, *Smart Set* published more poems by McClure than by any other author; Lee was its second-most-frequent contributor of verse during this period. His verse appears together with hers—on the same page—in *Signature of the Sun: Southwest Verse, 1900–1950* (University of New Mexico Press, 1950).

9. Alfred Kreymborg, *Troubadour: An American Autobiography* (New York: Sagamore Press, 1957), 172.

10. Sara Teasdale to Harriet Monroe, May 13, 1919, *Dear Editor: A History of* Poetry *in Letters,* edited by Joseph Parisi and Stephen Young (New York: Norton, 2003), 243–44.

11. Application for federal employment, January 6, 1949, copy in federal personnel file of Muna Lee, National Archives and Records Administration, St. Louis, Mo.

12. Lee to H. L. Mencken, January 15, 1922, H. L. Mencken Papers, 1905–56, New York Public Library, New York, N. Y.

13. Margery Swett, "Words That Fly Singing," *Poetry* (October 1923): 51–52.

14. *New York Times Book Review,* June 10, 1923, 12.

15. In 1925, in a review of the nation's regional literary activity, H. L. Mencken cheered the new "Oklahoma manner" in literature: "Oklahoma, though it came in before Arizona and New Mexico, is actually the youngest state in the Union. Until 1889 it was a sort of No Man's Land. Yet I can testify as an editor that it produces ten times as many likely manuscripts a year as Maine, which was admitted in 1820, or Delaware, which was one of the original thirteen colonies, and it has already thrown off such men as John McClure, the poet, and Burton Rascoe, the critic. The reason I don't know, but the fact is brilliantly plain that many young Oklahomans are taking to the pen, and that not a few of them have talent. There is almost, indeed, an Oklahoma literature, or, at all events, an Oklahoma manner" ("Geographical Adventure That Reveals More 'Saharas of the Bozart,'" *Baltimore Evening Sun,* May 9, 1925, 9).

   Comparing Oklahoma's literature to that of contemporary New England "writers who apparently pull down the blinds before they begin to write," Mencken lauded it for "the sharp sense of reality, the gusto in life as it is being lived by actual people, the feeling for homely beauty and everyday drama." His critique immediately became a source of great pride among Oklahoma's writers. Ever since he was editor of *Smart Set*, he had given much encouragement to several of them, whom he published in his magazines. Muna Lee was a leading figure among them. Her early development as a poet was much influenced by both her personal and literary experience in Oklahoma. For more on the Oklahoma manner, see the following two studies: Lawrence R. Rodgers, "H. L. Mencken and the 'Oklahoma Style' of Literature," *Chronicles of Oklahoma* 78 (Winter 2000–2001): 468–83; and B. A. Botkin, "The 'Oklahoma Manner' in Poetry," *University of Oklahoma Magazine* 15 (November 1925): 27–31.

16. *Boston Evening Transcript*, September 29, 1923, 3.

17. Lee, *Sea-Change*, inscription to Mencken, May 13, 1923; Lee to Mencken, May 13, 1923, Mencken Papers.

18. Mary Reid, "Muna Lee: Poet and Feminist," *Holland's, the Magazine of the South* 59 (April 1940): 25.

19. Lee, "Poetry Every Day," *Four Talks on Writing*, 14.

20. Private collection of the author.

21. Lee, "Brother of Poe," *Southwest Review* 11 (July 1926): 310.

22. Harriet Monroe, "Pan-American Concord," *Poetry* 26 (June 1925): 155.

23. As quoted in Marable and Boylan, "Muna Lee," 68–69.

24. Horace Gregory, *The House on Jefferson Street* (New York: Holt, Reinhart and Winston, 1971), 167.

25. *New York Times Book Review*, June 20, 1926, 28; *American Review of Reviews* 74 (July 1926): 110; *Boston Evening Transcript*, June 5, 1926, 5; *New York Herald Tribune Books*, June 20, 1926, 18.

26. "Address Made by Muna Lee of the National Woman's Party, Porto Rico Branch, and the University of Porto Rico, in Behalf of Equal Rights Treaty before Unofficial Plenary Session of the Sixth Pan American Conference" (unpublished text), *National Woman's Party Papers, 1913–1972*, edited by Thomas C. Pardo, Reel 38 (Glenn Rock, N. J.: Microfilming Corporation of America, 1977).

27. As quoted in Lee, "Pan-American Women," *Nation* 126 (March 14, 1928): 295.

28. As quoted in Carmen T. Bernier-Grand, *Poet and Politician of Puerto Rico: Don Luis Muñoz Marín* (New York: Orchard, 1995), 46.

29. Lee to Luis Muñoz Marín, November 3, 1927, Luis Muñoz Marín Papers, 1926–28, New York Public Library, New York, N. Y.

30. As quoted in M. C. Blackman, "Muna Lee, Poet Was Wife of Luis Munoz Marin," *New York Herald Tribune*, April 4, 1965, 38.

31. Lee, "On Not Writing about Mauna Loa," *New York Herald Tribune*, March 4, 1936, 15.
    Lee was often teased about her name. In the November 1916 issue of *Poetry*, in which Lee's Lyric Prize was announced, the Correspondence section included another name-tease, titled "The Retort Courteous" and signed "L. U." (Louis Untermeyer): *"An imaginary conversation between two lady poets on the plains of Arizona, after perusing each other's manuscripts. / Said Mina Loy to Muna Lee, / 'I wish your style appealed to me.' / 'Yours gives me anything but joy!' / Said Muna Lee to Mina Loy."*

32. Gerald Guinness—son of Maurice Guinness—recalls that in the late 1920s his father

and friends, including Lee, occasionally climbed Puerto Rico's famous El Yunque mountain, scrambling or hacking their way up through the tropical rain forest there, and at the summit (about thirty-five hundred feet above sea level) they would picnic and bathe in the mountain pools.

33. *New Statesman and Nation* 11 (February 29, 1936): 316.

34. Newton Gayle (Maurice Guinness and Muna Lee), *Murder at 28:10* (New York: Scribner's, 1936), 26–27.

35. Lee's "An Indian Territory Childhood," which she published in two installments in the *University of Oklahoma Magazine* in November 1929 and January 1930, is a remnant of her experiment with writing an autobiographical novel. Interestingly, the structure of her novel was modeled after that of Pío Baroja's popular work, *Juventud, egolatría* (1917; *Youth and Egolatry*, trs. Jacob S. Fassett Jr. and Frances L. Phillips, 1920). See also her "Luis—and an Episode," *Smart Set* 58 (April 1919): 117–20.

36. Lee, "Eugenio María de Hostos: After One Hundred Years," *Books Abroad* 14 (1940): 128.

37. Correspondence of Lee and Dudley Fitts, 1941–46, unpublished letters in private collection of family. The exchange described here took place between September and November 1941.

38. William Carlos Williams to Lee, July 26, 1942, unpublished letter in private collection of family.

39. Jorge Carrera Andrade to Lee, March 6, 1943, Jorge Carrera Andrade Collection, Frank Melville Jr. Memorial Library, Stony Brook University, Stony Brook, N. Y.

40. John Peale Bishop to Allen Tate, January 17, 1943, *The Republic of Letters in America: The Correspondence of John Peale Bishop and Allen Tate*, edited by Thomas Daniel Young and John J. Hindle (Lexington: University Press of Kentucky, 1981), 200–201.

41. Lee to Bishop, January 8, 1943, unpublished letter in private collection of family.

42. As quoted in Arturo Torres-Ríoseco, *The Epic of Latin American Literature* (Berkeley: University of California Press, 1970), 6.

43. Lee, "The *American Story* Broadcast by Archibald MacLeish," manuscript in private collection of family.

44. As quoted in "NBC University of the Air Opens Course in Literature," *NBC* (February 1944): 1.

45. Archibald MacLeish, foreword, *The American Story: Ten Broadcasts* (New York: Duell, Sloan and Pearce, 1944), xii.

46. As quoted in Hughes, "Lee, Muna," 292.

47. Barbara Haddox, "Muna Lee—An Envoy for the Americas," *Ohio State Journal*, May 18, 1944.

48. Lee to José Coll Vidal (director, *El mundo*), September 25, 1945, "a true copy of the signed original" (ML), unpublished letter in private collection of family.

49. M. L. Rosenthal, "By an Ecuadorean Poet," *New York Herald Tribune Weekly Book Review*, April 6, 1947, 2.

50. Babette Deutsch, "Lyrics from Ecuador and New England," *New York Times Book Review*, February 16, 1947, 4.

51. *Yale Review* 36 (Autumn 1946): 150.

More high praise of Lee's translation came from Donald Walsh. In December 1946, at the annual meeting of the American Association of Teachers of Spanish and

Portuguese held in Washington, Walsh delivered a paper in which he reviewed the year's publishing activity in terms of Spanish American literature, and he closed with the following statement: "I have not included in this paper translations from Spanish American literature, but I must mention one book that is a literary event in both languages: Muna Lee's *Secret Country*, translations of thirty poems of Jorge Carrera Andrade, Ecuador's most famous poet. [. . .] Muna Lee has translated him with perfect understanding and with a poetic skill that matches, and at times exceeds, that of the poet himself. This slender volume must be ranked with that small group of translations that are true re-creations of great literature in a new language" (Donald Devenish Walsh, "Spanish American Literature in 1946," *Hispania* 30 [February 1947]: 26).

52. MacLeish to Lee, no date; Carl Sandburg to Lee, March 3, 1952; unpublished letters in private collection of family.

53. Lee, "An Ecuadoran Observes His World," review of *Registro del mundo*, by Jorge Carrera Andrade, *Poetry* 59 (February 1942): 282.

54. Lee to Bishop, February 2, 1943, unpublished letter in private collection of family.

55. Gladys Cornell Irwin to Lee, June 19, 1962, copy in federal personnel file, National Archives and Records Administration.

56. Lee to Muna Muñoz Lee, November 18, 1946, unpublished letter in private collection of family.

57. Ruth Emily McMurry and Muna Lee, *The Cultural Approach: Another Way in International Relations* (Chapel Hill: University of North Carolina Press, 1947; Port Washington, N. Y.: Kennikat Press, 1972), 247.

58. Lee to Amelia Hines Walker (national chair, National Woman's Party), November 3, 1954, copy in federal personnel file, National Archives and Records Administration.

59. Lee, "Spain and U.S. Writing," review of *The Spanish Background of American Literature*, by Stanley T. Williams, *Américas* 7 (October 1955): 42.

60. Archibald MacLeish, *Archibald MacLeish: Reflections*, edited by Bernard A. Drabeck and Helen E. Ellis (Amherst: University of Massachusetts Press, 1986), 157.

61. Muna Lee de Muñoz Marín reading her poems in the Recording Laboratory (sound recording), Archive of Recorded Poetry and Literature, Library of Congress, April 25, 1960.

62. Lee, "Two Seventeenth-Century Women: Mistress Anne Bradstreet and Sor Juana Inés de la Cruz," Steinman Poetry Lecture, Tufts University, April 13, 1960, unpublished manuscript in private collection of family.

63. Lee to Mencken, September 8, 1924, Mencken Papers.

64. M. L. Spector (executive director, Bureau of Inter-American Affairs) to Honor Awards Committee, Department of State, February 4, 1963, copy in federal personnel file, National Archives and Records Administration.

65. Muna Muñoz Lee (1920–79) did much translating for Oscar Lewis's books, among other projects. She married the Puerto Rican painter Julio Rosado del Valle and with him had three children, a son and two daughters, one of whom continues the family's feminine tradition of working as a professional Spanish-English translator.

66. *Library Journal* 95 (February 1, 1970): 507.

67. "Miss Lee Ends Distinguished Years at State," *Department of State News Letter* (March 1965): 41.

68. Lee's grave is located in the seaside cemetery of Old San Juan, Puerto Rico: Cementerio Santa María Magdalena de Pazzis. Plain and unadorned, it simply states her name and the years of her birth and death. An astonishing feature of this white marble tomb—not to be described here—awaits the visitor who wishes to pay homage to Lee at her final resting place.
69. Esther N. de Calvo (executive secretary, Inter-American Commission of Women) to Dean Rusk (U.S. Secretary of State), April 5, 1965, copy in federal personnel file, National Archives and Records Administration.
70. Ernest Kroll, "Muna Lee (1895–1965)," *Texas Quarterly* 20.4 (1977): 152.

Muna Lee around 1919. Courtesy of family of
Muna Lee.

Luis Muñoz-Marín in 1918, the year before he
met Lee. Used by permission of the Photographic
Archive at the Luis Muñoz-Marín Foundation, San
Juan, Puerto Rico.

Lee (right) with friend in Oklahoma City in 1924.
Courtesy of family of Muna Lee.

Lee in 1930. Courtesy of family of Muna Lee.

Lee (center) with her son and daughter, Luis and Muna
Muñoz Lee, in Washington, D.C., in 1942. Courtesy of
family of Muna Lee.

Lee at her writing desk in 1942. Courtesy of
family of Muna Lee.

Lee in San Juan in the late 1950s. Courtesy of family of Muna Lee.

Lee at her retirement ceremony in 1965.
Courtesy of family of Muna Lee.

Poetry

Rich Port

This desperately tilted plane of land, our island,
Toppling from its gaunt sea-rooted pillar,
Tilted ever more definitely toward the sea-floor,
Toward that bottomless rift in the floor of Mona Passage,
Slipping,
    sliding,
        creeping,
            ever more surely
This doomed beloved rock edging inch by inch with the earthquakes
Toward implacable disaster,
Some day will lurch, will plunge, the long tension ended,
And the ceibas and the yellow fortress and the lizards and the palm trees,
The wild beauty of mountain cliffs hung with blue morning-glories,
Immaculate cane-fields and cool breath of coffee-groves,
Thatched hovels and trolley cars and Ponce de León's palace,
Tree-ferns and flame-trees and frail white orchises,
My love and your pride,
All, all will lie in crushed indeterminate wreckage for a thousand thousand years
In the crevasse beneath the floor of Mona Passage,
With aeons of sea creatures moving lightly through heavy masses of water
Far above the nameless shattered shards
That in a year forgotten were you and I
        And flame-trees and Puerto Rico.

American Mercury, January 1930; the version here conforms to that of Lee's 1960
reading at the Library of Congress.

Of Writing Verse

When the granite mountain wavers into shadow
    Or streams like a banner on the sky,
When the green corn waving makes an ocean of the valley,
    Or a night of blackbirds rushes by;

It is hard to watch the changes of the mountain
    Or hear the exultation of the birds,
And stubbornly to grip the patient pen between my fingers
    Setting down my littleness in words.

Literary Digest, April 11, 1925

Planet

This midsea rock set in water as the spinning earth in air,
This planet of the constellated tropical islands where
Each looks across blue ocean as the stars across blue ether,
This rock is our world and we its slaves and lords together.
And history dwindles to a point in time as earth to this point in space,
And one moment captures them both and it is the moment that we face.

Commonweal, September 11, 1929

Hacienda

Afternoon in Don Efrén's field
Tastes of honey and cinnamon and cassava root
And is drowsily heavy with yield
Of thickly fledged furrow and groves of wild fruit.
Sun-colored with mango, night-colored with cane,
Pungent with rose-apple, drowsy with water,
It smells of roasting coffee and jasmine and rain,
Of fields plowed by the oxen of old Don Efrén—
And is sultry and still as Don Efrén's daughter.

Original title, "Porto Rican Hacienda"; *Commonweal*, June 11, 1930

Dies Irae

Since this hour is the worst, since I have found
    The doom long-dreaded, and found it can be borne,
For all that hope is trampled to the ground
    And the force in which I trusted fled and torn:

Why, I am still what I was one hour ago;
    What I was then, with this knowledge for new power—
Though ruin is swift and resurrection slow,
    This hour being worst, I shall be better in an hour!

New York Herald Tribune Books, May 5, 1929

Moonrise

Night is a steep black mountainside
    Thick with jasmine strewn;
Wearily up the craggy slope
    Flees the tired white moon.

She has no heart for jasmine flowers;
    She has no mind to rest:
Day will assail her from the east
    Whom she fled last night in the west.

Original title, "Puerto Rican Moonrise"; *Commonweal*,
May 26, 1933

On Going Ashore

I who have shivered in the moon before,
And seen different Aprils whiten the same tree,
How shall I swear that this is ultimate shore,
And not an island in an infinite sea?

There may be other isles where moons will waken
A world-old, world-young tremor in my blood.
My sail months hence or years hence may be shaken
Along the reaches of an alien flood.

But this is land, firm land, not mist nor shadow,
Whatever else has been or comes to be:
Here are green slope, and trees, and blossoming meadow,
On rock thrust up from bed-rock of the sea.

Original title, "On Discovering Land"; *American Mercury,* September
1928

Acacia Island

All the island over acacia trees are blooming,
Shaking out blond tresses upon the quivering air;
The breezes stumble drunkenly beneath their load of fragrance,
The yellow starlight tangles in the tossing yellow hair.
The Caribbean albatrosses fly through cloud on cloud of incense,
Incense lifts in topaz smoke to smoky hyacinth hills.
All the island over acacia trees are blooming,
Through all our island pulses their desperate sweetness shrills.
Acacia like a whisper, acacia like a clamor, acacia on the lowland and the salt
    land and the highland—
Thought tosses in the shaken mind as the trees' blond blossom tosses.
Dizzy with acacia on an intoxicated island
We plunge through clouds of perfume as plunge the albatrosses.

New Yorker, March 15, 1930

Night of San Juan

Moonlight prints the trinitaria leaves
Velvet-brown on the white-plastered wall, and on the dark door-casing,
Velvet-black;
Moonlight makes a gyring series of shadowy planes
Of the flame tree's widespread, detached airiness of boughs;
Moonlight picks out a cheek, a lace-clad shoulder, glides across a shirtfront icily;
The porch is cool and clear with the tropical moonlight and the voices clear
    and cool;
Talk flows in eddying ripples, pleasant, discursive;
Now and again a silver wave of talk drowns the ripples;
And all is of a pattern with the moonlight, calm and lovely.
And I listen or answer and watch the swaying leaves
While my heart runs up St. Joseph's Street and flees down the Street of the Moon,
And along the Street of the Holy Christ to the wall by the moon-whitened sea,
And back down the Street of the Cross and past the narrow, dark Street of
    St. Francis,
To turn to the café window and stand there, in the Street of St. Just,
Peering in at round tables circled with smoke, spicy with chocolate and
    cinnamon, clamorous with argument;
While my heart turns despairing to feel its way blindly along the steep, yellow
    walls of the ancient, useless fort;
While my heart, like a town crier, rings its bell on every corner to find you
    not there,
And cries your name—your name—your name—
To the rolling, unresting, moon-smitten sea,
Calling in answer its long, inflected, meaningless syllable hopelessly repeated
As moonlight prints the trinitaria leaves
Velvet-brown on the white-plastered wall, and on the dark door-casing,
Velvet-black.

New Yorker, September 5, 1931

Atavian

And I, a woman of the twentieth century, am well aware
That all my love for you is an anachronism,
Something Byronic, Tennysonian, with even a dash of Felicia Hemans,
And something of "Friendship's Garland" and something of the Napoleonic wars.
> It is an anachronism, my love for you; it might be worked into mournful
> willowwreaths of hair, or expressed by a sonnet sequence in feminine
> rhymes and couplet ending:
> It might mold its desires chastely into a garland of waxen fruit, perfect in
> form and color, lifeless, ornamental, useless;
> It might be built into a pseudo-Gothic castle, turrets and ghost and
> drawbridge all complete;
> It might be Elizabethan-Arcadian or Victorian-Olympian; any sad, foolish,
> extravagant thing
> Of an age that took its sentimental folly seriously.
But you, product of this century,
Your mind a by-product of its mad towns, of New York and Madrid, London
and Paris,
What, in the name of the four cities, could you ever do with my love?
And why cannot I follow the mode of my great-grandmother closer still
> And lay the silly thing away
> With a silly tear in its folds,
> And in the riband neatly clasping it,
> One little, pompous, declarative immortelle?

New Yorker, August 22, 1931

Caribbean Marsh

Acres of mangrove, crowding the sea-streaked marsh,
Acres of mangrove, wading toward the beaches,
And here and there a milky-white bloom tossed
On fragile boughs above the flooded reaches.
　　Mangrove thrusts deep in salty mud,
Balances uneasily upon its three-pronged roots,
Huddles from wind in its dissonance of leaves.
Tempest and drought it has withstood,
This straggling orchard that bears no fruits,
This field where none will garner sheaves.
Sucking life up from the acrid marsh,
Drawing life down from the burning sun,
All the year offers of crude and harsh
There between sea and shore it has known.
　　Wave and glare, sea-urge, sea-drift,
It has been their victim, proved their power,
Persisting bleakly for one end alone—
　　Through an unheeded hour
　　Briefly, awkwardly, to lift
This frail, inconsequent flower.

New Yorker, January 7, 1933

Visitant

And have you seen Persephone
(No maiden, yet not woman quite),
Wrested from hell but yesterday,
Restored to earth, restored to light,
Lissom, lovely, young, and free—
Free to rejoice, as well she may—
Ah, have you seen Persephone?

So strange she is, so wan and slight.

She plucks a flower, she flings a ball;
Peers, curious, when the blackbirds call;
Curious, pores on blossoming grass—
Rescued from horror and dark alarms,
Torn last night from Pluto's arms—
Have you watched that lady pass?

Persephone among the flowers,
Persephone beneath the sun,
Moves pensively through honeyed hours,
Moves absently, as one aware
Of life's reality otherwhere.
Fleeing the hill, she haunts the glade
(So bright the sun, so keen the air);
Persephone seeks cedar-shade
As one too wearied of much sun—
Any would have sworn she said,
        "When will these dragging months be done!"

New Yorker, March 18, 1933

Deliverance

I am my own now, never need there be telling
Of the thought that lures and lingers and brightens the mind's dark crevice;
Nevermore the difficult choosing of words to make words plainer;
I am my own now, my silence a proud possession;
From the crags and crannies of silence never need there be dispossession.
If the awful apocalyptic vision flare and thunder about me,
Only within myself need I seek for a clue and a meaning;
I may pick windflowers in the fields, showing none how earth has stained purple
The underleaf close to the ground; I may walk in the rain and the dark.
I am my own, and no other can stand between me and the mountains:
Beauty savored slowly in quiet replaces the haste and the voices.

American Mercury, May 1933

Caríb Garden

So I shall plant wild-rose seed in my tropic garden—
Cherokee roses from Mississippi, ivory cups on a thorny hedge;
Pale pink roses from Oklahoma, trailers from the limestone ledge;
Prairie bushes, mountain climbers, rose-red, rose-white, single-petaled,
With the winy wild-rose smell.
In among my tropic lilies, by the frilly-bloomed hibiscus,
With camellias, frangipani, ylang-ylang, and stephanotis,
I shall plant my prairie roses, hillside roses, meadow roses,
The southland western Yankee roses
A prairie childhood knew so well.

New Yorker, January 13, 1934

Stalactite

In the heart's most stony cave,
Roofed from storm, floored from wave,
Stalagmites lift, stalactites drip
Mist and diamond, ice and flame
In forms intricate without name.
Blossoms of snow and jewel shine
By brink of fiery waterfalls;
Pendant clusters, gleaming lusters,
Sparkling tendril and gleaming vine;
Shimmering gardens along the walls,
Brilliant, airy, radiant, fairy,
Crystalline jungles bright and tall,
Delicate, durable, sculptural;
Glittering thickets of beauty grown
From mute eternal weeping of the stone.

New Yorker, June 23, 1934

Deserted Orchard

The gnarled and twisted orchard trees,
    Their years of bearing done,
Feel the thin sap rise and stir
    Beneath the April sun.

Oh, pitiful! they shake their limbs
    In the old ecstatic dance
And wreathe themselves in rose and green,
    And seize the breeze's chance.

They dance and toss their wizened boughs,
    Grotesque and tortured things—
Why can they not find calm at last
    After so many springs?

New Yorker, April 29, 1933

Albatross

Seventeen albatrosses rose from their wave-washed rock with thunderous wings
    outspread;
Together they crashed down heavily, shattering the sea's smooth plane.
Seventeen albatrosses veered and wheeled into intricate pattern overhead;
Then on the beach, hushed from our talking, we watched giant wings beat the
    waves into rain.

We have no memory of sorrow shared, nor mutual memory of joy we inherit;
Life has denied us everything but the intolerable sense of loss:
But through all the sundering years we shall meet, fleetingly, spirit with spirit,
When either sees dark, on the sea, in the sky, the splendid bronze wings of an
    albatross.

New Yorker, April 12, 1930

Wayfarer

Bewildered by calm, mazed by the plain,
I lack the rampart of hurricane;
In motionless air I am like to fall,
Who had leant on the blast as on a wall;
Accustomed to storm, I cannot find
Perfect balance without the wind:
Now I walk safe and now I walk warm,
But I was conditioned to storm, to storm.

New Yorker, December 19, 1931

Summertime Notation in a Troubled World

The crashing world is not enough
To wreak the raptured heart of love.
The smoking hills, the falling skies
Conceal love not from the lover's eyes.
Not unaware, not seeking cover,
Not led from reason by unreason,
Love flees no truth nor plots no treason,
But love is first fact to the lover.

Unpublished manuscript; original title, "Notation in Summer, 1948"

Apology for All That Blooms in Time of Crisis

Uninventive child of dust,
The flower, responding as it must,
Even under skies of doom
Finds no other way than bloom;
Catastrophic though this hour
When faith nor fact nor hope nor reason
Will alter rigors of its season,
It can no more, it could no less,
Than strive to be itself, a flower:
In that its fate, in that its pleasure,
Its only given way to measure
Existence as not nothingness.

Unpublished manuscript

Nightpiece

Fiery petals dimmed to ash, upon thick boughs the thick moon shone,
Color lost itself in form and form in shade—
White blossoms like white moths through tropic dusk were blown.
With stephanotis, clerodendron, silver lace vine overlaid,
Angled hedge and swerving terrace in a chequered pattern met;
Puff and whorl of alabaster, bars and lozenges of jet,
Sheathed gardenia in deep shadow, flared camellia in pale light,
Hour through silent moonstruck hour, white on black, black on white.

Unpublished manuscript

By the Caribbean One Remembers the Prairie

The prairie tossed about like a sea,
The little town, islanded in the vast
Of moving green, or, with the summer past,
Of bare brown levels empty of a tree.
North, South, East, West—far as the eye could see
Rolled dun monotony, until at last
Where hard planes dimmed, grew vague, were overcast,

The prairie plunged into immensity.
It was an island, self-contained and lonely;
A port that never saw the naked spars
Of a great ship beneath the gliding stars,
Nor crowding sail against the sunset flame;
In all an island, save in this thing only—
Across those seas no vessel ever came.

University of Oklahoma Magazine, November 1929

Mushroom Town

Composed in the months immediately after the publication of *Sea-Change*, this sequence of eight sonnets originally appeared in the April 1924 issue of H. L. Mencken's *American Mercury*. The title refers to Hugo, Oklahoma, where Lee spent several years of her childhood during the first decade of the twentieth century. In a letter sent to Mencken dated November 5, 1923, and written at her home in Teaneck, New Jersey, she expressed her gratitude for his interest and guidance that encouraged this particular poetic venture. An excerpt from the letter illuminates not only the sequence but also Lee's sense of herself as a poet and her ongoing relationship with Mencken as a mentor: "I am more glad than I can say that you found the Indian Territory sonnets worth working at: the characters and experiences they evoke are so vivid to me that it was impossible to judge them with any critical detachment; yet if they are not good, I can never do anything that is. [. . .] It is very hard to do them unsentimentally. Besides the ones you saw, only 'The Methodist Revival' is finished (it came out very well) and there is still to do—for instance—the sonnet on rain. It baffles me to express straightforwardly and convincingly what the long-expected, long-delayed tempests of rain meant to a child in a treeless prairie town far from the sea, far from lakes and mountains and rivers; a town to which water was brought in barrels and every drop was hoarded. What a child felt for rain in those towns and in those days was a passionate pagan adoration" (Muna Lee to H. L. Mencken, November 5, 1923, H. L. Mencken Papers, 1905–56, New York Public Library, New York, N. Y.).

I. THE DRUGSTORE

A door with blurred panes swung aside to show
The cavernous room, across whose muffled scents
Came sudden drifts, volatile and intense,
Of pennyroyal or tansy. A smeary row,
Cases of soaps and notions stood before
Long, gleaming shelves of jars in sapphire glass.
Below were drawers—salts, sulphur, copperas.
The soda-taps dripped sirops by the door.

And pent in every jar, a bewildering djinn:
Linden—among whose crackling light-brown leaves
Still clung small blossoms from a foreign tree;
Sesame—flat seeds known to the Forty Thieves—
A child for hours could peer and find within
Spoil of far lands and islands of the sea.

II. ELECTORS

The drugstore was a club, in whose talk took part
Tall men, slouch-hatted, neither old nor young—
Men who had failed elsewhere, and who had wrung
Stakes from scant capital for another start.
Not hopeless men: here was a junction which
Ensured a Harvey Eating House; next year
Congress would pass the Enabling Act; right here
Would be a metropolis: they would all be rich.

These consummations meanwhile they awaited
In the drugstore, talking politics till night.
Texans, farmers, and carpet-baggers they hated;
Feared the Negro—"This state should be lily-white,"
And arguments to damn whatever scheme
Were the epithets "Utopia" and "dream."

III. AUGUST

Day after day the treeless street was baked
By intolerable sun. The moulded wagon-tracks
Were rayed and rifted by the widening cracks.
Through wavering blurs of heat the red bricks ached.
Drouth made the plain stretch flatter and more wide.
There was no dew in August, there was no shade.
Upon the lake the Commercial Club had made
Hundreds of dead fish floated on their side.

Walking the sweltering street, "wet leaves," one said.
"Rainy leaves," "drenched leaves"—oh words like rillets stealing
Amongst the tortured brain's heat-tangled mazes.
"Drenched leaves," "wet leaves"—savoring the words of healing
For crisp forgetful moments the spirit fed
Upon cool freshness of the cress-like phrases.

IV. THE DUELISTS

On Landau's corner, the loafers saw them fall.
Meeting, each drew with an oath; they fired together,
And each fell dying without knowing whether
His enemy fell too. And that was all.
The town threshed through the story, nothing loath—
Simple enough, they told it over and over:
How Billy Ascham was the woman's lover,
The Doctor's wife's; the Doctor had warned them both.

Afterwards, when the town forgot at last,
Not nudging nor whispering even when the woman passed
With that hard, veiled look of hers, one child still thought
With dull, perplexing pain, for a long while,
Of a trick with matches that Mr. Ascham taught,
And of the red-haired Doctor's freckly smile.

Original title, "Murderers"

V. THE CARNIVAL

The carnival came late to town that year,
Tents pitched forlornly in the baseball park,
Where a cold wind extinguished every spark
Of merry-making. A ferris-wheel, austere
In skeleton loneliness, viewed vacant grounds.
It rained continuously, a dreary, chill
September drizzle. The merry-go-round was still;
Half-hearted spiels and catcalls the only sounds.

My brother and I, small, shivering wretches beneath
Our papery coats, stood with chattering teeth,
Drinking in pleasure desired through arid days
As we watched a draggled woman lift to our gaze
Grisly tentacles of the octopus, and explain,
"This one killed three sailors off the coast of Spain . . ."

VI. THE BLACKSMITH'S WIFE

Around Mrs. Hastings' house, verbena grew.
She coaxed her roses from reluctant earth,
And tenderly nursed jessamine to birth,
And through long drouth, her iris-plot was blue.
She told of an Irish childhood; of hopeless hours
Waiting tables in Dallas; of how the saints one day
Had sent Sam Hastings to snatch her far away
And build the yellow house amid the flowers.

Sam and her boy—coarse as the hides they tanned,
Gamblers and drunkards and foul-mouthed fools—no less—
Were tinged with romance by her tenderness.
"I would not die before them!" the soft voice said.
"How could I bear that an unloving hand
Should bathe and tend the bodies of my dead!"

Original title, "Mrs. Hastings"

VII. THE REVIVAL

When the throbbing drums of the opening hymns were still,
The preacher shouted, "Brethren! let us pray!"
And ardently he pled that God that day
Might bend an hundred sinners to His will.
The prayer ended, he touched a lighter note—
Joked with the choir, and merrily mocked the Devil;
Then flung God's curse at the drunken nation's revel
With a voice that sobbed and fluted in his throat.

"Oh, my beloved . . . !" he launched his passionate pleas.
A woman stood. "Praise Jesus!" shrieked another,
A girl ran sobbing and knelt beside her mother.
At a sudden word, again the music swept
The tent with thunder. Quivering, one wept,
Wretched, and shamed, and groveling on one's knees.

Original title, "Methodist Revival"

VIII. PRAIRIE SKY

Sometimes for days one can forget the sky
That god-like, indifferent, never fails to bless
With unflawed beauty our huddled littleness.
One can forget—the meddling breeze goes by
Piling vacant lots with waste to catch the eye;
Or mud, or dust, or merely the heat that shows
In quivering air, can make the senses close
To everything that is far or vast or high.

Then a scrap, a bird, the casual glance beguiles
Up, up, up!—till once more, swiftly, surely,
The clean, keen blade of ecstasy stabs purely:
Oh, glorious blue across which clouds are blowing,
Or lucent gray the far rain-tempests showing,
Or sunset blazing for ten thousand miles!

The Thought of You

The thought of you is taller than the sunset
Flaming up above the world's crumbling edges.
The thought of you is shyer than the lizard
In a cleft of the limestone ledges.

The thought of you is wilder than the wild birds
Whose only joy is in their own wild flying;
The thought of you is lovelier than starlight
And sadder than a young child's dying.

Sea-Change, 1923; *Smart Set*, January 1917

The Stars Are Colored Blossoms

The stars are colored blossoms on a storm-shaken tree,
The moon a wanton shepherdess that wanders apart.
Night spreads out before us like a dark gleaming sea,
And this glamour of the moonlight is a thing to shake the heart.

I cannot flee beyond you; you are waiting when I come,
Companion of the far white moon, comrade of the dew.
I shiver in the moonlight—though my lips are sealed and dumb,
My heart is torn asunder with desire and fear of you.

Sea-Change, 1923; *Smart Set,* November 1916

Lips You Were Not Anhungered For

Lips you were not anhungered for,
    And those that won your praises,
A century hence will blossom out
    In careless purple daisies.

Eyes that smiled lightly into yours,
    And eyes that wept for you—
Ah, soon, not Love himself might know
    The brown eyes from the blue.

For even he will come to dust,
    And even longing passes,
That crumbling flesh may feed the growth
    Of the hungry-rooted grasses.

Sea-Change, 1923; *Poetry*, January 1916

Survival

There would be no this year's flower there
    If we went back;
They have ploughed the anemones and bluets under,
    Wheat grows down to the track.

The stream is widened and dammed across,
    There's a house on the hill.
There is nothing left of the spring we found there,
    Wild and still.

It is all changed as you and I,
    Changed and torn away—
But cool and fragrant and fresh as rain
    Is the song I made that day!

Sea-Change, 1923; *Smart Set*, May 1920

April Wind

The wind-flowers fluttered purple and white
    The maple-leaves blossomed with sun;
The redbud blazed from the winding creek,
    And the willow's loose hair was undone.

And because I was in love with the sun and the wind
    And the spring blooming strange and new,
I stopped on the wind-ruffled crest of the hill
    And lifted my lips to you.

Sea-Change, 1923

I Have Had Enough of Glamour

I have had enough of glamour,
    Of dawn, and violet dusk, and stars,
Of crimson banners flaming and floating
    Over vague and perilous wars;

I am tired of moonlight and water,
    Of the violins and bugles of youth;
I have had romance and proud, pale sorrow—
    Now I should like the truth!

Sea-Change, 1923; *Smart Set*, February 1919; original title, "Song"

A Woman's Song

This is my wrong, if wrong I have done you—
    I who had all to give
And would have showered all on you
    That love might teach us to live—

When you asked for a loaf of my baking
    And a bit of blossomy spray,
Gave only these for your taking,
    And hid the rest away.

Sea-Change, 1923; *Poetry,* August 1917

Choice

I set on this barren board
    (Yours is the choice, not mine)
The bread and leeks for your hunger's ease,
    The unacknowledged wine.

No protests—no demands—
    Always there shall be
The driftwood fire that warms your hands,
    The stars you will not see.

Sea-Change, 1923; *Liberator,* October 1920

Gifts

These are but words, and I have more than these to give you:
    I have moments to give you, delicate as fern-leaves,
    Cloudy and clear as quartz,
    Colored like rose-hips and wild grasses,
    Various as the infinite rain.

    I have hours to give you like stretches of shell-strewn beach,
        (The sea within sight, within sound)—
And hours when there are no shells, no beach,
    But only sea.

    I have years to give you:

These are but words.

Sea-Change, 1923; Current Opinion, July 1923

Imprisoned

I

Do not chafe at your bonds, dear:
It is only my heart that holds you;
That is easily broken.

II

I was sent from a far country that I might bear one message:
You will neither hear it nor let me return.

III

I thought love would come gloriously,
With the blare of trumpets and ruffle of silver bugles,
Lighting the night with his pageantry.
And I found him in two sad eyes so tired they could not look on mine.

IV

In our town
There are painted wooden houses, one dusty park, and I.
Each year we grow more faded,
More hopeless,
More alike—
The houses, the park, and I.

Sea-Change, 1923; Others, May-June 1916

The Confidante

Has no one a gift to bring to you,
    My heart,
So wearied, so listless? Why,
    I shall sing to you,
      My heart,
        I, I!

Sea-Change, 1923; *Others*, May-June 1916

Mid-Western

Whatever Aprils I may know,
　　April will always mean to me
A wet bank dark with violets,
　　A whitely-blossoming locust tree.

And the rough furrows of the plain
　　Could call me laughing from defeat,
Remembering like a battle shout
　　The lyric of the winter wheat!

Sea-Change, 1923

Tropic Rain

The blue lagoon is a sudden gray,
    The tallest palm sways in the breeze,
And petals in sodden purple heaps
    Pile up beneath the China trees.

Rose and hibiscus droop in rags,
    The swift drops splash against the wall;
And on the courtyard's yellow tiles,
    One after one the almonds fall.

Then the gray lagoon is a sudden blue,
    The downpour stops, the wind is dead;
And from an oleander trunk,
    A jet-black lizard lifts its head.

Sea-Change, 1923

A Song of Dreams Come True

My love was born on a tropic coast
        And I, far from the sea;
But the ardent eyes of my lover
        Know the dreams that came to me
When I longed for wide blue waters
        And great winds flung out free.

And the magic words of my lover
        Are the songs I tried to sing
When my heart grew sick for green hill-tops
        In the midst of the arid spring
That brought no rain to the wheat-stalks,
        Nor brought me anything.

He is tall as a palm, is my lover.
        As a flame-tree, vivid is he.
Dusk and fire is his utterance;
        And about and over me
Are the warm soft wings of the trade winds
        That blow from the tropic sea.

Sea-Change, 1923

The Seeker

I who had sought God blindly in the skies—
Listening for heaven to thunder forth my name,
Waiting for doves descending to my head,
Looking to see the bushes burst in flame—

Went from the temple with a weary throng
Of questions in my soul, and told my grief
To the heart of the yellow flower with the scent
Of citrus clinging to its pointed leaf.

Sea-Change, 1923; *Poetry,* January 1916

Verse Translation

Running Water

ALFONSINA STORNI
Argentina, 1892–1938

Yes, I move, I live, I wander astray—
    Water running, intermingling, over the sands.
I know the passionate pleasure of motion;
    I taste the forests, I touch strange lands.

Yes, I move—perhaps I am seeking
    Storms, suns, dawns, a place to hide.
What are you doing here, pale and polished—
    You, the stone in the path of the tide?

Poetry, June 1925

You Say I Forget You, Celio

SOR JUANA INÉS DE LA CRUZ
Mexico, 1651–95

You say I forget you, Celio, and you lie
In saying that I remember to forget you.
For within my thoughts there is no place left you
Wherein—even forgotten—to stand by.

Forgetfulness must take some memory's place
As the ash must be preceded by the ember.
But you have never won so great a grace:
There's nothing to forget nor to remember.

If you could be forgotten you might find
Joy to have been once remembered—even glory
Might fleetingly have known of being loved.
But so far are you from any such proud story,
Unremembering you not forgetfulness is proved
But merely a negation of the mind.

Unpublished manuscript

The Rose

SOR JUANA INÉS DE LA CRUZ

Rose divine, of gentle nurture,
With fragrant subtlety you are
Beauty's crimsoned avatar,
Snowy lore for grace's culture.

Image of our human doom,
Loveliness born to be blighted,
In whom nature has united
Happy cradle, mournful tomb.

How proud, how arrogant, in your disdain
You scorn the thought that you might chance to die;
Then when your petals shrunk and faded lie
What withered symbols of your fate are plain!
Thus with wise death and foolish life you may
Living, mislead us, but dying, show the way.

Unpublished manuscript

Love

JAIME TORRES BODET
Mexico, 1902–74

In order to escape you,
stairs are no longer enough,
nor tunnels, nor airplanes,
telephones, nor ships.
All that accompanies
the man escaping:
silence, speech,
the trains and the years,—
avails not to flee
from this precise corner—
without clock or hours
or windows or pictures—
that goes with me
wherever I go.

In order to escape you
I need a weariness
born of you yourself:
a doubt or a rancor,
the shame of a weeping;
the fear that I felt
(for example) shaping
unfitly with my lips,
harsh and brusque,
your frail name. . . .

The hatred that I sensed
being born simultaneously
in you with our love,
will thrust me forth from your soul
sooner than light,
quicker than dream,
with greater precision

than the swiftest elevator:
the hatred which love
hides between its hands.

Anthology of Contemporary Latin-American Poetry, New Directions, 1942

Proletarians

LUIS MUÑOZ MARÍN
Puerto Rico, 1898–1980

A donkey
ascending a mountain,
slowly,
vibrating under the weight of the saddlebags.
  (His optimist ears
  slant toward the summit.)

A bricklayer
setting brick upon brick.
  (His humming is monotonous,
  interminable.)

God,
hard at work with the stars.
  (His silence is profound.)

Anthology of Contemporary Latin-American Poetry, New Directions,
1942

Pamphlet

LUIS MUÑOZ MARÍN

I have broken the rainbow
against my heart
as one breaks a useless sword against a knee.
I have blown the clouds of rose color and blood color
beyond the farthest horizons.
I have drowned my dreams
in order to glut the dreams that sleep for me in the veins
of men who sweated and wept and raged
to season my coffee . . .

The dream that sleeps in breasts stifled by tuberculosis
    (A little air, a little sunshine!);
the dream that dreams in stomachs strangled by hunger
    (A bit of bread, a bit of white bread!);
the dream of bare feet
    (Fewer stones on the road, Lord, fewer broken bottles!);
the dream of calloused hands
    (Moss . . . clean cambric . . . things smooth, soft, soothing!)
The dream of trampled hearts
    (Love . . . Life . . . Life! . . .)

I am the pamphleteer of God,
God's agitator,
and I go with the mob of stars and hungry men
toward the great dawn . . .

Anthology of Contemporary Latin-American Poetry, New Directions, 1942

Brother Dog

LUIS ANÍBAL SÁNCHEZ
Ecuador, 1902–22

In the enormous tragic silence of the night, Francis, the monk of Assisi, with
sunken eyes of immense tenderness, caressed the white body, the snow-white
body, of a poor dog that died in the war.

To that body which had no soul, but which felt much, loved much, suffered
much, Francis has given a tear and infinite pity.

Francis has wept, while afar nations made war.

It is the apocalyptic hour. Humanity is condensed into one long shriek. Hate
asserts its supremacy. The great red cataclysm sows earth with tears and
blood; tears of the child and of the beloved, and ancient crystallized tears of
the venerable mothers who weep in dark alcoves where the cat whines
sybaritically without knowing why.

Before the white body of the poor dog slain by chance bullets, the divine Francis
wept.

Poetry, June 1925

Horses of the Conquistadores

JOSÉ SANTOS CHOCANO
Peru, 1875–1934

The horses were strong!
The horses were eager!
Their necks finely-arched; and shining
Their flanks; and musical their hoof-beats.
    The horses were strong!
    The horses were ready!

No, not the warriors only,
With plumes and cuirasses and fire-brands and banners,
Conquered the primitive forests and the Andes:
The horses of Andalusia, whose sinews
Had sparks of the flying race of the Arabs,
Stamped their glorious hoof-prints
    Upon the dry lava-fields,
    Upon the wet marsh-lands,
    Upon shores of loud rivers
    And upon silent snows;
Upon the pampas, the mountains, the woods and the valleys.
    The horses were strong!
    The horses were eager!

A horse was the first among the parched thickets
When Balboa's followers awoke sleeping solitudes,
Who gave on a sudden the warning
Of the Pacific Ocean ahead
Because the breeze wafted to his nostrils
A salt whiff of the sea.
And the horse of Quesada that on the summit
Paused, seeing in depths of the valley
The brandishing whip of the torrent
Like an angry savage's gesture,
Saluted first with his whinny
The interminable savannahs;
Then descended with easy trot

The stony stairs of the Andes,
As if by a thousand steps
Creaking under the musical beat of the hoofs.
     The horses were strong!
     The horses were eager!

And he of the mighty girth,
Rearing as if to add to his stature,
Upon whom Hernando Cortez,
The knight of the glittering stirrups,
Measured leagues and weeks among rocks and woods—
     Worthier he of laurels
Than colts galloping in the triumphal songs
With which Pindar celebrated the Olympics
Among flying chariots and rushing winds.

     Worthier still of immortal odes
The horse upon which De Soto,
Dexterously controlling its capers,
Frightened, astounded, overcame
The chorus of Indians, among whom—
None daring a gesture—he pressed
To the very throne of Atahualpa,
And spattered with froth the royal insignia.
     The horses were strong!
     The horses were ready!

     The horse of the Bedouin,
     Swallowing the deserts;
The miraculous horse of St. George,
Which crushed with its hoofs hellish dragons;
     That of Caesar in Gaul;
     Of Hannibal in the Alps;
The Centaur of classic legend,
Half-steed, half-man, who gallops without tiring,
Dreams without sleeping,
Darts at the stars and out-strips the breeze:
     All these have less spirit,
     Less vigor, less nobility,
Than the epic horses of Andalusia

In the lands of the wild Atlantides,
 Enduring fatigue, spurring and hunger,
Under the weight of the iron armor,
Between the fringe of the great banners,
Like a procession of heroism, crowned
With Babieca's glory and Rosinante's pain.
In the midst of decisive clamors of combat,
Under their breasts the horses
Bore down the Indians and pressed forward.
Often—to the shout of "Santiago!"—
Amid the smoke and glitter of metals,
Was seen to pass like a vision
The horse of the Apostle galloping through the air!
 The horses were strong!
 The horses were eager!

An epic should be made of hero horses,
Who, as wingless hippogriffs,
Or as a river flung out from the Andes—
All of them come, weary, bedraggled,
From lands never seen
And from other, accessible lands;
And suddenly startled by a horn
Puffed out with hurricanes—
Give nervously such a deep neighing
That it promises to endure forever;
And then, on the boundless pampas,
View the solemn distances,
Feel the lure of far-off horizons, climb again the ages,
Crowd together, pawing and sniffing . . . and are off head-long!—
Behind them a cloud,
The cloud of glory rising in the air!
 The horses were strong!
 The horses were eager!

Poetry, June 1925

Nameless Islands

JORGE CARRERA ANDRADE
Ecuador, 1902–78

The canoe which returns
with its harvest of seaweed
on the sand relates
its salty adventure—

endless yawn of the oysters—
The pines talk together
and with all their eyes
peer through the bark,

but see only ravens,
since these are their islands,
the lands which hidden
corpses inhabit,

where days are that row
unhasting to the horizon,
and glowworms devouring
coiled sea-snails;

cities in ruin
besieged by their dead;
rains dressed in green,
sowers of insects;

and little women
who live upon eels
and the minuscule fishes
of the mild bays;

where the typhoon looses
wild colts of the sea,
overwhelming pines and not the worm,
small chain of dust;

islands where silence
is the highest offering
in a night that is leather and straining eyes,
coffins and seaweed;

isles deafened by the wind,
inhabited by shadows,
like a country lost
in gray marches of memory.

Secret Country, Macmillan, 1946

Sunday

JORGE CARRERA ANDRADE

Fruit-vendor church,
seated at a corner of life:
glass oranges of the windows,
organ of sugar-cane stalks.

Angels: fluffy chicks
of Mother Mary.

The little blue-eyed bell
runs out barefoot
to scamper over the countryside.

Sun-dial;
angelical donkey with its innocent sex;
wind, Sunday's good errand-boy
bringing news from the hill;
Indians with loads of vegetables
bound to their foreheads.

The sky rolls up its eyes
when the little barefoot bell
comes scampering out of the church.

Secret Country, Macmillan, 1946

The Guest

JORGE CARRERA ANDRADE

Against the huge black door of night
twelve knocks resound.

Men sit up in their beds:
dread glides over them with its scales of ice.

Who is it? Through the house
fear goes with bare feet.

Men see the flame of their lamps
go out at the sound of the knockings:

the unknown guest is calling
and a blue flicker runs along their eyelids.

Secret Country, Macmillan, 1946

Vocation of the Mirror

JORGE CARRERA ANDRADE

When things forget their form and their color
and, beset by night, the walls retire
and all things kneel, yield, or are confused,
you alone, luminous presence, stay upright.

You impose on the shadows your clear will.
In the darkness shimmers your metallic silence.
Like a sudden flight of doves
you convey to things your secret messages.

Every chair, grown taller in the night, awaits
an unreal guest before a plate of shade,
and only you, transparent witness,
repeat by rote a lesson of light.

Secret Country, Macmillan, 1946

Place of Origin

JORGE CARRERA ANDRADE

I come from the land where the custard-apple—
that brocade bag—with its rind prevents
the spilling of sweetness from its rounded snow;

where the avocado with its polished green skin
elaborates in secret within its oval enclosure
a substance of flowers, fibres and climates.

Land nurturing birds, apprentices at languages,
plants that yield brews of love and death,
the magic of dreams or joyous strength;

tender little animals full of flavor and laziness,
tiny insects of green flesh and music,
metallic light, or petals that fly.

Capulí—cherry of the mid-Andean Indians—
quail, the chasing armadillo, the tough frond
sentenced to fire, or to be net or garment;

the eucalyptus with branches like strings of fish—
soldier of health with an armor of leaves
deploying on the air his heavenly battalions;

they are the tamed allies of the man of the land
whence I come, free, with my lessons of winds
and my cargo of birds who speak all languages.

Secret Country, Macmillan, 1946

Nameless District

JORGE CARRERA ANDRADE

In my district there are groups of houses and cattle,
sacks of cloud that pour forth silver kernels of sleet,
a sky that suddenly opens and closes its showcases,
pumpkins heavy with dream that drowse by the roadside,
a torrent emerging from a counterfeiter's cave,
morning vegetables traveling to town on muleback,
all the insects escaped from the multiplication table,
and air that at every hour fondles the fruit.

In my district the flowers offer up in their tiny open hands
or in their little close-shut fists,
the essence of earth's silence.
A cascade juggles its mirrors,
hurling its lambs of water
like a flock over a mountain-pass.

In my district the neighbors know about horses,
the forge imitates the tones of a bell,
the sentinel frogs give warning
when the rain hops by on its stilts;
under the color-organ of the sky
kneel the innumerable barley
and the far-off horizon is an ox
meditatively ruminating distances.

Secret Country, Macmillan, 1946

Biography for the Use of the Birds

JORGE CARRERA ANDRADE

I was born in the century of the death of the rose
when the motor had already driven out the angels.
Quito watched the last stagecoach roll,
and at its passing the trees ran by in good order,
and the hedges and houses of the new parishes,
on the threshold of the country
where slow cows were ruminating the silence
and the wind spurred its swift horses.

My mother, clothed in the setting sun,
put away her youth in a deep guitar,
and only on certain evenings would she show it to her children,
sheathed in music, light, and words.
I loved the hydrography of the rain,
the yellow fleas on the apple tree,
and the toads that would sound from time to time
their thick wooden bells.

The great sail of air maneuvered endlessly.
The cordillera was a shore of the sky.
The storm would come, and at the drum-roll
its drenched regiments would charge;
but then the sun with its golden patrols
would bring back translucent peace to the fields.
I would watch men clasp the barley,
horsemen sink into the sky,
and the laden wagons with lowing oxen
go down to the mango-fragrant coast.

The valley was there with its farms
where dawn touched off its trickle of roosters,
and westward was the land where the sugarcane
waved its peaceful banner, and the cacao
held close in a coffer its secret fortune,

and the pineapple girded on the fragrant cuirass,
the nude banana her silken tunic.

It has all passed in successive waves,
as the vain foam-figures pass.
The years go without haste entangling their lichens,
and memory is scarcely a water-lily
that lifts between two waters
its drowned face.
The guitar is only a coffin for songs,
and the head-wounded cock laments.
All the angels of the earth have emigrated,
even the dark angel of the cacao tree.

Secret Country, Macmillan, 1946

On Someone's Death

EUGENIO FLORIT
Cuba, 1903–99

Here she is, in the gaze now empty of landscapes and clouds;
in the unshadowed brow, still wet with another's tear;
in the dry mouth, which let the bird of speech escape;
in this sunken breast,
in these cold hands which until yesterday gestured in agony
and which now do not feel the weight of the black hours.
Here in all this inert body fallen upon the bed,
crossroad of sighs and doves of mechanical prayers.
Here, and even more: in the closed bedroom,
and in the friendly sunny nook,
and at the place at the table where they forgot to remove the plate.
And even more: under the hat,
and hidden in the handkerchief's folds,
and even in the flower left in the book.
(What a pity, Lord, what a pity. She was so young.)
Away there in the distance, two doves join in flight.

Anthology of Contemporary Latin-American Poetry, New Directions, 1942

Mob of Mountains

JOSÉ VARALLANOS
Peru, 1907–97

A mob of mountains
is this our land,
and you are the sun,
the air and the water
of every bit of it.

Ah my *chola* girl:
firm as a white lily,
your body is a fruit,
a sweet-smelling fruit,
caprice of men,
sin that drives us mad.

Your eyebrows soar—
wingless swallows—,
reed-lily, lily bud,
blossom of the air,
blossom of the water,
always fresh, flowering ever,
since Time, for you,
Time passes never,
Time with his plowshares!

Say yes, my little one,
unguent of mallow,
eyes aglow,
thighs like stars,
two caramel feet.
But the air only,
only the air
senses your fragrance!

Anthology of Contemporary Latin-American Poetry, New
Directions, 1942

Andean Crossing

ALEJANDRO PERALTA
Peru, 1899–1973

Silence crumbles before the cavalcade
   Tides of neighing
Dawn leaps over the rocks
the hamlet strips its stone vertebrae
The churchbell sails toward the pampa
We drink the 1st morning alcohol
THE SUN IS CLEANING THE ROOF-TILES
The streets are cooking up their leftover words
Joy entangled in the horses' manes
   Day runs captive to the stirrups
                 FAR OFF
flies the framework of the town
   THE PAMPA
       opens up the shops of its mountains
We stuff our saddlebags with oxygen
The road unfolds its trails of firm ground
A dustcloud of doves blows from the north
       and aloft
       b u r s t
f i r e w o r k s o f p a r r o t s
     ON OUR WAY
Projectiles of dawn our eyes riddle the cloth of the horizon
The sun passes over the horses' rumps
A wedding party of Indians from the district
   makes a festive girdle around the hill
Geranium caps shawls like flames
   blaze
     flutes
   and tabors
Vicentina the bride sprinkles poppies and barley-stalks
     on the spangled
      morning
THE PLAIN IS GREEN WITH SONGS
  At full gallop

we carry the landscape on the croup like a manycolored poncho
    Indian wayfarers
    drub the crest of the road
The pampa sweats its noontime weariness
    Birds
        foreshortened
           inspect
           the stretched hides
    of the sleeping rocks
Afternoon straddling the slope
Belated travelers have walled in the sun
    The earth is suppurating through mudholes
Into the river we toss the stones from the gulch
The mountains form a compact line against the night
    The whip of the reins
        cuts off pieces
    of mountain mist
The wind raveled with voices
BONFIRES OF TWILIGHT
    HANG THE SKY WITH LANTERNS
Salvos of barking
    knock at the town's aching temples
THE ROAD SHRUGS ITS SHOULDERS

Anthology of Contemporary Latin-American Poetry, New Directions, 1942

Provincial Moment

ASDRÚBAL VILLALOBOS
Costa Rica, 1893–1985

It has been raining for days. People huddle together.
At the foot of the mountain, as though under eaves,
the silent city endures the bad weather,
waiting for the downpour to cease.

(The sky is a teat
swollen with pure water which in jets and in sprays
the month of October is monotonously milking
into its ample bucket of thirty-one days.)

Gross words are bandied inside the tavern:
a pretty girl crosses the street and shows,
lifting her skirt, a leg on which a pink
petticoat reflects its delicate rose.

Chasing a cat, a lapdog passes by;
a clock strikes five with the hourhand at three;
in your heart, secluded and pious city,
everything's the opposite of what it should be!

A drunkard goes stumbling through the park,
an idiot woman insults a cop;
(here's a fine theme for Luis Carlos López. . . .)
The girls troop forth from the Normal School.

And under the twisted eaves at the corner,
hands in my pockets, my beloved, I stay
until your bovine glance from the window
shall frighten this cold evening's loneliness away.

Anthology of Contemporary Latin-American Poetry, New Directions, 1942

Elegy to the Invented Woman

XAVIER ABRIL
Peru, 1905–90

A woman or her shadow of ivy
fills this solitude with empty lamps.

In the memory of the heart
a flower is withered,—
a woman's name.

The eyes of absence
are full of rain, of frozen landscapes without trees.

Who knows the name of that woman
who forgets her tresses in rivers of dawn?

How difficult to distinguish between the night
and a woman long-drowned in a pool!

The swooning of a flower can not compare
with the silence of her shut eyelids.

Anthology of Contemporary Latin-American Poetry, New Directions, 1942

Vision of Moth-Eaten Pianos Falling to Pieces

CÉSAR MORO
Peru, 1903–56

Incest represented by a frockcoated gentleman
Receives the congratulations of the hot wind of incest
A fatigued rose supports the corpse of a bird
Leaden bird where is your basket of song
And provisions for your brood of clock serpents
When you stop being dead you will be a drunken compass
A halter on the bed awaiting a moribund gentleman from the isles of the Pacific
    who sails on a musical turtle divine and cretinous
You will be a mausoleum for victims of the plague or a passing equilibrium
    between two trains in collision
While the square fills with smoke and straw and rains down cotton rice water
    onions and vestiges of high archaeology
A gilded frying-pan with my mother's portrait
A lawn settee with three charcoal statues
Eight sheets of paper written in German script
Some days of the week in cardboard with blue noses
Hairs from the beards of different presidents of the Republic of Peru nailing
    themselves like stone arrows into the causeway and producing a violent
    patriotism in those with ailing bladders
You will be a minuscule volcano more beautiful than three thirsty dogs bowing to
    one another and recommending a method of making wheat grow on disused
    pianos

Anthology of Contemporary Latin-American Poetry, New Directions, 1942

The Illustrated World

CÉSAR MORO

Like your window that does not exist
Like the shadow of a hand on a phantom instrument
With the same equality with the precious continuity that your existence ideally
     assures me of
At a distance
At the distance
In spite of the distance
With your forehead and your face
And your whole presence without closing the eyes
And the landscape that blossoms from your presence when the city was not could
     not be anything but the reflection of your hecatomb presence
The better to moisten the plumage of birds
This rain falls from on very high
And shuts me up alone within you
Within and far from you
Like a road which is lost on another continent

Anthology of Contemporary Latin-American Poetry, New Directions, 1942

Parable of Generosity

ANTONIO SPINETTI DINI
Venezuela, 1900–41

You, who have everything,
give!

Give yourself as the rain
gives itself to the parched earth.

Give yourself as the sap
gives itself to the tree.

Give yourself as trees give themselves in flower and fruit.

Give yourself as the earth gives herself wholly
in sheaves and roses.
And the sea in salt and fishes.
And the sky in its blues,
its sun and its stars.
And the prairie in horizons and roads.
And the mountain in curves and colors,
in green things and fountains.

You, who have everything,
give!

For even the harsh thistle
gives itself as an emblem of pride,
gives itself in its snow-flower or flowers of blood,
gives itself even though it be of its thorns,
but gives what it can, what it has.

Even the very stone
gives itself in its hardness.

You, who have everything,
will you be harder than the stone,

→ 153 ←   Parable of Generosity

harsher than the thistle?

You, who have everything,
give!

Anthology of Contemporary Latin-American Poetry, New
Directions, 1942

Man's Road

ENRIQUE PEÑA BARRENECHEA
Peru, 1905–88

I could not know
if it was your heaven or mine,
if it was my dream or your dream,
my delirium or yours.

A broad light on the water
was like a road,
and on the light a ship,
and on the ship a fate.

Garden of the air, garden
sunlit and shadowy;
the blue rain was like
the spirit of the landscape.

I could not know
if the sea was the sea: if I say
that it was the sea, the sea it was not;
if I say it was not, it was the very sea.

How long was the dream
from another dream suspended?
Little lily-flower of air,
lamp above the abyss.

I could not know
if it was your dream or mine.
Man who chooses his way
has to keep to his road.

Anthology of Contemporary Latin-American Poetry, New
Directions, 1942

Dregs

CÉSAR VALLEJO
Peru, 1892–1938

This afternoon it is raining as never before, and I,
my heart, have no desire to live.

This afternoon is sweet. Why shouldn't it be?
It is dressed in grace and sorrow; dressed like a woman.

It is raining this afternoon in Lima. And I remember
the cruel caverns of my ingratitude;
my block of ice crushing her poppy,
stronger than her 'Don't be like this!'

My violent black flowers; and the barbarous
and enormous stoning; and the glacial interval.
And the silence of her dignity will mark
in burning oils the final period.

And so this afternoon, as never before, I go
with this owl, with this heart.

And other women pass; and seeing me so mournful,
they take a little of you
from the grim convolution of my pain.

This afternoon it is raining, pouring. And I,
my heart, have no desire to live!

Anthology of Contemporary Latin-American Poetry, New Directions, 1942

Aboriginal Mother

ANGELINA ACUÑA
Guatemala, 1905–

Aboriginal mother, mother of ancient heritage
and of new lineage;
you are full of world, furrows, and dawns
in you blooms the jubilant blossoms of fruits
torn from earth by hands of your brood.

Indian mother, arrayed in bright colors
even though your soul may wear mourning,
you croon to the child of your blood,
cradled on your sweaty shoulder,
in the to-and-fro of your tasks
as you lean over the washing-stone
above languorous murmur of water
that kisses your knees as it passes;
as you bend to the grinding-stone
and keep time to your lullaby,
tossing the tortillas back and forth.

The mountains and valleys know you,
and the lakes cherishing your image,
and all the roads measuring your weariness,
that long sorrow of your footsteps
which is the barefoot motherland!

You are the total voice, voice of the land,
with your burden, your anguish, your hope;
when grief and delight overwhelm you,
with one child on your shoulder,
another maybe asleep in your lap—
a bundle on your head like a crown,
hung from your waist, a jar spilling over . . .
so weak and so strong,
so small and so great!

You are heroic symbol of the destiny
your ancestry bequeathed you;
you go brimmed and overflowing,
still bearing in your eyes
your sky and your landscape!

Indigenous mother, penniless and wealthy,
so that nothing more may burden your shoulder
nor a jot more weigh on your spirit,
I shed the petals of this poem, sensitive
as a flower, before your bare feet.

Unpublished manuscript

Prose

Poetry Every Day

For one who like myself has come back to Blue Mountain College after long years of absence, nothing could seem more natural than a Literary Festival on its campus. To my mind it is much nearer the fortieth such Festival than the tenth, for it was in 1909—thirty-eight years ago—that I came here as a girl of fourteen and found Blue Mountain what I have ever since recognized it to be: the place of all the places I have known in the world where culture is most generally and most truly cherished, where the achievements of the mind and the spirit are most ardently regarded as the natural aim of the normal mind.

I wish that for those of you who are students here today, and young now as I was then, and for those others here present who come from other centers of learning, as well as all these others who as visitors share with me Blue Mountain's hospitality, I might evoke the college as it was in 1909. There were fewer buildings then, and a campus more rustic and spacious. The library was small, though I shall never forget immortal passages of poetry and prose that I first met with from its open shelves. Blue Mountain College was not a wealthy school, though it was a beautiful one; but even four decades ago it had already struck root deep in the state and in the South, and it was already lifting aloft the flower and fruit of its learning.

Over all the campus then, the living presence of Mrs. Berry was a great spiritual force, as her living memory is today. And poetry was as much, as integrally, a part of the day's experience at Blue Mountain then as the classroom was, or college friendships, or the tulip trees and beech trees growing from these red clay hills. I recall that when I myself arrived here, it was to find that my highly gifted cousin, Nell Owen, had just won the Blue Mountain College Poetry Prize with a lyric which—after all these years—I can still repeat and still know to be a good lyric. Poetry indeed was in the air. No one who was privileged as I was to be in Professor David Guyton's classes will ever cease to recall him as a great teacher who made great literature quicken into actuality within the classroom's walls. In those days when Professor Guyton was teaching so memorably the courses in English and in French, Professor Ellett, dead, alas, these many years, was likewise a stimulating critic and commentator, ever generously interested in encouraging a talent for letters or an appreciation of them. And in those days Perrin Lowrey used to come up now and then from Mississippi College and bring his own new poems for the reading.

The climate of Blue Mountain then was very propitious to poetry, and this Tenth Literary Festival being celebrated here and now proves that it is no less propitious today. It is very fitting that on this campus where culture has so long been a part of daily living, one who owes much to Blue Mountain should be speaking to you of poetry as daily fare—of poetry as being as much the daily bread as the white hyacinths of life.

There is nothing to be afraid of in the name of poetry, though it is in all languages and in all ages a name for wisdom and beauty. Whether we know it or not, poetry is a part of the everyday life of all of us. It is about us, and inside us, all the time. More often than not, we do not recognize it. Even when it is most present, we may not realize that what we are seeing or hearing or even saying is poetry. But we can learn to recognize and realize it: and to the extent to which we may do so, we ourselves become poets. In an essay familiar to most high-school students, Carlyle declared that everyone who reads a poem understandingly becomes a co-creator of the poem, and so a poet. We are creators in greater degree; and, therefore, poets the more, when we open our eyes and ears and minds to the innumerable little things as well as the big things that make life.

One of the deeply interesting and exciting things about the world—the world of three stout dimensions—is the way in which the same patterns are found over and over again, without apparent relationship. We marvel as we ask: "Why Nature loves the number five / And why the star-form she repeats."

Many writers have commented with wonder and awe on these strange identities. Olive Schreiner, for example, was struck in childhood with a new vision of the world when she saw one day, as a chicken was being prepared for dinner, that its branching blood vessels were the same shape and design as the many-branched thorn tree outside the kitchen window. In a universe where things at first thought seem scattered and unlike, poetry is our search for meaning, purpose, and unification, or, to put it into one word, for *identities*.

"The acutest end of speech," according to Wallace Stevens, is:

> To pierce the heart's residuum
> And there to find music for a single line
> Equal to memory, one line in which
> The vital music formulates the words.

Milton, in declaring that it was his purpose in *Paradise Lost* to reconcile the ways of God to man, expressed this search for essential truth which is poetry's chief concern. In our own day W. H. Auden voices a similar confidence in the poet's power to find answer and meaning for the riddle of existence:

> Follow, poet, follow right
> To the bottom of the night,
> With your unconstraining voice
> Still persuade us to rejoice . . .
> In the desert of his days
> Teach the free man how to praise.

All our lives are made up of what we call hard facts and of what we call imagination, which is the quality that enables us to understand facts by seeing their relationships one to another. This working partnership of facts and imagination gives us reality, which I think is another word of poetry. I do not believe that poetry can ever be anything but truth. When poetry speaks in parables, or in metaphors or in similes, it is not to lead you away from what is real to what is unreal, but rather to lead you by the quickest path to the very core of reality. Poetry does not give us fanciful falsehood instead of truth: poetry is a shorthand for truth itself. When we depart from truth, we depart from poetry. It has been my privilege to know some of the famous poets of our time, from several countries, and there is not one of them who has believed that the language of poetry can be anything but truth.

So here we have an essential test for poetry: it must be *true*. Prose may lie if it likes; but if a poem lies, the poetry is gone from it, and what is left can be nothing more, at best, than an exercise in verse. It is poetry to see (as Edna Millay saw) the purple chalk on a blackberry briar in the fall, or to hear (as Thomas Wolfe heard) the coral cry of the cock. It is poetry to make a plain statement of fact which transports us at once to its own time and place, as Tennyson did by saying merely, "The lights begin to twinkle from the rocks."

It is poetry to express an entire philosophy in simple words, as does a four-line Spanish folk song translated by Salvador de Madariaga:

> The stars run and run.
> I need not run as they do.
> Wherever night overtakes me,
> There I shall find the dawn.

It is never poetry to use a forced or a false figure of speech: to say that one thing is like another, or is another, unless the likeness is real, is true. Few things are duller and less convincing, nothing is farther from poetry, than a far-fetched attempt to establish an identity that does not exist. The imagery of a poet of today is drawn from the world about him, the life he knows, from the world of the atomic age: the imagery of Tennyson and Browning was born of the Darwinian theory and the machine; the imagery of Shakespeare was from the voyages of Elizabethan adventurers; the imagery of Chaucer was from the English countryside and the French court and men who long to "go on pilgrimages." But each in its own age was fresh, vivid and real; and each in the long perspective of time is true. And basically all are surprisingly and reassuringly harmonious, one with another.

For the world, which seems so various, is made up to a large extent of a few patterns used over and over again in innumerable combinations. We need not falsify in order to find the identities. We need only to look with comprehending eyes. Poetry is this recognition, and expression, of identities. The common words of our language, and of the language of every other people, is full of such poetry—the familiar names of flowers, for instance: "larkspur" (how plain the lark's spur shows on the blossom once we look for it!); or another kind of identity, "California traveler," the trailing vine with purple cups that became a familiar companion, almost the only thing that stayed with the pioneers on the hard journey, when the covered wagons creaked westward. Homesickness and unflinching determination to journey on, both are in the flower's name. "Daybreak" and "crack of dawn" are two phrases which express the same vision of the sun thrusting through the wall of dark.

What I have been taking so many words to explain, Archibald MacLeish expresses in the shorthand of poetry: "A poem must not mean / But be." Once the poem "is," we often wonder why its words were needed in order for us to see. That discovery and expression of enduring truth is what makes folklore poetry and is part of the universal treasure of mankind. It is also what makes "The heavens declare the glory of God / and the firmament sheweth His handiwork" [Psalms 19:1] an eternal hymn of the human spirit.

Four Talks on Writing; Delivered at the Southern Literary Festival, Blue Mountain, Mississippi, 1947

Contemporary Spanish American Poetry

Pegasus is content, leaping and playing,
For Pegasus through fields of the Inca is straying.

—Darío

Contemporary poetry in Spanish America is essentially lyric poetry; and its multi-colored profusion had led to the comment—true enough, so far as my own knowledge goes—that there is no Latin American who has not written at least one good lyric. Poetry, however, is far from being confined to the written page. As in Spain, where the folk-poetry, the anonymous voice of the *pueblo* [people], is perhaps the most interesting phase of contemporary poetic activity, one hears from the lips of *payo* [peasants] in Mexico or *jíbaro* [peasants] in Puerto Rico a spontaneous love-song:

> Oh mother, I went to the market,
> To the booth where love was sold—
> I bought but a trinket, mother,
> And it cost me dearer than gold!

Or caustic political comment equally spontaneous:

> Now that the sapling has fallen
> Where the peacock slept the night through,
> On the hard ground he must slumber
> As other animals do!

In Spain the leading modern poets have long recognized and turned to their own uses the popular method; and in South America, too, the anthologies begin to be enriched with the charming pattern of the *cantares*—four-line songs, two unrhymed lines alternating with two in assonance or rhyme:

> Ah, the hard stones of the highway
> Keep the print of my footsteps;
> But of all my suffering
> Not a trace on your heart is left!

Naturally, the poet born into such an environment is assured of his audience; and it is not strange that the Latin American finds in poetry even a means of professional and political advancement; with poet-presidents as the rule rather than the exception. The result of this emotional debauch—as the Spanish intellectuals who oppose the phenomenon like to call it—is undoubtedly to exaggerate the more romantic and fantastic traits of the Latin temperament, and to postpone the general acceptance of the scientific attitude toward life: but that some very fine poetry is also the result is equally demonstrable.

Take the two following sonnets, for instance, by authors practically unknown even in their own small countries: sonnets which are not better than a dozen others to be encountered in a month's casual reading, and yet which, once met with, one does not care to let quite slip from the memory. The first is by a San Dominican, Armando Alvarez Piñeiro:

> In my hammock indolently reclined
> After the rough toil of the day I lie,
> While in the soft transparency of the sky
> Likewise in my brunette's warm eyes I find.
>
> The stars their quiet brilliance display;
> The atmosphere its warmth and calmness yields.
> I breathe the pleasant odor of the fields
> And, "Life is good!" half-dreamily I say.
>
> In this settled peace that Fate bestowed,
> The Strange and the Withheld are past my knowing;
> Far-off the dog barks and the wind is blowing:
> While the light breeze to my ears is bringing
> The rough voice of a farmhand who is singing
> A folk-song, in the moonlight, down the road.

And the other, as I discover with some difficulty, is by O. Cerna Sandoval, of San Salvador:

> You make me desperate: what forces shall I bring
> To bear that you at last may come to see
> That your soul will have everything in me—
> Torment and joy, life, love, and suffering!
>
> How would you be loved? Name your desire!
> With a sweetness as of Christian light on all,
> Or with the delectable bitterness of gall,
> Or with a vanished pagan grace and fire?
>
> Of all love's stairs the ascent I divine;
> And for your love, if yours shall equal mine,
> My every energy to the one end bending,

How easily shall I do your behest:
Baring my talons, or my wings extending,
To love you as a dove or a wild beast!

One finds, then, poetry everywhere in the Southern republics. What of the voices that sound most clearly above the chorus? What is their method, and what its results? These are questions that it is fascinating to attempt to answer.

A poet may express his environment in either of opposite ways: by an interpretation of it or by a reaction against it. Certainly the best contemporary example of the former method is José Santos Chocano; of the latter, Rubén Darío. Darío, born into the tropical luxuriance of volcano-dominated Nicaragua, in the old Spanish city where the *Cristus* of dark wood stands among the silken-robed saints of the great cathedral, within sight and sound of the tropical forest vibrant with "wind and axes and birds and wild bulls in chorus," longed passionately for the ordered and formal elegance of the eighteenth century. His dreams were of marquises and abbés at Versailles; of the prim beauty of gardens; and of marbles through a dusk of cypresses. He was as surely formed by Nicaragua as Ezra Pound by Idaho; but Darío had the advantage of being a great poet. This nostalgia for a vanished period resulted in some very beautiful poems—in the greater part of *Azul* [Blue], the book that made his reputation, as well as in *Prosas profanas* [Profane Hymns], and in the revelatory lyric that opens *Cantos de vida y esperanza* [*Songs of Life and Hope*, trs. Will Derusha and Alberto Acereda]; though it is quite true that, once in Paris, he discovered Nicaragua, and found inspiration for some of his noblest work in the somber and gorgeous complexity of the tropics. In spite of his early prejudices, his range was wide; and if toward the last—he died in 1916—his poetry narrowed somewhat, as is natural with a maturing poet, it deepened as well. He himself said of this later phase:

Poor tree that I am, the light wind's caresses
In youth made a vague, sweet sound through the bough.
Now the time of the youthful smile has passed over—
Leave it to the hurricane to move me now!

Darío's first book was the formal challenge to Romanticism, which in Spain had early hardened into a spiritual mold into which were almost invariably wrought Byronic despair and contempt for life. Metrical versatility had been lost, though old Spanish is metrically very rich; and poets, in a welter of apostrophe, were painfully concerned as to "poetic" and "non-poetic" words. Latin America, for all the patriotic feeling engendered by her various revolutions, had accepted the poetic formulas thus developed with little protest until Darío sounded in *Azul* the tocsin to which the youth of a dozen countries eagerly responded. His succeeding volumes

were a rising series of triumphs; and he lived to see his doctrines of absolute free-
dom in theme and diction, of individual and personal beauty, themselves hardened
into dogma among his disciples and become the object of attack by his rebellious
juniors. To a turn for unexpected phrase and an unusual—almost a unique—gift of
music, Darío united passionate vitality and a fine discrimination: there is tropical
luxuriance in his poetry, but rarely a fault of taste; although, strictly in accordance
with his theories, he does not hesitate to interrupt the organ-music of "The Litany
for Our Lord Don Quixote" with jeers at poet's prizes (which he was continually
winning), doctor's prescriptions, and the Spanish Academy:

> King of all cavaliers, lord of the sorrowing,
> From warfare your sustenance, from dream your cloak borrowing,
>> Crowned with illusion's golden crest:
> Of whom none has ever beat down the daring,
> As the shield on your arm, all vision bearing,
>> And all heart, as your lance in rest;
>
> Noble pilgrim, all pilgrims surpassing,
> Who sanctify all roads by your passing,
>> With tread heroic, august, uncouth;
> Against certainties and against consciences,
> Against the laws and against the sciences,
>> Against falsehood and against truth. . . .
>
> Pray for us, generous, pious, and most proud one;
> Pray for us, chaste, pure, heavenly, unbowed one,
>> Pray for the worthless, intercede for our sod!
> Since we are now without vigor or glory,
> Without soul, without light, without life, without Quixote,
>> Without foot nor wing, without Sancho nor God! . . .
>
> From so many sorrows, from griefs heart-wringing,
> From supermen of Nietzsche, from aphonic singing,
> From the prescriptions that doctors give to us,
> From epidemics of horrible blasphemies
> Of the Academies,
> Good Lord, deliver us! . . .

Darío's followers have been many, and they have produced shining and honied
things: yet perhaps the most interesting of the poets he aided in developing is his
talented and vigorous opponent, the poet who attacked his theories of beauty with

the energy of rebellious youth, Enrique González Martínez, of Mexico, who cried out against Darío's favorite poetic emblem:

> Wring the neck of the lying-feathered swan
> That lends a white note to the fountain's blue!
> Its prettiness is well enough, but on
> The soul of things it cannot say much to you!

The idea of poetry as a decoration—an idea undoubtedly held by many of Darío's followers—infuriates the Mexican poet. His own work is thoughtful, terse, vivid, whether in a brief lyric, "The tree was a dome above the miniature garden / An emerald heaven over a little world"; or in one of the solemn odes wherein "the strange eternal voices / over desert vastness speak."

Alfonso Guillén Zelaya, in Honduras, is another poet whose work presents at its sincerest and best the revolt against Modernism; though it is in his case rather a resolute and tranquil turning away from what is extravagant and transient in the movement. With a simplicity at times approaching naïveté, he writes quietly of quiet lives, observing to the letter Fantasio's advice to "write in a low voice." The flavor of this poet's temperament pervades even his briefest love-lyric:

> Impossible now that frivolous thought return:
> The Universe has caught me into its rhythm now anew.
> There is kindness in thorns, fresh water in the sea,
> And the tree has blossomed to shed fragrance on my verse.

Meanwhile, in Guatemala the perturbed spirit of Arévalo Martínez walks by night, launching its indictment against the age when "Sancho Panza criticizes, Sancho Panza writes verses."

José Santos Chocano, of Peru, was born to glorify his environment, as Darío to transcend it. That the traditions, topography, and potential future of Latin America constitute excellent subject matter for poetry was, perhaps, discovered by Andrade; it was certainly brought before the world in bold relief by Chocano, who lost little time in announcing, "Walt Whitman has the North, but I have the South." The implication is misleading: he is more like Vachel Lindsay in method than Whitman. His widespread popularity is due to his splendid rhythms, gorgeous splashes of local color, and insistence on the twin splendors of the Aztec and the Castilian heritage. At his sonorous best, he is not far from being what he declares himself to be, "the primitive spirit, / the primitive spirit of the forests and the Andes." He indicates his own scope and limitations in "Blazon":

> I am America's singer, autochthonous and wild:
> My lyre has a soul, an ideal my singing.

My verse does not rock with the motion mild
Of a tropic hammock from low boughs swinging.

When I feel Inca, the Lord Sun invoking,
Into my hands his royal powers spring;
When I feel Spanish, the Conquest evoking,
My strophes then like crystal trumpets ring.

My imagination comes from the Moor.
The Andes are of silver, but gold the Lion glows,
And the two I mingle with an epic sound.
Spanish is the blood that to an Inca measure flows:
Were I not poet, I might have been renowned
As a white Adventurer or an Indian Emperor.

Chocano suggests, though he does not resemble, the handful of poets who in countries so far apart as Colombia and Uruguay attempt to picture the familiar details of homely life; those whose intention, shall we say, most nearly approximates that of Robert Frost—though the vision of a Latin Frost does, I admit, seem rather richly humorous. Best known of these is Luis C. López, a Colombian, the distinctive characteristic of whose work—apart from its very singing quality—is the juxtaposition of the beautiful and the repulsive. He delights to shock the reader; a youthful trait he may outgrow. He is at his best in picturing night in a tropical village, when—

> the breeze
> Wafts down the street what an odor
> Of yucca-bread and chocolate, of camphor and cheese!—

almost permitting one to forget the revolting metaphor that follows. Less celebrated than López, more even in workmanship, and promising a considerable performance, is his young compatriot, Jorge Mateus, who says of himself:

> I learned song among the paths
> By which the white sheep browse;
>
> I learned song upon the hill-top
> Where go the country girls with startled eyes;
>
> And my verses know—oh, poor child-songs!—
> About red carnations pinned to the blouse.

Still another Colombian, Cornelio Hispano, has succeeded admirably in rendering the village life of the Cauca. In Puerto Rico, Virgilio Dávila, a middle-aged

Puerto Rican farmer, has given in *Pueblito de antes* (A Village of Yesterday) a sonnet series picturing with sympathy and unfailing good humor small town types not so very different from our own; and the most melodious and popular living Puerto Rican poet, Luis Llorens Torres, has written a charming series of Creole sketches dealing with life on the haciendas; while a young Uruguayan, Pedro Leandro Ipuche, published last year in his first book, a vivid interpretation of the Uruguayan cattlemen—poems with more than a passing resemblance to our own cowboy songs.

These poets are reporters, not primarily critics, of manners; but the spirit of criticism is not lacking. The Colombian, Guillermo Valencia, one of the most widely read of contemporaries, has written in "Anarchs" a powerful poem of social protest, developing his theme by a series of images sometimes brutal, sometimes very delicate, but always striking:

> Dogs, miners, artists,
> The arid enclosures that shut you in
> Consume your livid flesh;
> And in the world's dusty Sahara
> You find the water—of tears only!

The poetry of protest seems to belong inherently, however, to Chile, which ranks with Argentina as the most progressive and material of the republics. In Samuel A. Lillo, in Manuel Magallanes Moure, even in Gabriela Mistral, who is more often concerned with the invisible than with the visible world, we find the awakened social consciousness that reaches its most flaming expression in "The New Marseillaise" of Victor Domingo Silva:

> The egoistic poet who keeps silent before
> Earth's pain and her infamy is a knave—and no more!
> In supreme epochs the harp-strings should teem
> With impassioned notes of an anger supreme.
> The great poet his standard must unfurl,
> And across the trenches his strophes hurl! . . .
> And in the same storm, the same madness come
> As his brothers, to triumph or martyrdom!

There is, too, the poetry of the revolutionists—poetry written in exile or in prison against a specific tyranny; the poetry that Díaz Mirón, "the old Mexican lion," wrote in his youth, and that Blanco-Fombona (Venezuela) is writing now; the vigor of which compensates for what it frequently lacks in finish: "There is yet something good despots cannot imprison / Nor load irons upon!" In justice to the poets just mentioned, it should be stated that each of them has produced some very finely-finished lyrics as well; a fact not to surprise us when we remember the kind of song uttered in time of peace by that grizzled warrior, Ben Jonson. What Darío said of Fombona is true of the three of them: "In the mouth of this lion you will often find the Biblical honeycomb."

And there is the poetry that escapes the world entirely, and finds the compensations so often and so nobly celebrated in Spanish—by Santa Teresa; by St. John of the Cross; by Fray Luis de León; by that lovely and dauntless and irresistible seventeenth-century Mexican nun, Sister Juana Inés of the Cross; by her biographer, Amado Nervo, just five years dead; and at the present moment in Chile, by the mystic who prefers to be known as Gabriela Mistral, whose sonnets ran across a continent like wild-fire upon publication two or three years ago. Her poems for children are also very lovely, and they are unique in Spanish literature, which has often sung of childhood, but never before with the convincing simplicity achieved by Gabriela Mistral in her "Song for a Children's Round":

> The sky of December is pure,
> > Holy nectars the spring's basin fill,
> And the shivering grass started up
> > To dance a round on the hill.
>
> The mothers gaze from the valley
> > And past the tall grasses, until
> They see a great white daisy
> > Which is our round on the hill.
>
> They see a great white daisy
> > That lifts and bends and is still,
> That falls apart, comes together,
> > And is our round on the hill.
>
> Today there blossoms a rosebud,
> > Wild pinks their fragrance distil,
> A lamb was born in the valley,
> > And we danced a round on the hill.

"Whoever wishes to have something by which to distinguish Uruguay from its many sister republics," said James Bryce in his book on South America, "may remember that it is the smallest of the South American States, and that it has neither mountains, nor deserts, nor antiquities, nor aboriginal Indians." These facts merely make it harder to explain why, in the last half-century, Uruguayan literature has produced Spanish America's profoundest and gentlest philosopher, José Enrique

Rodó; her one analytical and brilliant dramatist, Florencio Sánchez; her most popular and very talented woman-poet, Juana de Ibarbourou; and the strange genius whose influence on the younger generation of poets is that today most marked, most widespread, and most easily traceable, though he died fifteen years ago at the age of thirty-five—Julio Herrera y Reissig. One may explain Darío as a reaction against environment and Chocano as its apotheosis, but the influences that made Herrera y Reissig lie deeper, deep as the roots of being. His world was the invisible world that he carried about with him, his stage the interior of his own consciousness, where the drama might reach its climax in inaction:

> Conning you close with a suggestive surmise,
> The epilogue of all my dreams I learned;
> And the gray messenger doves of your eyes
> Most quietly then from the skies returned.
>
> I was to have said the last word—and I kept
> A frightful silence without one lament.
> My lost Aprils I was to have wept—
> And I smiled, fierce and indifferent.
>
> The moon, like a good sister, understood,
> For my sake hushing her own pain as well:
> Not a movement, not a gesture, not a mood.
> A frozen kiss there was—a frozen word—
> A kiss, a word; there is no more to tell.
> All occurred in nothing's having occurred.

His love-sonnets in general give a detached, half-mocking analysis of a situation trivial in its outward aspect, and yet, in his own phrase, with implications that approach "the glacial wall / that marks the utmost boundaries of existence." His technical contribution was the perfection of a subtle and intricate harmony in such of his longer poems as "Armando," and a brilliant use of precise and unexpected metaphor, as this, of a summer dusk: "Across rose-scented silence, a cricket scratches"; or, of waters at sunset, "The lake dreams of a crime."

His imitators have been more successful in achieving his effect of brilliancy and his unexpectedness than his precision. During his last years his work became incoherent—he had fallen a prey to morphine—but even then it was never shoddy or dull. One confronts in it at all times a mind skillful and relentless in probing its own motives. His influence, which has spread slowly but unceasingly since his death, and is today perhaps at its highest level, may be traced in every one of the countries of South America; frequently, in the work of the most promising of the younger poets. Lugones in Argentina is a well-known example; Caballero Mejías in Venezuela and Palés Matos in Puerto Rico, neither of them yet thirty, are others who will be well-known in the future. The interesting work of the Cuban, José Manuel Poveda, while individual and striking, has, in its strangely haunting harmonies and almost weird choice of words, much in common with that of Herrera y Reissig.

Although the work of the woman poet mentioned, Juana de Ibarbourou, is less subtle than that of Alfonsina Storni, on the other side of the River Plate; though she is more easily moved to light responses than Gabriela Mistral; she has, at the age of thirty, achieved her own very widely applauded manner: the brief, passionate lyric with a fragrant blossom and a bitter seed:

> I shall suffer for you.
> Blessed be the evil that your love will do!
> Blessed be the blade, the net I shall feel!
> Blessed be thirst and steel!
>
> Instead of diadems in my hair
> Seven long thorns shall I wear.
> Instead of ear-rings I shall don
> Two burning coals vermilion.
>
> And you will weep and pity me.
> Then more than ever mine you will be.

Alfonsina Storni's work, while sometimes carelessly finished, seems to me of firmer texture and more original quality than Juana de Ibarbourou's. Both, however, show a new insight—new, at least, in the literature of their race [ethnicity]—into feminine psychology; the young Argentine speaking characteristically in "Running Water":

> Yes, I move, I live, I wander astray,
>   Water running, intermingling, over the sands;
> I know the passionate pleasure of motion;
>   I taste the forests; I touch strange lands.
>
> Yes, I move—perhaps I am seeking
>   Storms, suns, dawns, a place to hide.
> What are you doing here, pale and polished,
>   You, the stone in the path of the tide!

Are these all? Not all, nor half. Each country has its own packed and overflowing anthology—its *Parnaso*—and not all the poets can be found even therein. I have simply offered a footnote to a richly interesting literature of which we think too seldom. This ferment of creation to the south of us, in conjunction with our own quickened interest in poetry, is perhaps helping in the achievement of the Pan-American character prophesied by Antonio Pérez Pierret (Puerto Rico), who sees "aboriginal copper, carbon of Ethiopia, Latin dream, and stark Anglo-Saxon reality" fusing at last into a personality synthesizing the trinity of force in a profound unity:

> And he will be brain,
> And he will be arm,
> And he will be poet.

It is a vision worth pondering.

North American Review, May 1924; all translations by Muna Lee

A Charming Mexican Lady

Juana Inés of the Cross was thirty-eight years old when her poems were published in Madrid in 1689, the title-page hailing her as "the Unique Poetess, the Tenth Muse, who in various meters, languages, idioms, and manners, enriches various matters with elegant, subtle, limpid, ingenious, and profitable verses."

"Subtle, limpid, and ingenious" are apt adjectives to describe the complex personality of a wise and passionate woman, capable of complete detachment in the analysis of her own emotions. The poetry is the exquisitely ironical record of the adventures of a soul. It is neither colonial nor provincial, although, at the time when her book appeared, she had been a nun in the Convent of San Geronimo in the City of Mexico for more than twenty years, and had never seen more of the external world than the capital and the neighboring villages.

Born in the hamlet of Nepantla, between the flame and smoke of Popocatepetl upon the one hand and Ixtaccihuatl upon the other; taken as a child to Mexico City so that the viceroy might witness the prodigies of her learning; educated there, a part of the gay and cultivated vice-regal court and a favorite of the vicereine; she was only sixteen years old when the viceroy, the Marquis de Mancera, declared that the responsibility of measuring the depth and scope of her talent was too great for him alone. He called in a committee of forty—poets, painters, theologians, courtiers, and, as the old chronicler is careful to tell us, several famous beaux and wits—to question the beautiful, brilliant child, and come to some agreement as to what should be done for her.

For several hours the examination continued, Juana de Asbaje—as she was in the world—confounding them all, especially the beaux and wits, by the discretion and justice of her responses. "As a royal galleon defends itself from the canoes that assail it," says the contemporary record, "so Juana Inés extricated herself from the questions, arguments, and responses that the assemblage propounded, each in his own department."

Shortly afterward, the vicereine, the "Laura" of much of Sor Juana's verse, offered to make her a lady-in-waiting. For whatever reason, the young girl refused. The mysterious love affair which colors her poetry, and which according to tradition ended unhappily because of her lover's exalted station, must have taken place about this time. Mystical by nature, she turned to religion, and at once the viceroy's confessor urged upon her the advisability of entering a convent. She records her initial recoil from the idea; but at last she let herself be persuaded, years later explaining the step in an illuminating comment: "I thought to fly from myself, but alas! I brought myself with me."

She spent part of a novitiate in the order of the Carmelites. That discipline proved too severe, and upon the recommendation of her physician she withdrew. A year and a half later she was admitted to the convent of San Geronimo. She seems never to have regretted her profession, and certainly the brilliancy and color of life were hardly dimmed for her because of it. She did not go out from her retreat, but the world came to her.

Life in the Mexican monasteries in the seventeenth century was anything but monotonous. Between court and convent flowed a constant stream of little notes, of music, of verses and compliments, of presents such as embroidered slippers or those delicate light pastries called "nun's sighs," or richly blended confections of yucca or wild orange. Did distinguished visitors stop at the cloisters? There were apartments regally furnished for their reception, and a play was sometimes arranged for their entertainment. A dance, even, might be held in the great hall where the Velásquez or the Ribera hung. Afterward, upon cloths weighed down with fringe of gold, spiced wines would be set out, and that ancient Mexican refreshment of chocolate and honey whipped together, and dry cakes fat with citron and almond; and there would be conversation, very learned and witty.

They loved good talk, these sisters with their pale, ascetic faces and slender hands—they shone at repartee, and quoted the classics appositely, and made puns in lisping Latin. Even when visitors did not come, they met at stated hours and fenced in gallant argument with one another. The number of their servants was a scandal, one convent counting six attendants for each sister; but their learning was a matter of national pride.

As for Sor Juana Inés, her brilliancy in conversation was a legend, and her industry passed belief. She made verses in Spanish, in Latin, in Aztec; she composed music and sang to the harp; she lined her cell with volumes on mathematics and astronomy, physiology, philosophy, and canonical law; she understood the principles of medicine; she was famous as a grammarian; she painted upon wood and ivory; she wrote enchanting occasional verses upon the birthday of her patroness, upon the festivals of the saints. Beneath all this and around it flowed the stream of her serious poetry, simple and passionate and marvelously restrained, like the poetry of no other woman in Spanish, like none in English till Christina Rossetti; although in its unrest, its bitterness, its mockery of its own pain, and its sudden, thrilling laughter, it belongs less to the period of the pre-Raphaelites than to our own.

II

Spanish culture thrust its deepest roots into Mexico, and established there the first institution of learning and the first printing-press of the New World. It had grown old before the Pilgrims landed at Plymouth. There was continual contact with

Madrid, socially and artistically as well as politically. The musicians for a single banquet were sometimes brought from Spain on one vessel to return upon the next. The literary period was that of Góngora, the Euphues of Spanish verse, who was distorting with gorgeous ornament a style just simplified by Cervantes and Calderón. It is one of the amazing things about Sor Juana that she yielded so slightly to Gongorism. In an age when poetry was esteemed in proportion to the elaborateness of its figures, her lines are stripped and bare, achingly direct. Her dramatic work shows the unwholesome influence to some degree, at times, in the *autos* [one-act religious allegories], becoming a glittering tangle of inversions; but even here, the most famous of her dramas, *Los empeños de una casa* [The Trials of a Noble House], is comparatively simple in treatment, a delicious comedy of manners, pithy with proverbs after the Spanish tradition.

This comedy contains Sor Juana's well-known discussion of her own fame, in the mouth of her heroine:

> I went to my studies
> From earliest childhood
> With such sleepless ardor,
> With such rapt desire,
> That I reduced to brief period
> Fatigues of much compass . . .
> In such manner that people
> Revered as inherent
> Laurels hardly acquired.

"The sublime style" was easy for her. All methods, indeed, seem to have been easy for the facile pen which glided from a sarcastic madrigal upon a pretentious and unlovely "Queen of Beauty" to the impassioned feminism of her "*Redondilla*" [poem of quatrains rhyming *abba, cddc,* et cetera]:

> Stupid men, who accuse
> Women, in and out of season,
> Never seeing you are the reason
> Of the faults that you abuse! . . .
>
> With vain pretensions rife,
> You would a She discover
> Who is Thaïs as a lover,
> And Lucretia as a wife. . . .
>
> With whom shall blame begin,
> However evil they—

With her who sins for pay,
Or him who pays for sin?

While her poetry, at its best, has the somber, reticent beauty of the sonnet on her own portrait:

This which you gaze upon, a painted lie,
Blazoning forth with niceties of art
False syllogisms that the hues impart,
Is a shrewd snare, the sense being ta'en thereby.
This, wherein the flatteries try to cover
The horrors of the years, and to erase
The rigors Time has left upon the face,
Age and forgetfulness to triumph over:
Is an artifice most vainly wrought,
Is a frail flower carried on the wind,
Is a shield against a sure Fate borne:
Is the idle labor of a vagrant mind,
Is a solicitude ponderous and out-worn,
Is corpse—is dust—is shadow—and is naught.

When the Marquise de Mancera died, Sor Juana wrote three sonnets which, as Amado Nervo—most devoted of her adherents—has pointed out, evidence the depth of her grief by their mediocrity. She had the consolation, however, some years later, of finding in another vicereine, the Countess of Pareda, whose "little name," Lysi, sparkles through an entire volume of Sor Juana's verse, a friend who seems to have fulfilled to admiration the role the nun ardently desired for her friends, that of smiling benignly as they received the myrrh with which she bathed their feet. In verse as deft as Matthew Prior's—and the resemblance extends to subject-matter so strikingly that some of Prior's poems are more like Sor Juana's than most translations are like their ostensible originals—she celebrates Lysi's beauty: Lysi, whose hand should receive the rose which surely blossomed from the impress of her foot; Lysi, who needs no Easter greeting, because she has only to look into her mirror to see Paradise and glory; Lysi, who could never be adequately portrayed, since the "unfortunate and vain" century offered only outworn phrases and metaphors soiled with use, leaving the poet to envy her peers of the springtime of poesy, when to say for the first time, "'Those locks are a golden treasure,' / Was worth another beyond measure."

The *villancicos* [carols], which she delighted in writing, are charming carols, light and musical:

Between the stars and the flowers
A dispute began to loom:
How wisely they used their powers,
The first with the voice of light,
The others with shrieks of perfume.

One turns always with a feeling of relief, however, from this lighter work to the spring from which flowed her beautiful "Sonnet of Hope":

But I, in my condition wiser much,
Am holding both my hands before my eyes—
I see only those things which I touch.

Her moods vary, but the prevailing tone of her work is a deep tenderness. She was, says her chronicler, the gentlest and best beloved of the sisters; though there is a mischievous story of her once having silenced her mother superior with an impatient, "Oh, don't be silly, Mother!" When the Mother complained, she received only the satisfaction of having Don Fray Payo de Ribera write himself into legend by saying, "When the Mother Superior disproves the accusation, I shall be glad to reprimand Sor Juana Inés."

Very characteristic of her tenderness, and very beautiful in the original, is the following sonnet:

This evening when I spoke with you, my love,
From your face and gesture well I knew
That with words I had not persuaded you
Of what you saw my heart desired to prove.
And love, who aided me in what I willed,
Achieved what seemed impossible to attain,
Since in the tears wherewith I clothed my pain,
All my heart was melted and distilled.
Enough of rigors, beloved: let them end!
No more shall tyrant jealousies intervene,
Nor vile suspicions your quietude offend
With hideous shadows and with vain demands;
Since in liquid essence you have touched and seen
All my heart melted here between your hands.

She took all knowledge for her province; but she loved to embroider and garland her serious studies with playful verse. When a comet came to Mexico with the Conde de Pareda, whose vice-regency was certainly ill-starred enough, Sor Juana celebrated the wisdom of the astronomer who explained the nature of comets to the frightened populace by writing a Gongoristic sonnet to him "who gives more light to the stars." She had a Latin fondness for courtly generalities: "One suffers for the good fortune of a neighbor / Much more than for one's own hardship!"

III

It is hard to see how she found time for all this varied production after her fame began to spread. She never refused to hear and advise the stream of visitors who sought her advice in the convent, nor to read critically the manuscripts with which importunate authors besieged her; and she did not relax her studies.

These activities were to end, nevertheless, before her death, while her enthusiasm still was high. About the time of the publication of her book, Sor Juana became engaged in a theological controversy with a famous Portuguese preacher of the time, Padre Vieyra. They argued courteously but impassionedly [her criticism, written in 1690, was actually of a sermon he preached in 1650]. The attention attracted by the controversy, and the public delight in the nun's agility in argument, and the frequently expressed popular opinion that she had met the padre on his own ground and overcome him, drew a remonstrance from the Bishop of Puebla. In a suave but severe letter, after praising her skill and polish in the theological interchange, he suggested with an irony perhaps unconscious that she leave off the study of profane letters and devote herself wholly to religious writings. He did not ask, he added, that Sor Juana give up entirely the study of poetry, for the examples of Santa Teresa and Fray Luis de León, as of several others, had proved poetry not incompatible with piety; but he should be glad to see her imitate those holy personages in meter and manner as well as in matter.

The effect upon Sor Juana was immediate and disastrous. For several months after receiving the Bishop's letter she remained in her cell, overcome with humiliation and distress; then she answered with what was to all effect an *apologia pro vita sua* [defense of her life], tracing her career from childhood, and her spiritual development. This document, the most striking example of her prose, and enough in itself to have secured her fame, closed with the expression of her desire to comply in all things with the Bishop's wishes. Shortly afterward, she sold her library, gathered through so many years, and devoted the proceeds to charity.

Without her books, cut off from poetry, she shut herself up for the few years she was still to live; and, finally, nursing others of her sisterhood through an epidemic, she "sickened of charity," as her biographer puts it, and died in her convent in the City of Mexico on April 17, 1695, in the forty-fifth year of her age; "not only with serene conformity," adds the chronicle, "but with lively indications of eagerness."

She was even then to the popular mind what she seemed to Menéndez y Palayo when he came to write his history of Spanish American literature two centuries later, a being "supernatural and miraculous." The crowds surged about the chapel and beat upon the doors and windows in their eagerness to look upon her for the last time; and she was celebrated in memorial verses by the poets of two hemispheres.

"What shall they say in my praise?" she had asked in her last poem, "What should they say except that fancy / Has dominion over the mind?"

American Mercury, January 1925; all translations by Muna Lee

Brother of Poe

Poe, who was fortunate in little else, was almost without exception fortunate in his foreign interpreters—the rarest good luck to befall poets. That the French acclaimed his genius long before it was recognized by his fellow countrymen—if, indeed, we may say we have ever recognized it—was due as much to Baudelaire's sympathetic and haunting versions of his poems as to the beauty of the originals. Poe's Spanish interpreter and occasional translator, José Asunción Silva, was, no less than Baudelaire, qualified by tragic experience of life as well as by sympathy and surpassing ability to embody in liquid and lingering Castilian the conception of poetry that was to help in altering to some extent the South American picture of the United States as a land where genius could not exist. To some extent only, unfortunately, for whenever a *norteamericanófilo* [yankophile; in other words, an admirer of the United States, its people, and its culture]—a creature as rare as the name—has cited Poe as an example of what we might rise to artistically, there has always been a chorus ready to shout, with discouraging truthfulness, "Yes, but they let him die in beggarly obscurity!" Poe is much more alive today south of the Rio Grande than in Virginia or New York: more loved, more reverenced, more often read and beyond comparison more often quoted—both as to his poetry and his theory of poetry.

His was a theory to which Silva passionately subscribed. The influence of Poe is everywhere in the Colombian's bitter, haunting music, it is shown in selection of subject, in treatment, in the very mannerism of lengthening rhythms and deepening echoes. For Silva, like every other good translator of poetry, was a poet first and a translator second, and like every other great translator, he was able to be both at once. However, it was as interpreter rather than as translator that he rendered most service to Poe; the incidental versions of several of the poems, happy as they are, fade into insignificance before the tremendous compliment that Silva paid his North American predecessor in taking over his method bodily, and exemplifying it in some of the most beautiful lyrics in modern Spanish.

Silva's life might well have furnished material for one of Poe's tales of the fantastic and arabesque. He was born in Bogatá, loftiest and remotest of capitals, even now a week's difficult journey by steamer and muleback from its port, and fifty years ago practically a bit of seventeenth-century Spain, walled off from softening exterior influences. By nature he was poet and mystic. He found himself, when hardly more than a boy, however, left as sole support of his idolized sister, and he turned his energies to the task of conserving and managing their property. He was, like Poe, one of those beings born under a dark star. Grief and misfortune dogged him. The property of the family vanished in a business failure. His sister died, and he lost in her the only human being for whom he cared passionately. With all his dreams and ambitions diverted into the intense and rapid channel of his poetry, he poured forth his grief in a series of sonnets which he believed to be his best work—he was his own severest critic—and a novel of which the theme had haunted him for years. The manuscripts of both novel and sonnet sequence were lost in a shipwreck. He had no copies of the works, and found himself completely unable to rewrite either. He sank into deep melancholy, finding little upon which to fix his dreams in the chill, wind-swept city amid its mountains; and in 1896 he shot himself. "He died of hunger," said Unamuno tersely.

Silva's work has a remarkable technical range, though he was too much under Poe's influence—or perhaps it would be more accurate to say that his point of view was too much akin to Poe's—for him to care greatly for treating a large number of widely differentiated subjects. Love, death, most frequently of all Poe's cherished combination of these themes, the death of a beautiful woman, are Silva's chosen topics; and about his loveliest lyrics there is always a faint odor of decay. He voiced a gospel drawn partly from Whitman to the effect that art excludes nothing of the truth, and is without prejudice as to subject; but his own work is highly selective, unmistakably showing that what art really meant to him, apart from theories, was the deification of ideal beauty and the mournful recognition of its impermanence. There is no novelty in the attitude; but his expression of it was charged with an intense and quivering magic.

His broad-minded theory is adequately set forth in the subtle assonances of "Reality":

> Nature is an Anywhere—
> She suppresses distances—in Japan or Genoa.
> And Triptolemus and Dombesle
> Are the same: toga and petticoats.
>
> La Vallière with her Louis in the royal
> Blazoned carriage
> Is primitive as the Cyprian Venus
> In her white shell's chalice.
>
> O my sons! O brothers! O poets!
> If the deed, the word, exist, decide.
> Be pure spirits and act, always;
> For noble spirits nothing is vile.
>
> In Poestum the language of Silenus
> Becomes a gloomy hiccup. Horace

Sings to Priapus; and Bottom, the grotesque,
Crosses over Shakespeare's drama.

Truth has no boundaries, brother!
Great Pan's, the goat god's, beard
And twisted horns emerge
From the pale countenance of the Ideal!

But that is, after all, theory; and Silva's practice is more adequately represented by
one of the most musical and most frequently quoted of his lyrics—a poem which
is, in effect, his rendering into Spanish verse of Poe's dictum that the perfect lyric
should be brief, should be melancholy, and should be beautiful, and consequently
will in all probability have as its subject the most melancholy of all themes, the
death of a beautiful woman. Silva, as will be seen from the following translation,
treated the subject with a seriousness across which flickered like phosphorus the
extraneous humor of the Latin:

To devise a poem was then all my dream,
Of art sensitive and new, a work bold and supreme.

I sought among sources grotesque and tragical,
I called all rhythms to me with conjury magical.

And the headstrong rhythms trooped one with another,
Joining in the shadows, seeking, fleeing each other,

Powerful rhythms, or grave or sonorous,
Some like arms clashing, some like birds in a chorus;

From Orient to Occident, from the South to the North,
The meters and forms came marching forth.

Champing golden bits beneath harness fragile
Crossed over the tercets, those chargers agile;

And opening a path through the gathering horde
In purple and gold strode the Sonnet, the Lord.

And all sang together! The crowd forgetting,
My soul was enchanted by the coquetting

Of some slender strophe that caught my desire
With soft music trilling like bells from a spire.

I chose of them all; for a bridal gift, glowing
Rhymes of crystals and silver bestowing.

I wrought a tale with them, all model evading,
Tragic, fantastic, and subtle in shading.

The history mournful, neglected, and true, they said,
Of a beautiful woman, beloved and dead.

And that one savor the bitterness of this,
I joined syllables sweet as the taste of a kiss,

Phrases broidered with gold, with music endowed
Like that of mandolins accompanying a shroud.

I let a vague light in the distance play,
Melancholy and misty-gray.

And in the rear, in the orchestra's view,
As graceful dominos in carnivals do,

(Words like a veil about them wearing,
Masks of black velvet and satin bearing)—

In the background I let cross vague suggestions
Of mystical beliefs and vague temptations.

Pleased with my poem, with an artist's pride
With heliotrope I perfumed it, in amethyst dyed.

And I pressed it into a great critic's hand.
He read it four times and said: "I do not understand. . . ."

It was during the period of his intensest preoccupation with the work of Poe, the period following the death of his sister, his romantic attachment for whom has become one of the legends of Hispanic literature, that Silva met Baudelaire and Mallarmé in Paris. The result of this meeting has been very important in the literature of his language, because Silva produced, partly in consequence, his greatest poem, surely one of the beautiful elegies of the world, written in free verse, in a full-toned Castilian that dies along wailing repetitions into ineffable echoes—a technical feat that opened heaven, as the Spanish say, to the other Spanish poets, and was the first great single impulse toward the *modernista* movement, the movement which has done more than any other to revivify Spanish poetry, and by which poetic leadership was temporarily transferred from Spain to Spanish America.

This poem, the third "Nocturne," is unrhymed; and it is only partially translatable—that is, so much of its beauty depends upon the intricately braided jet and silver of its cadences that a great deal is necessarily lost by translation into a less liquid tongue. It has strength enough, however, to remain a poem even though some of the music vanishes—a poem which, even in translation, more than any other that I know, really chills the listener, across whose consciousness seems to blow the cold wind of mortality:

> One night,
> One night filled with murmurs and perfumes and the music of wings,
> One night
> When fantastic fireflies blazed in the moist nuptial shadows,
> By my side slowly, clasped to me, pale and silent,
> As if a presentiment of infinite bitterness
> Agitated the most secret depths of your heart,
> Over the blossomy path through the plain
> You wandered;
> And the full moon
> Scattered white light over bluish skies, boundless and deep.
> And your shadow,
> Frail and languid,
> And my shadow
> By the rays of the moon projected
> Over the gloomy sand,
> Joined together
> And were one,
> And were one,
> And were one,
> And were one long shadow,
> And were one long shadow,
> And were one long shadow. . . .
>
> Tonight,
> Alone: my soul
> Filled with the infinite bitterness and pain of your death,
> Separated from you by time and space and the tomb,
> By the black infinity

Whither the voice cannot reach:
Silent and alone
I wandered along the path,
And I heard the dogs baying the moon,
The pallid moon,
And the chirrup
Of frogs. . . .

I was cold, with the cold of your cheek and your brow and your beloved hands
Among the white snows of your shroud.
It was the cold of the sepulcher, the ice of death,
The chill of nothingness. . . .
And my shadow,
By the rays of the moon projected,
Went alone,
Went alone,
Went alone over the lonely plain.
And your shadow quick and slender,
Frail and languid,
As in that warm night of vanished spring,
As in that night filled with murmurs and perfumes and the music of wings,
Came close and walked with mine,
Came close and walked with mine,
Came close and walked with mine.

Oh, the shadows knit together!
Oh, shadows of the body joined with shadows of the soul!
Oh, shadows which seek one another in nights of sorrow and tears!

To enumerate the poets who have been influenced by this poem—whether to accept the theories of art implicit in its technique or whether to react violently against them in a passionate demand for poetry that faces and grapples with daily life—would be practically to call the roll of poets in South America. In Colombia, where there are reputed to be more poets than voters, every poet seems to have written at least one poem on Silva in addition to the innumerable variations upon and imitations of the third "Nocturne." The best of these is "Reading Silva," by Guillermo Valencia, himself generally regarded as one of the two greatest living Spanish American poets. "Leyendo a Silva" [Reading Silva] is included in most modern Spanish anthologies, among them *The Oxford Book*.

Valencia knew Silva, of course, and he has succeeded in informing with reality his sketch of the young romantic whom he calls "the last-born of Leda and the swan"—who was fated, he says,

> Loving its details, to hate the Universe;
> To sacrifice a world to ornament a verse;
> For an eagle's wings, a lion's claws to plead
> (To conquer the storm, to make hearts bleed);
> To follow close on ideals Quixote knew
> When he set his steed galloping toward the blue;
>
> . . . .
>
> To feel deep in his soul April breezes respire
> Before a scarlet missal or an old friar;
> To have a brow crowned with flame, feet in the mud;
> To long to make all seen, felt, understood. . . .

A dark, morbid, passionate poet with a thrillingly beautiful gift of song; a poet self-centered and pridefully chanting his own sorrow; a poet bewildered and overcome by the tragedy of death even more than by life: such was the poet who nearly thirty years ago in the old Colombian city flung himself violently out of a world which had grown cold and empty past endurance. A strange story and a strange being! José Asunción Silva was fit brother to the North American with his alien nightingale's tongue and the bitter alien draught of wormwood in his honey.

Southwest Review, July 1926; all translations by Muna Lee

Pan-American Women

SIR: Sandino was kept out of the Sixth Pan-American Conference at Havana, but the Woman's Party of the United States got in. The conference had a definite program to work from, and a definite plan for dealing with it. The question of equal rights for women was not in that plan. When the Fifth Pan-American Conference in Santiago de Chile in 1923 recommended on vote of Maximo Soto Hall, delegate from Guatemala, the inclusion in the agenda for the succeeding conference of a study of methods for obtaining equal rights before the law for the women of the twenty-one American countries, no one—probably not even Sr. Soto Hall himself—expected much.

The Sixth Conference, assembling in Havana this January [1928], certainly did not dream of a feminine invasion. Women never had disturbed the Pan-American delegates by so much as a petition, and it would have seemed highly unreasonable to expect such disturbance in Cuba of all places. In Cuba the new constitution grants women the vote, then automatically nullifies it by a joker in another article, but the women had it protested. When the delegates arrived, they found with some amusement that two members of the National Woman's Party—Doris Stevens, chairman of the Committee on International Action, and Mrs. Clarence Smith, chairman of the National Council—had been in Havana for a week, and had established headquarters in the Hotel Sevilla Biltmore, where the purple, white, and gold Woman's Party flag fluttered from the balcony along with the flags of the twenty-one sovereign American states, and a few days later Mrs. Valentine Winters arrived from Ohio and Muna Lee from Puerto Rico. Little by little the delegates became aware of an activity and a controlled excitement, a constant concentrated challenge.

Miss Stevens and Mrs. Winters, on the day after their arrival, called upon Dr. Bustamante, head of the Cuban delegation and soon-to-be-elected president of the Sixth Conference. They told him what they wanted: that the conference recommended the negotiation of a treaty which when ratified would give equal rights to men and women before the law in all the countries of America. Dr. Bustamante, although friendly and interested, pointed out the difficulties of such a course.

"And we want a chance to present the case for equal rights to the Pan-American Congress in plenary session," flashed Doris Stevens, waving difficulties to one side.

Dr. Bustamante murmured something about "the rules." Miss Stevens and Mrs. Smith had the rules with them and turned to the paragraph stating that the congress might invite whom it pleased to speak on any subject about which the members wished to hear.

Mr. Hughes, likewise, assured the women that so far as he was concerned there would be no objection to having the women appear before the conference. Obviously, the thing to do was to get invited! People began to drop in at the Sevilla headquarters, invitations to speak began to come too, and none of them was ever refused. Organization after organization of Cuban women heard and eagerly responded to the plan for a treaty granting equal rights to the women of the Americas. Detailed press stories were sent out daily in Spanish and in English. An increasing army of women lobbied every delegate. The poor men opened any one of the five leading Havana dailies to find an equal-rights story staring at them from the Spanish headlines. They drove up to the university where the conference was in session and were amazed to meet women coming to them with the same quiet demand. They went out to dinner in the evening and sat next to a woman who asked pleasantly in Spanish or English or Portuguese or French: "How soon will women have their hearing?" There was no escape—not at the Yacht Club or the Jockey Club, not by the roulette wheel at the Casino or on the golf course, not even when presumably safe in their offices or at their hotels. Whenever there were women there was that insistent question: "When shall we have our hearing?" In the Law Building—the *Edificio de Derecho*—which was the center of the conference, a table draped with the Woman's Party's purple, white, and gold was a center from which radiated many currents of activity. These women received lobby assignments, discussed methods of getting the treaty before the congress, distributed literature, and answered questions about "the first treaty, in the history of the world," as Doris Stevens explained through the columns of a hundred papers in half a dozen languages, "proposed by women on behalf of women."

The enthusiasm and energy of the Cuban women was unequivocal answer to all who had ever said (and how many they have been!) that the Latin woman does not want her rights; that the Latin woman will not speak in public; that the Latin woman is bound by customs which she cannot break.

Help began to come from within. Dr. Enrique Olaya Herrera, Colombian Minister in Washington, Dr. Bustamante, Dr. Ferrara of Cuba, Dr. Amézaga of Uruguay, Dr. Alfaro of Panama, Dr. Guerrero of Salvador, Dr. Garcia of Mexico, all declared themselves heartily in favor of an open hearing. Then entire delegations fell into line—Mexico, Guatemala, Panama, Cuba, Salvador, Costa Rica, Nicaragua, Paraguay. The day when Dr. Varela Acevedo, president of the Uruguayan delegation and ex-Minister of Uruguay in Washington, proposed in the Committee on Initiatives that the open hearing be granted, Dr. Pueyrredon of Argentina seconded the motion, and it was carried without dissent. The open hearing which "could not be granted" became an accomplished fact, at the cordial invitation of the Pan-American Conference itself.

The women presented their case briefly and urgently. For the United States,

Doris Stevens and Mrs. Clarence Smith spoke; for Cuba, Dr. Julia Martinez, Sra. Maria Montalvo de Soto Navarro, Sra. Angela Zaldivar and Sra. Pilar Jorge de Tella; for the Dominican Republic, Sra. Plintha Wos y Gil; for Puerto Rico, Muna Lee. That was Puerto Rico's only appearance at the conference. Fifteen hundred women who had crowded into the Aula Magna of the university and had been standing, waiting, an articulate, swaying mass, for more than three hours, burst repeatedly into joyous applause which was echoed here and there from the places where the delegates listened with divided emotions but unified attention. Outside, thousands were crowding up the splendid flight of white stairs, while the radio amplifiers carried the speeches through the bright Cuban air. It was a larger and far more responsive crowd than that which had heard Presidents Machado and Coolidge some weeks earlier.

"We are glad the conference granted the women that hearing," *El pais* remarked editorially that afternoon, "else we should likely have seen something comparable to the storming of the Bastille!"

The result was immediate. The conference unanimously voted to have the report on equal rights received and discussed in plenary session rather than in one committee. When that report was made, a resolution was voted declaring that an Inter-American Committee of Women be constituted, to prepare information to enable the next Pan-American Conference to study constructively the civil and political equality of women. This committee is to consist of seven women, appointed by the Pan American Union, the number to be increased by the committee itself until each republic is represented thereon.

At least in this hemisphere no more international codes are to be written concerning women without consulting women. The struggle for equal rights has become an inter-American movement. The women of no country will look upon the cause as won until it is won for all. Here at last is a unity of ideal and effort which establishes a real, a spontaneous, a spiritual commonwealth of Pan America.

Nation, March 14, 1928

In Behalf of the Equal Rights Treaty

Honorable Delegates:

Today is the seventh of February, 1928. In the minds of our children and our children's children, this date may flame with significance. It may mark the birth of a new freedom, and the beginning of a new world. That depends on you.

Many temples have been built to shelter Pan-Americanism. Some of them have been built with marble, some with words. But deep and true friendship is no less rare than beautiful. It does not come even to temples merely because it is summoned, nor even because each country of our continents may sincerely desire its coming. International friendship to be real must be unselfish, and complete unselfishness is hard of attainment when interests differ; as hard for nations as for individuals.

But here, today, you have before your eyes a concrete demonstration of that very thing: a Pan-Americanism that includes all, that excludes none, that makes not the slightest difference between one and another. The women of all the Americas have one need. Every enlightened woman of this hemisphere desires for her sister of another country, the same good which she craves for herself. The woman of no country of our Americas believes that equal rights for herself will in any way give her or her country an advantage over her sisters to the north or to the south. She does not wish such advantage. She does not ask for one thing and pay with another; she is not carrying on a barter of power, of friendship, of advantage. She asks for herself and for every other woman in all of our countries, one thing, for the good of all—and for the good of those countries which we women have helped upbuild and are helping uphold.

The woman of colonial times displayed the same splendid traits in Latin America and in Saxon America. She worked and fought beside her men; gaily and gallantly she dedicated her strength of body and spirit to building the Americas. And now, with one impulse of the heart, though in the ringing accents of four languages, she reminds you of this, of which you should never have forced her to remind you. She asks that the countries she has helped to create recognize in her the powers by which they have benefited during four centuries.

Our petition as women, amongst you free citizens of Pan America, is like the petition of my Puerto Rico in the community of American States. We have everything done for us and given us but sovereignty. We are treated with every consideration save the one great consideration of being regarded as responsible beings. We, like Puerto Rico, are dependents. We are anomalies before the law.

We, the women of the Americas, ask for a treaty granting us equal rights before the law. We ask this not for one woman, not for one country, not for one race, but for the women of Pan America; for the women who are proving to you here to-day by their solidarity and mutual trust that Pan-Americanism is a fact.

We offer you a new definition: Pan-Americanism is the deep desire of every country for the common good of all, favoring none and slighting none. It is the oneness of purpose that makes of us all responsible citizens of the spiritual commonwealth of Pan America.

We offer you a definition and we offer you an opportunity; the opportunity of acting with unparalleled generosity and vision.

We, the women of America, ask of you, the men of America, a treaty guaranteeing us our equal human rights.

Address delivered before the Unofficial Plenary Session of the Sixth Pan-American Conference, Havana, Cuba, February 7, 1928

Paulina Luisi, Internationalist

Greatly gifted and greatly beloved, Dr. Paulina Luisi, Representative of Uruguay on the Nationality Committee of the Inter-American Commission of Women, brings to the Commission not only a richly dowered and highly trained mind, but an international experience of amazing breadth and fruitfulness. It is in great part due to Paulina Luisi and her unwavering feminism that the women of Uruguay have achieved so great a degree of equality. Dr. Luisi through her own efforts has founded practically all the feminist organizations in her native country. She has represented the women of her country at innumerable international gatherings, and has been the delegate of her government with equal frequency.

Several years since, without previous consultation with her, the King of Spain awarded her the Commander's Cross of the Order of Alfonso XII. Shortly afterwards, she was offered by the Portuguese government, and in true democratic spirit declined, the decoration of St. Jacques de l'Epée. I was a few weeks ago in Madrid, and found abundant evidence there of the affection and admiration with which feminist leaders of what is now the youngest republic regard Paulina Luisi.

She was the first woman graduate of the University of Montevideo, the first Uruguayan woman to obtain a medical degree, and the first woman on the faculty of the university. She was also—among other posts which she held as a pioneer— the first woman to be elected Chief of Clinic of the Faculty of Medicine in Montevideo. The mere enumeration of her more important offices and honors requires a paragraph in itself.

First Latin woman delegate from her government to the League of Nations and the International Labor Office; delegate to the Fourth International Labor Conference; member of the Committee of Experts against white slavery at the League; delegate from Uruguay to the Permanent Consultative Commission of the League of Nations for the Protection of Children and Youth and against the traffic of women; president of the Uruguayan Alliance of Women; founder and honorary president of the National Council of Women of Uruguay; member of the Bureau for the International League for Women's Suffrage; president of the Commission of Unity for Morality and Against Traffic in Women; delegate from her government to the Congress of Social Hygiene in Paris, where she was nominated *rapporteur* for the question of sexual education; honorary member of the Sociological Congress at Rome and of the Congress on Moral Education in Geneva, also of the International Congress of Medicine and Medical Pedagogy and the International Conference on Syphiligraphy at Buenos Aires. Dr. Luisi also represented the Municipal Council of Montevideo at the International Congress for the Protection of Children, being nominated president at the first of these congresses. Dr. Luisi at the present time takes an active part in the International Committee for Scientific Preparation and the International Institute of Anthropology; and holds the Chair on Social Hygiene in the National Normal School of Uruguay.

The foregoing list only begins to enumerate her public services. The bibliography of her published works is no less imposing—titles scientific, literary, economic, showing a great range of interest, yet all pivoting about the one great central theme, feminism. It is Paulina Luisi's sustained and ardent belief in equality which illumines and emphasizes all that she writes and all for which she strives.

Her human personality is one of the greatest assets of her campaign: vigorous, abundant, warmly responsive, with a practical sense of how to do what her idealistic vision sees must be done. She is a large-hearted person, sane and sunny; and her popularity at Geneva reflects the affectionate admiration which has greeted her in a dozen different lands. In Uruguay, she was several years ago the recipient of such an ovation on the part of press and public as is usually reserved for foreign potentates, but rarely bestowed on prophets in their own country and almost never on feminists! In Cuba, also, that stronghold of feminist endeavor, birthplace of the Inter-American Commission of Women, the Club Feminino carried through impressive exercises honoring Paulina Luisi *in absentia* in 1923.

Her work, so effective and so firmly planned and executed, is one of the most heartening phenomena among the women of the Americas. Representing as she does a country which is one of the five in the world with absolute equality in nationality for men and women, and embodying in herself so many valiant forces for the establishment of justice, Paulina Luisi is eminent among feminists of our hemisphere and of the world.

Equal Rights, August 6, 1932

Harriet Monroe

⇝ Poet and Pioneer ⇜

"Our work is not so far apart as it may seem," Harriet Monroe told the feminist group at a Woman's Party dinner preceding the opening of the Republican National Convention in Chicago in June [1932]. "Freedom and equality of opportunity are basically the same in all aspects of life." And she added, "I hope that the Equal Rights Amendment may come in my lifetime!"

When Harriet Monroe was a young poet entering upon her twenties, she was invited by the Committee on Ceremonies of the World's Columbian Exposition in Chicago to write an ode for the opening of the exposition. Her "Columbian Ode," produced in response to this invitation, was partly read and partly sung before an audience of one hundred and twenty thousand persons in the vast hall, on the four hundredth anniversary of the discovery of America. It was one of the most magnificent festivals in the history of the world: never on any other occasion in history has a woman poet been so signally and imposingly honored. All nations and all States of the Union were represented with delegations and troops, and before this assemblage the slender, lovely, gifted girl, concluding the golden strophes of her ode, was called to the front of the platform to receive a laurel wreath from the vice president of the United States.

It is interesting to note that she recovered from the New York *World* $5,000 damages for a premature publication of the poem. The whole episode was a remarkable and not uncharacteristic introduction to what has been one of the richest and most influential careers in the realm of contemporary literature. Harriet Monroe's service in her chosen field of poetry should be a motive of pride to all feminists as to all poets; since it is a daring, unique, and highly successful adventure planned by a woman in generous dedication to an ideal, and carried out in calm disregard of indifference, criticism, and hostility.

The history of this adventure is quite largely the history of American poetry since 1912; and its ramifications, national and international, are manifold. In 1911, after a trip around the world to visit her sister at the American Legation in Peking, Miss Monroe decided that something must be done to raise the status of poetry in America, in her own words, "to break down the stone wall of public apathy which made the lot of American poets desperate in the extreme." She resolved to start a magazine which should be dedicated exclusively to poetry, welcoming experiments and new forms and new names. Since October, 1912, the magazine has been endowed by more than one hundred persons, and in the twenty years ensuing has played an ever increasing part in the cultural life of our times. "To have great poets there must be great audiences too," Whitman had said, and these words, quoted on the back-cover of every issue of *Poetry: A Magazine of Verse,* have set forth the aim of the magazine: to increase the stature of poet and audience, making each worthy of the other.

The magazine has been an extraordinary success artistically from the first. It introduced Vachel Lindsay to the public; printed Carl Sandburg's first poems; published H. D.'s first rare and lovely imagist pieces; printed the first poems of Rabindranath Tagore to appear in English. The list of accomplishments is too long to give even in fragmentary fashion. But Rupert Brooke's famous sonnets were first published in *Poetry;* and now familiar and well-loved poems of Edna Millay, Edwin Arlington Robinson, Robert Frost, Elinor Wylie, Leonora Speyer, Constance Lindsay Skinner, Sara Teasdale, and many others which are permanent possessions of our literature have enriched its pages. "Thanks to a rare coincidence of poise and generous imagination, of sense and sensitiveness, *Poetry* ranks easily as the best vehicle of poetry in the English language," the *New York Herald Tribune* remarked editorially not long ago; and the *Chicago Tribune* said: "*Poetry,* more than anything else in America, has brought poetry from its despised position to one of first importance in the literary life of our country." The late William Marion Reedy summarized these conclusions tersely: "Probably Harriet Monroe has done more for the high art of poetry than any other person in the United States."

It is possible that this may be the last year of the magazine's existence; now that *Poetry* has lived out twenty proud and successful years, attained its majority, Harriet Monroe may leave off being godparent to all poets and cultivate her individual life and art once more. She has, of course, written much and well while editing, but never with that freedom from preoccupation with the interests of others that should be the poet's inherent right. Her first book, *Valeria and Other Poems,* was published in 1893; her second, a memoir of her brilliant brother-in-law, *John Wellborn Root, Architect,* in 1896. In 1904, she published a volume of five modern plays in verse, *The Passing Show.* Later works include *You and I* (poems), 1914; *The Difference and Other Poems,* 1923; *Poets and Their Art* (essays), 1926. Her incomparable anthology of twentieth-century verse, *The New Poetry,* was first published in 1917 and enlarged in 1923, with a new further enlarged edition in press. Of *The Difference and Other Poems,* May Sinclair commented, "These poems are beautiful, delicate and individual. She takes these modern forms and does exquisite things with them. It is exciting to see what she has done!" "Miss Monroe lives in a realm of 'new power,'" declared Edgar Lee Masters. "She reaches it through an inspiration of freedom, and her art is its expression." Witter Bynner said in a recent lecture that Harriet Monroe's prose is the best being written in the English language.

No brief article could begin to express what Harriet Monroe has meant as editor, critic, and friend, to her fellow-poets. Her twenty years' devotion to securing greater freedom in art is a contribution to the all-embracing movement of greater freedom in life. To end upon a second quotation from Edgar Lee Masters: "The idea through Harriet Monroe's book is that of diverse experiences, sorrows, joys, tragedies, struggles, failures, falling into appointed places of human fate—a fate that is working toward more liberty, more strength, more enlightenment, more democracy."

Equal Rights, August 27, 1932

Notes from a Feminist's Travel Diary

I. CLARA CAMPOAMOR

"She will be busy!" warns the old concierge as he opens the elevator door and pushes the button that sends us jerking upward. She *is* busy. Clara Campoamor's anteroom and outer office are filled with waiting clients, men and women. From the inner office comes a steady hum of conversation, with a feminine voice, clear, pleasant and emphatic, audible now and again in an energetic phrase. She is standing by her desk, not sitting, as one enters at last, summoned by a pretty secretary with a notebook in her hand.

Clara Campoamor stands during much of our talk, moves about, returns. The effect is of intensity and force. She is a vivid person, with dramatic black eyebrows above large brown eyes with a level gaze. Even in repose she gives the impression of being on the alert.

Her father was a well-known journalist, but he died when Clara was hardly more than a child. She was faced with the necessity of earning a living in a country which made small provision for such necessity then on the part of its women. A painful period of struggle ended when she obtained a position as telegrapher and journeyed to Saragossa and San Sebastian. Later she held a position in the Ministry of Public Instruction and Fine Arts; later still, as teacher of stenography and type-writing in the State schools. She studied law, was admitted to the bar in 1925, and opened her law office in Madrid.

Feminist and revolutionist, she was working to build the republic while she worked to build her own life. The republic once established, she has organized an association of women of all parties who are united for safeguarding "its liberal and democratic principles."

She is famed for her eloquence. When the constitution of the republic was being drawn up, Clara Campoamor and Victoria Kent clashed on the floor of the Cortes. Both believed in suffrage, but Victoria Kent believed that the women of Spain were not ready for the vote; that education for republican life should precede it. Clara Campoamor answered her with all the eloquence of passionate conviction reinforced by the bitter experience of hard years of struggle.

"We cannot hesitate and compromise!" she cried. "If the republic is to endure, Spain must trust her women!"

And so votes for women on equal terms with men was written into the basic law of the new Spain.

II. MARGARITA NELKEN

Margarita Nelken's apartment looks out over the Paseo de la Castellana, Madrid's fashionable drive, flanked with embassies and great houses, with the shaded promenade down the center where nurses with enormous frilled bonnets like huge white gillyflowers walk solemnly up and down with their small charges.

"If I were not sick I should not have been here today to see you!" says Margarita Nelken. We both smile. I have been trying to see her for a week. When not actually in the Cortes, she is always away—lecturing on the purposes and obligations of the republic to voters in the cities along the coast, in small mountain villages, in the arid upland towns. "Will you permit me to finish dictating this letter first?" she asks. I look at her appreciatively while I wait. Hers is an alien, tawny-haired loveliness. Her parents were German, I recall. But her room is wholly and delightfully Spanish, furnished discriminatingly with the best of that satisfying Spanish folk-art which is so simple in outline and so rich and subtle in coloring. A hanging in magenta, violet, and electric blue is the background for a carved oak chest. Charming pottery animals walk across the mantel. A dark oak table with iron braces gleams with two centuries of wax.

Margarita Nelken finishes her letter and is swiftly the gracious charming hostess. She asks about the women in North America; in South America. And what are women doing in the Antilles? With difficulty I focus our conversation on herself. Will she tell me why her election to the Cortes was contested and how she won her seat?

She makes an expressive gesture with the long slender hand of an artist.

"Nationality!" said Margarita Nelken. "Nationality! I was born in Madrid of German parents. They registered me at birth as a Spanish citizen but I had not registered again on attaining my majority, though I had held a government appointment given only to Spanish citizens. But when the voters of Badajoz elected me to represent them, there was a great campaign against permitting me to take my seat."

"And how was the matter settled?"

"Oh, very simple!" laughed Margarita Nelken. "The Cortes voted that I be a citizen, and that's how I became the only person who has acquired citizenship by vote!"

III. VICTORIA KENT

Tall and slender, with dark eyes and dark hair, a wholly Castilian charm and distinction, Victoria Kent has little obvious connection with her English surname. The remote British ancestor who bequeathed it to her, bequeathed nothing apparent to the eye. Spanish of the Spanish, Victoria Kent sat down beside me upon the sofa in her office in the Ministry of Prisons, and talked with me about women in her country and mine.

"We must have realities!" was the underlying theme of her talk. "We have had rhetoric so long!"

She is Director of Prisons, this earnest low-voiced woman, and her work in reforming the Spanish prison system has been news in the headlines of the world.

The first woman to be admitted to the bar in Spain, Victoria Kent was one of the lawyers who defended the revolutionists when they were on trial for their lives. She has the popular and official confidence to a remarkable degree.

"You would better see what Victoria Kent says about it," is a remark one hears often.

Her office is in the Ministry of Justice, a grim building on a noisy cluttered street. Her anteroom is filled, always, with petitioners; old peasant women in dusty sandals who have walked from southern Spain with a plea for Victoria Kent to save a son from prison; women with strained faces, in fashionable street suits; men of all classes. It is a tense atmosphere, that of Victoria Kent's antechamber; but the tension relaxes unconsciously when Victoria Kent herself appears for a moment in the door, a pale, grave woman with a smile of great sweetness, who with a quiet word makes them welcome and promises to see each one in turn.

One may disagree with Victoria Kent on questions of policy; one could never doubt her sincerity and intellectual integrity. She has the practicality of the Spaniard, that realistic race [ethnicity] so romanticized and falsified by most foreign commentators. Her first act as Director of Prisons was to revise the diet of the prisoners and see that it was balanced and adequate. Her second was to cut down expenses by consolidating prisons and abolishing those that were unsanitary or superfluous. The good of the prisoner and the good of the State; efficiency and economy: the dual purpose motivates her official life.

"Will you tell the women of the United States for me how touched and surprised I was by their generous enthusiasm when I was named to office?" she asked me. "It overwhelmed me to receive so many messages of congratulation and good wishes from the United States. Tell them," she added, with the sudden warm smile which erases the weariness from her face, "that they gave me a sense of friendship and companionship which has made your country seem very close to mine."

Equal Rights, March 26, 1932

Puerto Rican Women Writers

⇥ The Record of One Hundred Years ⇤

One hundred years ago [1833] Puerto Rico was a remote outpost of Spain, to which a Spanish sailing vessel would come once every month or so bringing news from the outside world. Very few other vessels came. The nearest port of call was Cadiz, across thousands of miles of Atlantic. There was one weekly newspaper printed on the island, and there was the *Government Gazette*. There were no colleges. The few books published by Puerto Ricans were printed in Spain. To Spain or to France the wealthy families sent their sons to be educated. Daughters were educated—those who were educated at all—in convent schools which made no attempt to give anything but rudimentary instruction. Literary effort on the part of women was not encouraged; yet it is only fair to say, it was not actively discouraged; and the first one, then two, then later increasing numbers of women began to write. One hundred years ago, in 1833, Bibiana Benítez, the island's first dramatist, was fifty years old. She had formed her taste by reading Calderón and Lope de Vega, and her themes were the themes of her day—independence and freedom. Her chief work, the first play by a Puerto Rican author, is a cry for liberty, a fitting way to usher in woman's contribution to Puerto Rican letters.

The second woman writer owed much to the first. Alejandrina Benítez, niece and foster child of Bibiana Benítez, was fourteen years old in 1833; and a decade later she had published a volume of simple and passionate lyrics whose musical intensity has not dulled in a century. In the year in which Alejandrina Benítez's book was published, Lola Rodríguez de Tió, best known and best loved of Puerto Rico's women poets, was born; and from that day to this the continuity of woman's contribution to Puerto Rican letters has been unbroken. The pioneers were all poets, but toward the third quarter of the century woman's intellectual unrest showed itself most forcibly in a demand for better educational opportunities. The local papers—it was before the epoch of dailies—began to burgeon forth in letters and articles demanding what was then known in all countries as "female education." The Puerto Rican woman discovered herself as a polemist; and she has never since ceased to employ the talent then put to use.

The first woman's magazine, *Brisas de Borinquén* [Breezes of Borinquén; the latter term being a variant of the aboriginal name of Puerto Rico]—"dedicated to woman," as it declared itself to be—was published in San Juan in 1864. It encouraged women contributors, dug up the records of prominent women in the past, and along with the usual inanities of mode and sentimentalism, offered a real forum of which Puerto Rican women timidly at first, then with increasing confidence, took advantage.

During the last period of the Spanish governors, patriotism was an increasing theme of women writers as of men. The stirring poems of Lola Rodríguez de Tió, already mentioned, did much to foster the spirit of revolt and the demand for freedom.

During this period, and following the American occupation in 1898, right down to the present, the demand for the right to vote also occupied the minds and the pens of women. A large proportion of the contributions made by women writers to the local press in the past decade has dealt with the civic disabilities of women; and with the granting of suffrage last year [1932], these contributions have become able interpretation and criticism of political issues.

In the fields of research and of science, as well, Puerto Rican women are making definite contributions to knowledge; as for instance, Raquel Ramos de Dexter, in biology. Conchita Meléndez—herself a poet of distinction, many of whose poems have been translated into English—is author of a scholarly and authoritative work on the development of the novel in Spanish America [*La novela indianista en Hispanoamérica, 1832–1889* (1934)]. Carmen Gómez Tejera, in her work on the novel in Puerto Rico [*La novela en Puerto Rico: apuntes para su historia* (1929)], has given us a genuine adventure in historical criticism, the first in the field. Angela Negrón Muñoz is author of invaluable historical sketches of Puerto Rican women [*Mujeres de Puerto Rico: desde el período de colonización hasta el primer tercio del siglo XX* (1935)]; and of a no less interesting series of contemporary interviews, covering the leading personalities in Puerto Rican affairs and the chief visitors to the island during recent years, soon to be gathered into a book. Isabel Andreu de Aguilar, Marta Robert, and Ricarda L. de Ramos Casellas are commentators on current politics. Margot Arce writes sensitively and arrestingly of art and literature. The poems of "La Hija del Caribe" [Daughter of the Caribbean], Trina Padilla de Sanz, have been celebrated far beyond the borders of the island. A year or so ago a commentator in the *American Mercury*, discussing Spanish American poetry, singled out her poems for praise. A volume of her short stories was published in Paris; and she has contributed prodigiously to the insular newspapers and magazines. An ardent believer in Puerto Rican independence, her work is instinct with local color, simple, intense, and vivid.

In addition to these and other representative writers in Spanish, there is a small group of continental American women resident in Puerto Rico whose themes are drawn from the island to so great an extent that they too should be classed as Puerto Rican writers, writing in English. Among these are Ellen Glines, whose arresting and lovely poems, anthologized, have appeared in *Harper's, Voices, Poetry,* and other periodicals, and Elizabeth Van Deusen, author of a charming series of children's books consisting of Puerto Rican poems, sketches and short books; contributor of articles on the island to leading magazines; and co-author with her husband of *Puerto Rico: A Tropic Isle.* Maude Walters, of the University of Puerto Rico faculty, has written a useful work on puppet shows and made various collections of short stories for children of school age.

It is also interesting to note that this year [1933] has seen the local publication of a book of English verse by a young woman of Puerto Rican birth, Ismael Casalduc. This is the first time that a native-born Puerto Rican woman has published a volume originally written in English.

It is not all a triumphant forward sweep, however. Indicative of the kinds of opposition with which the talent of women sometimes has to contend in Puerto Rico are two of our contemporaries.

One is María Cadilla de Martínez, an interesting example of the modern spirit in Puerto Rican letters, whose struggle for education and recognition has just been crowned with success after almost a lifetime of endeavor. A grandmother, with years of writing and teaching behind her, she has worked as hard as any toiler in the fields for what she has won; this spring receiving her doctor's degree from the Center of Historical Studies in Madrid. Her study of Puerto Rican folklore [*La poesía popular en Puerto Rico,* 1933], recently published and widely commented upon by the Spanish press, indicates the increasing trend of present-day Puerto Rican writing: a trend toward the Puerto Rican past and the Puerto Rican environment, and toward the understanding and interpretation of the "jíbaro" [peasant], the Puerto Rican representative of so much that is indigenous.

The other is a young woman whose work reveals unusual originality, charm and power, but whose name I am not privileged to give. I can only say, in evidence of good faith, that personally acquainted with her poems and reading them in manuscript, with increasing delight, over a period of years, I would stake my reputation as a critic on their merit. This woman, still in her early thirties, is married to an Hispanic gentleman, of the old school, himself cultured, brilliant and delightful, who believes that for a woman of birth and position to write, and what is worse, to publish her writings, is nothing short of disgraceful. His wife does write, and her manuscript is one woman's authentic footnotes to life; but she has never published one of her poems, nor read them to more than a chosen handful of people. The notable fact is that she continues to write them, with increasing power and maturing technique.

Woman's leadership in and contribution to public education in Puerto Rico has been notable and significant. It was a woman, indeed, who made the first donation of a building for public school purposes, and that during the Spanish régime. She was Doña Antonia Martínez, of San Germán, who presented to that town her aristocratic old home, which had once belonged to a branch of the Quiñones family, prominent in insular affairs through many generations. During Spanish times also, women began those contributions to educational literature which have flourished so richly on the island during our own period. Lola Rodríguez de Tió, already mentioned as poet and patriot, Ana Roqué de Duprey, and Clementina Albéniz de Ruiz are among those who made such contributions previous to 1900. The list during the first third of the twentieth century is imposing, and includes a long list of authors of valuable textbooks besides innumerable commentaries. Among these—and there are many more—we may mention Herminia Acevedo, Monserrate Deliz, and Beatriz Lasalle.

A fitting climax to any study of this kind is Doña Ana Roqué de Duprey, whose life bridges the gap, so brief in years, and so great in circumstance, between the period when Puerto Rican women were just beginning to exert their powers outside the family circle, and the present, when their intellectual curiosity and their literary aptitude is one of the most admirable features of insular life. The writings of Doña Ana—as she is referred to affectionately the island over—would fill at least a five-foot shelf of books; short stories, novels, treatises on botany, textbooks in geography and grammar. She was described last year at the Commencement Exercises of the University of Puerto Rico, on the occasion of being granted an honorary doctorate in letters, as "the grandmother of the present generation," but there is no decrepitude in her spirit. For more than fifty years Doña Ana was a teacher. She studied astronomy and botany, and while still a young girl, had her researches cited by Camille Flammarion. Her *Botánica antillana* [Botany of the Antilles] classifies some six thousand specimens. Her mind has been drawn moth-like to mathematics, geography, and philosophy as well. During a half century she has founded and edited five magazines devoted to the advancement of woman. She is author of a series of social studies and of several novels, and throughout her work she has preserved a style that is flexible, colloquial, and distinctive.

The attempt to deal with immediate realities and with the Puerto Rican past is an attempt to make manifest the Puerto Rican personality, the special flavor of the little island. On its Caribbean rock, self-contained and lonely, it has had always a personality of its own. To reveal and enrich that personality is the deliberate purpose of most of Puerto Rico's woman writers today.

That conscious growth of a sense of nationality, that development of a recognizably Puerto Rican character, is shown by the steadily increasing number of works delving into the insular past and attempting to interpret it in the light of modern developments. We find, for instance, women—as also men, of course—reporting Puerto Rican folklore; making studies of Puerto Rican music and the typically Puerto Rican "danza" [dance]; investigating moot points of Puerto Rican history; analyzing the work and characters of distinguished fellow citizens of the past and the present; making copious political commentary and thorough-going and very valuable sociological studies; as well as writing the fiction, the essays, and the poetry of Hispanic literary tradition.

Beyond all question, the work being done at the present time by the women writers of Puerto Rico affords abundant proof that this small tropical island with an area two-thirds that of Connecticut, for generations under attack by pirates and pestilence, with hurricane still a recurrent enemy and poverty a constant companion, is succeeding, in spite of difficulties at home and consistent indifference abroad, in achieving a literary tradition and a national personality.

Paper read at the "Sweep of the Century" Round Table of the International Conclave of Women Writers, held in Chicago in connection with the International Congress of Women, July 1933; *Books Abroad*, January 1934

Cuban Literature

"We see generals of thirty, poet-swordsmen spending themselves equally on their battles and their verses," the Peruvian García Calderón wrote of revolutionary, nineteenth-century Cuba, "indomitable guerrillas, orators brimming with tropical eloquence, passionate pilgrims roaming the Americas to proclaim the miseries of Spanish domination." Those revolutionary years that burn like an ember in the long history of Cuba glow with equal brilliance in the Cuban literary chronicle. Juan J. Remos y Rubio, indeed, in the three-volume "History of Cuban Literature" under review, lays such stress upon these years as to make them dim all that came before and all that has come after.

Concretely, *Orígenes y clasicismo* [Origins and Classicism], which is Volume I of Señor Remos' *Historia de la literatura cubana*, deals with the sixteenth, seventeenth, and eighteenth centuries and the first third of the nineteenth, in 276 pages of text, not including Dr. Chacón y Calvo's prologue and the author's general introduction. Volume II, *Romanticismo* [Romanticism], allots 735 pages to the years 1835–1895. Volume III, *Modernismo* [Modernism], gives account of the literary scene from 1895 to 1944 in 582 pages. (This volume includes also a general index and a valuable 50-page inclusive bibliography.) In short, to the sixty years from 1835 to 1895 Sr. Remos devotes 735 pages of a work which disposes of the remaining four and one-half centuries in 858.

It should be remarked, however, in this connection, and this will explain the relative slimness of Volume I, that for Sr. Remos Cuban literature is literature produced by Cubans, and does not necessarily include literature produced by Cuba; which is to say, the narrations, letters and reports by the discoverers, the conquerors and the colonizers—those fiery sparks from the impact of America on the quickened mind of Europe which help illuminate the annals of this hemisphere and of the human spirit. Hatuey as Siboney hero and the *areytos* [Indian songs] as aboriginal composition have place in Volume I—but Juan Díaz, the priest with Grijalva's expedition who found the island "beautiful and charming . . . giving forth when we were ten miles away the sweet-smelling fragrance of trees and shrubs," is not in the record at all; while Fray Bartolomé de las Casas is there only in passing mention because he inveighed against Hatuey's execution. As may be seen, Juan J. Remos y Rubio is not in accord with Archibald MacLeish's argument in *The American Story*:

> But was there not, from the beginning of the New World, an American literature—a literature more certainly American at least than it was anything else?
> What, after all, is the literature of a nation or of a continent? Is it a library full

of books written by men who were born in a certain place—and if they, why not their fathers, and if their fathers, why not their grandfathers? Does a literature become a literature because of the race [ethnicity] or geography of its writers? Or is the literature of a nation or the literature of a continent the words, however written, which are the chronicle of its life; its life inward and its life outward; the life which belongs to it . . .

If the texts of the American discovery are not ours as literature, if they belong as literature to the Genoese because Columbus was a Genoese, and as literature to the French because Cartier was a Frenchman, and as literature to the English because Captain Gosnold and William Strachey were Englishmen, then so much the worse for literature, which belongs to an owner like a suit of clothes. If the great American texts are not ours as literature, they are ours as something better. They are ours in deed. They are ours because our past is in them.

Señor Remos, however, omitting all such texts (which to do his critical judgment justice, were less abundant in Cuba than in some other New World centers), states uncompromisingly that "during the period extending through the first three centuries of colonization, the literary production of Cuba has nothing of autonomous character, but is a reflection of Spanish letters; only at the end of the eighteenth century a spirit of its own begins to creep in tenuously." Beyond question, nothing of great literary merit was written by a Cuban-born author during those centuries. Cuba produced no Inca Garcilasso de la Vega, no Sor Juana Inés de la Cruz; and possessed Bernal Díaz del Castillo only inarticulate and in transit.

The earliest poem extant written in Cuba dates from 1608, Silvestre de Balboa Troya y Quesada's *Espejo de paciencia* [Mirror of Patience]. A relation in *octavas reales* [eight-line stanzas with regular pattern of rhyme: *abababcc*] of the kidnapping of Bishop Fr. Juan de las Cabezas Altamirano by the French pirates, and of his rescue and the dire fate that overtook his captors, this poem foreshadows, in its intense concern with immediate problems, much that is characteristic of Cuban poetry to the present day.

The *Espejo*'s intrinsic merit, however, is rather historical than literary; and Sr. Remos quite properly, in writing of the period of colonization, lays less emphasis on such productions than on the efforts to establish schools in Cuba. Franciscans and Dominicans were the Island's earliest educators in both religious doctrine and the classics. In 1571, Francisco de Parada, lieutenant governor of Bayamo, left a legacy to spread Christian teachings "among slaves and humble people." Toward the beginning of the seventeenth century, the municipal council of Havana contributed to sustaining the Tridentine Seminary which trained for the priesthood. From the same period dates mention of certain dramatic representations on feast days of the Church, with students taking part.

Luis de las Casas becomes a beneficent actor in the Island scene with his inauguration as governor in 1790: "the purest, most humane, most conscientious, most able head the country ever had under Spanish rule," says Señor Remos. Las Casas encouraged science and the arts, established schools, and sponsored cultural development in all its aspects. He is held in especially grateful remembrance for his service in founding the *Papel periódico de la Habana*, a newspaper in which Cubans had for the first time a vehicle for timely articles and commentary of general literary, scientific and political interest. Yet, it should be noted, it was not on absolutely unbroken ground that such seeds were cast. Printing had been introduced into Cuba in 1707; and while that was nearly two hundred years after introduction of the printing press into Mexico, it was a full century before it was to reach Venezuela and Puerto Rico. The first public theatre had been built in Havana in 1776, fourteen years before Las Casas became governor.

When at long last Cuban literature did come into flowering, the phenomenon was swift and glorious. Everywhere the singing of birds was heard in the land. "In no epoch and in no country," Rafael Montoro wrote fifty-seven years ago in his *Estudio del movimiento científico y literario en Cuba* [Study of the Scientific and Literary Movement in Cuba], in a passage which our author quotes, "was there ever constituted amid such unfavorable circumstances and institutions a literature like the colonial literature of Cuba, which notwithstanding its natural subordination to foreign models, especially the Spanish, gave to the plaudits of the world of culture in a mere thirty or forty years of productivity such names as those of Heredia and la Avellaneda; such hopes as those of Orgaz, Mendive and Luaces; a figure so sublime in its steady contemplation of the eternal as José de la Luz y Caballero; a publicist so profound and wise as Saco; such writers as del Monte and Echeverría; and even of the lowest levels of a society vitiated by slavery, such plebeians as Plácido and such servants as Manzano, upon whose brows humbled by injustice God set the spark of inspiration to redeem their souls from ignominy and opened to them wide and splendid the door of immortality." Two of Cuba's greatest names are lacking from Montoro's list, though when he drew it up in 1890 José Martí was thirty-seven years old and Enrique José Varona forty-one, and both had produced work which today, with the advantage of more than a half century's perspective, is easily recognizable as work of genius.

Among the leaders in Cuban science and scholarship toward the first half of the nineteenth century were José Agustín Caballero (1762–1835) and Father Félix Varela (1787–1853), philosophers; Francisco Arango y Parreño, economist (1765–1837); and Felipe Poeg (1799–1891), zoologist. Of Father Varela, Luz y Caballero said, "He was the first who taught us to think." Also the first eminent separatist, Varela in 1822 was elected deputy to the Cortes from Havana and presented measures for acknowledging the independence of the Americas and for the abolition of slavery.

It was in lyric poetry and the drama, however, that Cuba first wrote the Island into world literature. The first Romantic poem in Spanish, "En el teocalli de Cholula" [On the Temple Pyramid of Cholula], was written in 1820 by the Cuban José María Heredia, and antedated by ten years (as Arturo Torres Ríoseco has noted energetically) the appearance of Romanticism in Spain. The first Romantic play of the Americas, *Don Pedro de Castilla* [Peter, King of Castile] by the Dominican-born Cuban dramatist Francisco Xavier Foxá (1822–1883), was produced in Havana in 1838. Meanwhile Domingo del Monte (1804–1853) had found in the country life of the Cuban interior a fresh theme which he was developing in *poesía criollista* [Creole poetry]; and Cirilo Villaverde (1812–1894), chief of the Island's novelists of manners, was making notes for his masterpiece, *Cecilia Valdés; o, la loma del ángel* [Cecilia Valdés; or, Hill of the Angel] which, though not to be published entire until 1882, depicts with melancholic intensity colonial life in Cuba from 1830 to 1840.

The Cuban-born Gertrudis Gómez de la Avellaneda, whose work was acclaimed as no other woman's in Spanish had been since Sor Juana's, and who, in her own day, was hailed "even by Juan Valera" (as Pedro Henríquez Ureña commented dryly) as the greatest woman poet the world had ever known, won fame for her plays as well as her lyrics. Perhaps the greatest gift of la Avellaneda to her native country was less her work itself, of which neither the colors nor the textures withstand very well the wear and tear and the changing modes of a century, than the sense of pride, of achievement, of Cuba articulate and applauded, which she gave her countrymen in her own generation. It can hardly be doubted that because of Gertrudis Gómez de la Avellaneda and her affirmation of the spirit of her native land, better Cuban poets than she wrote better than they would have done had her voice been silenced or unheeded.

José María Heredia (1803–1839) has been called "the poet of frustrated independence." His gifts were undeniable, producing poems classical in outline but wholly romantic in spirit; but with him also, as with Gertrudis Gómez de la Avellaneda, his significance is even greater in the work of those whom he influenced than in his own. "The men of my generation learned to love Cuba in Heredia's poems," Varona said. "Not Varela, nor Saco, nor del Monte, nor Luz y Caballero, made us aware of our own nascent country as did José María Heredia."

Because of revolutionary utterances, Heredia, like his fellow poet Royal Mendive, spent years in exile; while Plácido—Gabriel de la Concepción Valdés—and Clemente Zenea were sentenced to death and shot. José Martí (1853–1895), fulcrum of the revolution that made Cuba free, died in the struggle, but not before he had bequeathed the country which in so large part owes him its independent existence a record in poetry and in prose which is testimony to one of earth's noblest spirits. Federico de Onís has said of him that his life is among the purest in the history of mankind. Martí's poetry has the seemingly effortless spontaneity of the born lyrist. His prose, as P. Henríquez Ureña has pointed out, was always written either to promote the liberation of Cuba, or earn him enough to live on so that he might continue promoting the liberation of Cuba, and "is thus journalism, but journalism raised to an artistic level that has never been equaled in Spanish, nor probably in any other language."

As poet, Martí, with the lesser genius, Julián del Casal—likewise a Cuban, and one whose work in many ways exemplifies the transition from Romanticism to Modernism—was one of the five leaders in the Modernist school which dominated Hispanic poetry for a generation and gave it a new orientation. The three other leaders were of course the peerless Rubén Darío of Nicaragua, Manuel Gutiérrez Nájera of Mexico, and José Asunción Silva of Colombia. Casal, akin in manner to the French Parnassians and enamored of the pseudo-Japonesque, introvert and mournful in temperament, nevertheless dipped his pen into occasional unexpected acid to write of Cuba's ills.

Since Martí is first among his country's heroes, and in the first rank also of her poetry and of her prose, it is not surprising that more has been written about him— more books, more poems, more essays, more documents of every kind—than about any other Cuban who ever lived. For the same reason, every scrap of his multitudinous writing is treasured and published. Martí's acknowledged pre-eminence is, in fact, such that Sr. Remos asserts that even in his own country, "the truth is, hardly any Cuban writer is known but Martí; the other leading figures in our literature are unfamiliar. A little is known here and there about one or another—Heredia, la Avellaneda, Plácido, Zenea—and that with a certain sense of distance; real acquaintance is lacking." Even Martí, he adds, is more read about than read; those who had really read Martí, he avers, becoming acquainted with him at first hand, would have been drawn naturally to "consult and familiarize themselves with those other figures whose work was interwoven with Martí's: Arango, Varela, Saco, del Monte, El Lugareño, Pozos Dulces, Luz, Montoro, Varona, Sanguily, and the rest."

Enrique José Varona, philosopher and educator, who when the independence for which he labored was won reorganized Cuba's educational system from kindergarten through university, served one term as vice president of the republic and then in 1917 retired from active politics to function "as a national mentor." Varona's long and fruitful life, which ended in 1933, his eighty-fifth year, exemplifies integrity and consistency, according to one of his most discerning biographers, Medardo Vitier; and his dual contribution as teacher of philosophy and leader of public opinion is a vital influence in Cuba today.

An interesting development of Cuban letters after World War I was along the lines of poetry on negroid themes: *"poesía negra"* [Black poetry], or "Afro-Antillean poetry." This genre was cultivated first and notably on his native island by the Puerto Rican poet Luis Palés Matos, who as yet has received due credit for neither his pioneering nor his inventive genius and great rhythmic gifts; but in Cuba, *poesía negra* achieved a somewhat later but important manifestation in the work of Nicolás Guillén and of Emilio Ballegas. Guillén told an audience at the University of Chile in January of the present year [1947] that while the African theme pervaded music, poetry, and the plastic arts in Europe during the nineteen-twenties, it did so as an outward style, a passing vogue; while in Cuba Afro-Antillean poetry is based deeply on negro folklore—its story, its song, and its ritual dance—which, together with Heredia's genius and Martí's, has been a determinant of contemporary Cuban literature.

A valuable contemporary Cuban collection is the anthology edited by the great Spanish poet, Juan Ramón Jiménez, and published in Havana a dozen years ago, *La poesía cubana en 1936* [Cuban Poetry in 1936]; valuable not only for the poets represented, among whom the distinguished editor has a predilection for the subtle and evocative work of Eugenio Florit, but also for Jiménez' discerning commentary.

As will have been observed from preceding pages, poetry in Cuba has been from the beginning closely, even integrally, associated with political life. This is true even of many compositions in which the political relevance is not readily discernible by a non-Cuban reader. The present reviewer, for instance, some years ago, read, liked, and translated Enrique Hernández Miyares' well-known sonnet, "La más fermosa" [Most Beautiful One], taking it for an Hispanic and more suave "Miniver Cheevy" [Edwin Arlington Robinson]. But according to Sr. Remos, the poem was purely political in intent, a tribute to Manuel Sanguily for an eloquent speech in the Cuban Senate opposing the Treaty of Reciprocity with the United States which was no less eloquently defended by Antonio Sánchez de Bustamante. In the contemporary scene, one of the leading poets, Juan Marinello, and one of the leading essayists, Jorge Mañach, are more often in the news as politicians than as writers. Political coloration of one party or another is made the more evident throughout Sr. Remos' *Historia* (without evident partisan bias of his own, it should be added) by his conscientious determination to leave no gaps in the literary panorama. Consequently he includes data regarding not only scientists, educators, economists, and historians, but also editors, columnists, radio commentators, and orators. Under the last heading appear both President Grau San Martín and former President Batista.

Naturally, the political impulse evident in much Cuban poetry is equally apparent in Cuban prose, and very especially in the Cuban theatre. Throughout the nineteenth century, fiction, drama, literary criticism, economic treatises, and philosophy alike were arms of the Revolution. "First Félix Varela, then Luz y Caballero, and finally Varona were the leaders of the philosophic opposition," as Pedro Hen-ríque Ureña puts it. Cuba has made distinguished contribution to the development of the Hispanic American novel, as of the theatre (especially in "creole" pieces for the stage), and even more particularly of the short story; but the genius of Cuban prose seems most at home in the realms of philosophic thought and of penetrating critical analysis, exemplified strikingly by the essay, incisive and witty. Sr. Remos justly calls attention in this respect to Medardo Vitier's *Las ideas en Cuba* [Ideas in Cuba] (1938), which considers the origins and evolution of Cuban culture, in its political and philosophic as well as literary aspects. A more recent work, *Contra-punteo cubano del tabaco y del azúcar*, by Fernando Ortíz (just published in English translation by Knopf as *Cuban Counterpoint: Tobacco and Sugar* [1947]) interprets Cuban "transculturation"; that is to say, the racial interplay and fusion of elements Hispanic, African and aboriginal, and of the modifying factors, tobacco and sugar-cane. Fernando Ortíz himself, multiform and various, and enormously prolific as ethnologist, historian, critic, essayist, editor, orator and politician, is cited more often by Sr. Remos, and in more different connections, than any other living writer.

Carlos Loveira (1882–1928), a day-laborer on the railroad, developed into a novelist of sociological themes. His posthumous *Juan Criollo* relates with insight a politician's climb from the lowest economic level to a seat in the congress. Miguel de Carrión (1875–1929), in whose work Sr. Remos finds affinities with both Zola and Juan Valera, produced in *El milagro* [The Miracle] and *Las honradas* [The Honest Ones] "naturalistic" novels. Carlos Montenegro (b. 1900), a short story writer of radical ideology who began life as a miner, is probably most successful in *Cuentos de la manigua* [Tales of the Wilderness], vivid semifactual studies of characters in the War for Independence. The best-known name in Cuban fiction, however, is that of Alfonso Hernández Catá, whose work is distinguished by high imaginative qual-ity, sympathetic insight into human suffering, and an intricately wrought but smoothly patterned style: attributes kept in the public mind by the International Hernández Catá Short Story Prize awarded annually by the Instituto His-panocubano.

José María Chacón y Calvo in his prologue to Sr. Remos' *Historia* makes note of the author's somewhat arbitrary chronological classifications of writers as Classical or Romantic. Heredia the Romantic, he says, is discussed by Sr. Remos under Clas-sicism; while Varona, whose work affords "perhaps the highest example in Cuba's literary history of classically designed prose, is analyzed (in masterly fashion, to be sure!) in the section dedicated to Romanticism. . . . But undoubtedly what the au-thor has wished is to designate by these terms the characteristics predominant in the literary environment of a period." As a matter of fact, Sr. Remos amply docu-ments his discussion throughout; so that the reader, while he may differ on occa-sion from the conclusion, is hardly likely to be confused by the presentation.

Sr. Remos has, above all, gone to extraordinary pains over what must have been a period of years in order to give as full a picture as possible. If he has been generous to a fault in his inclusions, the generosity should not be deplored in a work which is concerned with reaping the harvest, not threshing it. His main purpose, as he states it in the introduction, is even more to make the public aware of Cuban literature than to write its history. That literature, he goes on to say, is scattered in books, pamphlets, and magazines (and as a rule is out of print in the several media), with copies preserved in some cases in public libraries and not infrequently in private collections, so that it has been extremely difficult to get access to many essential works; especially, he adds sadly, "in view of the ungenerous attitude of many of those who have old, out-of-print Cuban books in their possession." In spite of all difficulties, however, Sr. Remos has in his three volumes made available a mass of information of value and interest to every student of Hispanic American literature. Thanks to his pioneering efforts, the land is mapped and surveyed. Let others clear away the underbrush and build the roads.

Review of Juan J. Remos y Rubio's *Historia de la literatura cubana* (History of Cuban Literature), 1945; *Americas,* April 1947

Cultural Interchanges between the Americas

Many of the agencies which are helping to draw the Americas closer together either work so quietly that the general public rarely hears of them, or else are individually small, seemingly of little importance, though of great significance when one discovers how numerous and how constant and how effective these small factors are.

Since Puerto Rico is Spanish American in its past, Anglo-Saxon in its present, and, I trust, in the deepest sense Pan-American in its future, I shall note briefly some of these unofficial cultural interchanges as we in the University of Puerto Rico have seen them actually at work on the island. The university with its bilingual and bicultural program has been especially active in fostering such interchanges, and, to use a time-honored metaphor, we have been able to observe through the press of the Americas, how the ripples have continued widening from every pebble tossed into the Caribbean. Some of you may remember, for example, the accounts of the bilingual debate between Yale University and the University of Puerto Rico, which took place this spring. On that occasion the young men from Yale, North American all of them, spoke brilliantly in Spanish against imperialism, which was defended by the Puerto Rican debaters. On the following evening these latter youthful American citizens whose native language is Spanish, attacked imperialism, in English, in their turn, and were answered by the Yale group. The delight and interest of the audience, and their equal pleasure in both groups of debaters, were apparent at every moment. The four days during which the young visitors from the North were in Puerto Rico were of real importance, both on account of the impression which they left and because of the impression which they carried back north with them.

We have a regrettable tendency in most parts of the modern world to underestimate the importance of methods of cookery. Yet, how often international misunderstanding is complicated by preparing the right food in the wrong way! The University of Puerto Rico is doing its best to forestall any further such complications as regards the Americas by preparing a series of bulletins on tropical foods, under the direction of its Department of Home Economics. We have in the tropics many fruits and vegetables which should be a valuable addition to your diet; you have many which we need and are beginning to acclimatize as well as import. Moreover, recipes should be both interchangeable and adaptable. When I speak of your familiarizing yourself with our fruits and vegetables, I am not thinking of the more spectacular varieties—the pink coconuts, for instance, which are found in a few spots in Puerto Rico and the Philippines; and the white egg-plant, with fruit the color and size of an egg, a native of our part of the world and the variety which gave the familiar name to the species; and the rose-apple which is almost as much a flower as a fruit. I refer rather to such everyday practical vegetables as the yautia, which is—how shall we describe it?—like a potato that grows already buttered, with none of the potato's drawbacks and all its advantages! It is nourishing and delicious, but does not make one put on flesh. The university's bulletins on tropical vegetables give methods of preparing these and many others. Some of them are traditional tropical recipes, brought into accordance with modern knowledge of dietetics; some are frank and delightful exportations from the United States. Our adaptations of Northern recipes might amaze you, at times; just as we are amazed to see you making salads out of alligator pears. We use the alligator pear for almost everything else, but the mere thought of adding more oil to that oiliest member of the vegetable kingdom seems to us eccentric beyond words. Have you ever cut it into little cubes and scattered them over a clear soup with which they blend deliciously? Out of the dozen satisfying ways in which it may be eaten, won't you try this one, next time, in the interest of international understanding?

The purpose of the University of Puerto Rico has been not merely to introduce what is best from our university system in the States, but to conserve the rich Hispanic culture of the Puerto Rican past; to make the island a point of confluence of these two magnificent currents. It is a North American university in a Spanish American environment. We feel each of these two factors to be an advantage. To the university have come, for instance, some of the greatest figures in the intellectual life of contemporary Spain· men such as Dr. Tomás Navarro Tomás, Américo Castro, and Fernando de los Ríos. I mention them not merely for their own eminence and the benefits they have conferred on our university, but in order to speak of an important cultural agency developed by Spain, whose example in this the United States would do well to adopt.

Spain has never reconciled herself to the loss of her Spanish American colonies, and in many ways, indeed, has never lost them wholly. And now, Spain has decided to reconquer them. Not as colonies, not as territories, but as the inheritors and developers of that culture which made the Golden Age of Spain magnificent beyond any other triumphant epoch of the world. And as agents of this reconquest, the *Instituciones Culturales Españoles*, the Spanish Cultural Institutions, are being established throughout the Hispanic world. Ours in Puerto Rico was the third to be established; they exist also in Chile, Argentina, Santo Domingo, Mexico, Cuba, New York, and elsewhere. Their purpose is purely cultural; they take no part, no interest, in politics, commerce nor anything other than the conservation and growth of what is legitimately Spanish in Spanish America. The *Cultural* in Puerto Rico, for example, has been generous in giving the aid which has made it possible for our university, a young school confronted with great financial difficulties, to number among its faculty those men I have mentioned, and others; men who have filled chairs at Oxford, Cambridge, Columbia, Hamburg and Vienna, and whom we could not have called to us for years to come, without this aid. One of them, explaining their role in this hemisphere, said simply, "We are missionaries"; and all who have been benefited by their mission will, I am sure, agree with me in hoping that such missionaries may continue to come; and to wish that the United States might establish similar cultural agencies. If we had a cultural center for the United States in each of the countries mentioned, distinct from politics and commerce, a center such as these Spanish *Culturales* which ask nothing but an opportunity to contribute to the enrichment of the national life, I am sure we should feel the benefit in every way—even commercially and politically. I might add that these are not established by the Spanish government but by the voluntary association of enlightened Spaniards resident in the different countries.

That, by the way, indicates a very important source of mutual friendship or misunderstanding; the North Americans resident in Latin America and the Latin Americans resident here. One need not go into details of the criticisms usually leveled against such groups. Basically, criticism reduces itself to the elemental fact that a resident in a foreign country is generally a transient and adopts the viewpoint of a transient—which does not make for good fellowship. The important thing in such a relationship is to do away with foregone conclusions and keep an open mind. If to this may be added a real interest in one's environment, no problems are likely to arise.

The lack of understanding that comes from actual ignorance is notorious. Most North Americans know nothing even of Puerto Rico, which has been under the Stars and Stripes for thirty years; so it is hardly surprising that they are apt to confuse Uruguay with Uganda. Only last week, in Washington one of the most eminent scientists of the United States, a man whose name is known all over the world and with whose achievement we are all familiar, said to me, speaking of our recently appointed governor: "I suppose he has a hard task ahead in Puerto Rico, with all those scattered islands having no settled government." Puerto Rico is one island, one very small island almost exactly the size of Long Island, and its government house, still in use, was already hoary with age when the Pilgrims landed at Plymouth! It has, moreover, a long tradition of obtaining legislation by peaceful methods; it was the only Spanish colony of the New World which in all its history never had a revolution. Yet, though Puerto Ricans have been citizens of the United States for more than a quarter century, I have heard a very distinguished Southern writer ask my husband with keen interest, "What do you people think of your king?"

One important and too little recognized factor in removing or in creating misunderstanding is fiction. The North American in a Spanish story is apt to be tall, uncouth, and childish in everything except his ability to strike a bargain, if a man, and arrogant, domineering and ugly, if a woman. The Latin American of the North

American films and the blood-and-thunder novel is like something that never was on land or sea. Our novelists who write about Spanish America have usually spent only a few months there at the most; and even the Spanish phrases supposed to give color to their books are almost always wrong in grammar and in spelling. Too many are like the traveler who saw Latin America on foot, and in his book about the trip, bitterly criticizes the inhospitality of the "Latin Americans" because an Indian family in a stone hut high up in the Andes were afraid to let him in when he suddenly appeared at their door one night demanding food from their inadequate stores. And yet, even according to his own story, he was ultimately given not only food but shelter in spite of the natural lack of enthusiasm of his involuntary hosts.

There is at least one American writer who is doing golden service in helping to break down these barriers of ignorance. Constance Lindsay Skinner has written a delightful book for boys, *The Tiger Who Walks Alone*, in which the hero is a South American revolutionist who is a gentleman and a patriot and, what is more, displays that sense of humor which all Spanish Americans have in real life, but which they all seem to lose in fiction. She also has a book on California, *The Ranch of the Golden Flowers*, in which the interaction of Spanish and Anglo-Saxon traits is sympathetically portrayed. The same author's publishers announce a new novel for fall publication, *Red Willows*, with North American and Latin American characters, in which we may confidently expect a similarly faithful discerning and illuminating portrayal.

Translators, again the most abused and patient lot of folk on earth—are helpful in making us better acquainted; though we hope the time will soon come when citizens of the twenty-one republics will no longer need translators. There is no reason for our not speaking each other's language. Among these translators we may mention Alice Stone Blackwell, Isaac Goldberg, the late Thomas Walsh. We may recall also such friendly gestures as that of Harriet Monroe, who dedicated an entire number of her magazine, *Poetry*, to poets of Spanish America, and Mr. Goldberg's services in writing and Knopf's in publishing his studies of Latin American poets. Ernesto Montenegro, on the other hand, has introduced Sandburg, Frost, Robinson, Masters, and many other North American poets to the Spanish reading public. In fact, there are a dozen translators of our writers into Spanish for every one who translates from Spanish into English. "Babbitt" and "Main Street" have become familiar terms in Spanish America; and many commentators in the Spanish press have called gleeful attention to the fact that gentlemen prefer blondes but marry brunettes.

Harvard University has just initiated an investigation which will undoubtedly prove to be a valuable contribution to knowledge, and incidentally to friendship. A committee has been appointed, with five years to work in, to complete a bibliography for each of the Latin American republics. One of the members of this committee, Dr. Waxman, visited Puerto Rico, Santo Domingo, and Cuba, a short time ago, and the reception which he received in these places evidenced their appreciation of the interest shown in their writers by the great Northern university. These investigators may well prove to be cultural missionaries in the sense in which our visiting professor from Spain used the word.

Again, the Inter-American Commission of Women is a very vigorous and very friendly force in promoting friendship and understanding. It is the illustrious offspring of an agency, at first purely unofficial—a committee of four of the National Woman's Party—which won popular and governmental approval resulting in the official creation of the present body. It consists of one representative from each of the countries of the Pan American Union, appointed by the Sixth Pan-American Conference to determine the present status of women in these twenty-one countries and to make a report to the Seventh Conference when it meets in Montevideo in 1933; together with recommendations looking toward the establishment of equal rights for men and women in this hemisphere. The commission's first year has largely been devoted to the vexed question of the nationality of married women and their children, a subject so vital and immediate that it has claimed the attention of the press all over the world, thereby serving to introduce the purposes and methods of the commission under highly favorable circumstances. The consequent friendly and widespread response throughout the Americas has been overwhelming proof that women—and, I assume, men—in our different countries can cooperate quickly, efficiently, and delightfully, once their interest is really aroused and they are convinced of the need of action.

Another example of such cooperation is the Institute of Public Affairs of the University of Virginia. The growth and increasing interest in the round table on Latin American relations is proof of the general desire for accurate knowledge, the determination to do away with old barriers of ignorance and misunderstanding. Williamstown has for some years past been proving the same thing.

Last year, in another section of the institute mentioned above, some one made a stirring plea for fewer and better billboards. The reason was the wholly adequate one of delivering our landscape from defacement. But how many have stopped to think in how great part billboards and other advertising represent us and misrepresent us abroad? Too often our advertising is written for that mythical Latin American of the cheap novels—the one who, fortunately, has never existed in human form. But many pages of advertising matter carry material written for his presumable taste and down to his presumable level. It is another way of offending Latin taste and creating an unconscious prejudice against the United States. In our advertising in English here in the States, we often show a fine imagination, poetic and practical at the same time. It would be helpful in many ways if we employed those qualities in the matter sent to advertise our products in Spanish America. Even matter which is excellently presented in English may not prove effective nor even intelligible in Spanish. This is particularly true of that favorite device of our advertisers, an appeal based on a pun, which of course loses all effect in a foreign language.

"I cannot understand," a puzzled Dominican said to me as he studied a large and striking billboard, "why the fact that that extremely attractive child wants to go to bed should presumably induce me to buy a new tire for my car!"

Science of course is the great international bond. Especially has medical research helped to unite investigators in this hemisphere. It has been prophesied that the next quarter century will be the greatest yet known in the history of tropical medicine, and American research, North, South, and Central, is already playing a very important part in making it great. Men like Ashford in Puerto Rico, Lutz in Brazil, Iturbe in Venezuela, by their organized work of investigation and their generous interchange of information and ideas, are of the noblest type of international mediator.

I have mentioned almost at random a number of different agencies, some large and some small, but all helping to make up the sum total of influence. These, and dozens of others, are unceasingly at work. And the rest of us will benefit by their work if we permit ourselves to do so.

When my little sister was ten years old, I gave her a Spanish first reader and began teaching her Spanish. After a week or so of the book with its stories and pictures of children in the Spanish countries, she exclaimed one day, "Why those people speak differently but they are really just like we are!"

It was the most important lesson she learned that summer.

Address delivered before the opening session of the Round Table on Our Latin American Relations, of the Institute of Public Affairs of the University of Virginia, August 1929; *Pan-American Magazine*, October 1929

The Inter-American Commission of Women
✦ A New International Venture ✦

Few international questions present such conflicting and perplexing aspects as that of the nationality of women. It is a modern question, because only within the last generation or so have women, generally speaking, begun to travel widely and carry on diverse activities in a complex and ever-changing world. Women might lose their nationality fifty years ago, as indeed they did often, without ever becoming aware of the fact. Not only were they less likely to leave their own country, but they were less likely to marry foreigners. Now they have been forced into a rude awareness of the completely chaotic conditions of existing nationality laws. A woman may find herself possessing several nationalities or none! In some countries, a married woman takes the nationality of her husband in all cases. Sometimes, she loses her nationality on marrying a foreigner, providing that her husband's country gives her her nationality. Again, she loses it only if she goes to her husband's country to live, and if that country gives her his nationality. In other countries, the law works both ways: a native woman who marries a foreigner takes his nationality; a foreign woman who marries a native man takes his nationality. But in still others the law works only one way. In other cases, which give rise to lamentable and even tragic situations, a woman has no nationality. An Englishwoman, for example, married to an Argentine, ceases to enjoy British nationality according to British law, but does not become Argentine by Argentine law; she is cast off by her own country and not accepted by her husband's.

The above merely skims the surface of the whirlpool. Little wonder, then, that when the Inter-American Commission of Women was created, the brilliant and far-sighted young chairman, Doris Stevens, decided, after prolonged consultations with jurists and feminists, to make this vexed question of the nationality of women the first subject of research by the commission. More than a year ago, Miss Stevens, as chairman, began to assemble material on this subject to be presented to the first plenary session of the Inter-American Commission.

The subject of nationality is one of the three topics on the agenda of the proposed conference on the codification of international law, which has been called under the auspices of the League of Nations, to meet at The Hague in 1930. It seemed advisable that the Inter-American Commission of Women should be in a position to consider what recommendations as to nationality, if any, should be made to The Hague Conference by this official body of women, representing the twenty-one republics of the Western world. Miss Alice Paul, Ph.D., D.C.L., author of the Equal Rights Treaty, and a founder of the National Woman's Party of the United States, is chairman of the committee on nationality of the Inter-American Commission of Women, and to her indefatigable labor in research and the compilation of material is due the commission's monumental report now ready for presentation at the first plenary session. This report covers the nationality of women throughout the world. In every case, it gives actual excerpts from the law in the original language, with translation. This applies even to laws in Japanese, Greek, Siamese, Bulgarian, Russian, etc., with the original text in the original script facing the translation on the opposite page. Synopses of the laws are included also with important original chapters by Miss Paul so that the juridical information is made easily understandable to all readers, whether familiar with legal terms or not. Comprehensive tables on nationality prepared by Miss Stevens and Miss Paul are another novel and important feature of this report which is as plain as daylight, as thrilling as an air race, and as fascinatingly involved as a detective story.

Last year, in order to inform herself for the benefit of the commission as to the plans of other women regarding nationality proposals, Miss Stevens spent three months in Europe gathering material. To this end, she conferred with Viscountess Rhondda, chairman of the Six Point Group (Great Britain); Miss Chrystal Macmillan, chairman of the Section on Nationality for the International Alliance of Women for Suffrage and Equal Citizenship (Great Britain); Madame Maria Vérone, president of the Ligue des Droits des Femmes (France); the Marquesa del Ter, distinguished Spanish leader of women (Spain); Dr. Luisa Baralt, Ph.D., of the University of Havana, distinguished Cuban feminist, now living in Paris; Mlle. Hélène Vacaresco, delegate to the League of Nations (Roumania); Dr. Ellen Gleditsch, professor in the Oslo University and president of the International Federation of University Women, and other officers of the Council of the Federation of University Women; and others.

The chairman not only conferred with these women leaders, but the question of nationality was discussed at public meetings in London, Paris, and Geneva. The London meeting was held under the auspices of twenty-four affiliated societies of women of Great Britain, presided over by Viscountess Rhondda. The Paris meeting was held in the Salle des Sociétés des Savants under the auspices of the Ligue des Droits des Femmes, presided over by Mlle. Vacaresco. In Geneva, the chairman discussed the subject at a banquet given in honor of the Latin American delegates to the league, under the auspices of the Union of Societies for the League of Nations.

In September, Miss Stevens went to the meeting of the Assembly of the League of Nations in Geneva, to seek a resolution encouraging governments attending the forthcoming codification conference to include women in their delegations. She drew up a resolution which was submitted to the First Commission of the League of Nations by Ambassador Ferrara of Cuba and seconded by Sr. Diogenes Escalante, Venezuelan delegate to the League, and it was included by Mr. Rolin of Belgium, rapporteur to the commission, in his report to the commission. The resolution passed by the First Commission, and subsequently adopted unanimously by the Assembly of the League, is as follows: "7. The Assembly, considering that the question of nationality which is on the agenda of the Conference is of special interest to women, and that Article 7 of the Covenant embodies the principle that all positions under or in connection with the League shall be open equally to men and women, expresses the hope that the members of the League, when invited to the forthcoming conference, will consider the desirability of taking those considerations into account in composing their delegations."

In presenting this resolution to the Assembly for its approval, Mr. Rolin, rapporteur, made the following statement:

> Lastly, we propose that the Assembly should earn the lasting gratitude of our women colleagues by expressing the hope that—at all events with regard to one question, that of nationality—States should consider the desirability of including women in their delegations. The Committee was struck by certain communications from women's organizations, *in particular by a communication from a committee of women jurists, appointed by the Pan-American Conference on International Law.* We considered that, as regards questions of nationality which directly concern personal status and are thus of special interest to women, it was only natural that they should pay special attention to the position of their sex under international law, and that in those circumstances, in countries where women have already acquired the necessary legal knowledge, they should be called in when the question of nationality came up for discussion.

In October, the chairman conferred in Paris with Señor C. Zumeta, Venezuelan Minister to Paris, in his capacity of Venezuelan member of the Council of the League of Nations, to enlist his support in securing from the council an invitation to the Inter-American Commission of Women to send women consultants to advise on the question of nationality as it affects women at the forthcoming codification conference at The Hague.

On April 16th, Miss Stevens conferred with Dr. Gleditsch, professor of chemistry at the Oslo University of Norway, and president of the International Association of University Women, on occasion of the latter's visit to the United States. The conference was held in the Pan American Union to discuss plans of cooperation between the women of this hemisphere and the women of Europe at the forthcoming codification conference at The Hague. There were present at this round table the following persons, besides Miss Stevens and Dr. Gleditsch:

Dr. James Brown Scott (leading the discussion), president, American Institute of International Law, president, Institut du Droit International, etc.; Dr. Leo S. Rowe, director general, Pan American Union, formerly professor of political science, University of Pennsylvania; Dr. Henry B. Hazard, assistant solicitor, U.S. State Department, professor, American University, specialist on nationality; Dr. Thomas H. Healy, assistant dean, School of Foreign Service of Georgetown University, professor, Hague Academy, 1925 and 1929; Mr. William C. Dennis, ex-legal advisor to U.S. State Department, formerly legal advisor to Chinese government, professor of international law, American University, Harvard Research Committee; Miss Isabel Keith Macdermott, managing editor, *Pan American Union Bulletin*, author and editor of many Spanish textbooks, trustee of Santiago College of Chile; Dr. Alice Paul, authority on legal position of women, author of study of world law on nationality as it relates to women; Dr. Emma Wold, chairman, Committee on Nationality of Women's Bar Association, D.C., author of analysis of world law (U.S. House Document) on nationality as it pertains to women; Mrs. Burnita Shelton Matthews, attorney, author of research on legal position of women; Miss Margaret Lambie, international lawyer.

It will be seen from the foregoing that the Inter-American Commission of Women has not merely begun but has carried steadily forward the work of investigation with which it was entrusted. It will be recalled that the governing board of the Pan American Union at the meeting of April 4, 1928, created the Inter-American Commission of Women, following the terms of the resolution passed at the Sixth Pan-American Conference in Havana, Cuba.

On March 4th in Havana, Dr. Bustamante, erstwhile president of the Sixth Conference, Dr. Maúrtua of Peru, and Dr. James Brown Scott, drew up a resolution setting forth their interpretation of the official status of the commission. When this resolution was presented to the director general to the governing board of the Pan American Union at its meeting on April 3rd, the governing board passed the following resolution:

> As part of its important work, the Sixth International Conference of American States resolved, "That an Inter-American Commission of Women be constituted to take charge of the preparation of juridical information and data of any other kind which may be deemed advisable to enable the Seventh International Conference of American States to take up the consideration of the civil and political equality of women in the continent."

> The same resolution provided that the Inter-American Commission of Women should be composed of seven women from various countries of America, appointed by the Pan American Union, the number to be increased by the

commission itself until every republic in America has a representative on the commission.

The governing board of the Pan American Union, at its meetings on April 4th and May 2nd of last year, complied with the duty entrusted to it by the Sixth Conference and chose by lot Panama, Argentina, Venezuela, Haiti, Colombia and Salvador, as the six countries from which six representatives were to be appointed who, with Miss Doris Stevens, initiator of the idea and chairman of the committee, would form the commission of seven women who in turn are to elect the representatives of the other countries of America.

The members of the board, representatives of the countries named in the foregoing paragraph, have already given the names of the women who are to represent their countries, and to conclude the intervention which the resolution of the Sixth Conference gave to the Pan American Union in this matter, there only remains to hold the meeting of the commission of seven women in order that they may take the steps which they deem expedient to complete the Inter-American Commission and perform its work.

Consequently, and in performance of the duty which the chairman of the board entrusted to us, we have the honor to propose that the governing board authorize the director general of the Pan American Union to invite the seven members already appointed on the commission of women to hold a meeting, themselves or through the medium of representatives resident in the United States, in the city of Washington on a convenient date, for the purpose of completing the organization of the commission and undertaking its work with entire independence, in order to prepare the material which the commission is to present to the Seventh International Conference of American States on the subject that it was entrusted to study.

The commissioners who have been appointed to date are Dr. Ernestina A. Lopez de Nelson for Argentina, well-known author and educator, former professor in the University of La Plata. She has been sent by her country to various international conferences, and is well known for her active interest in all movements toward the improvement of social conditions. Dr. Lopez de Nelson was for some years president of the *Club de Madres* (Mothers' Club) of Buenos Aires.

Sra. Lucila Luciani de Pérez Díaz, editor and historian, whose "Battle of Carabobo" has been crowned by the Academy of History of Venezuela, is commissioner for Venezuela. Sra. de Pérez Díaz is editor of the interesting feminist magazine *Iris*.

The representative from Panama, Srta. Clara González, L.L.B., is the first woman lawyer of her country and was founder of the Partido Nacional Feminista. Miss González was sent to the United States by her government to pursue her studies in law, and also to inspect women's prisons and juvenile courts. Plans and reforms for similar institutions in Panama are to be drawn up with Miss González' report as a basis.

Sra. María Alvárez de Guillén Rivas, commissioner from San Salvador, is a distinguished author. She won fame for a novel published anonymously and has since contributed widely to the Spanish press.

Mme. Teligny Mathon, sister-in-law of President Luis Borno, and Haitian commissioner, has always been deeply interested in social and economic questions.

Sra. María Elena de Hinestrosa, who has recently been named commissioner of Colombia, is a woman of great charm and distinction and member of a family famous in Colombian history.

Miss Stevens, chairman of the commission and representative of the United States, was called recently by a Spanish commentator "the best known feminist in the world." Her brilliance, charm and courage have afforded texts to the journalists of all countries whose press is interested in the activities of the modern woman. "For daring, skill, and brilliant technique, her record is unequalled," says *Time and Tide* of London. "She knows how to handle the enthusiasts and galvanize the half-hearted. She understands the importance of the press, the value of drama and the hour for swift action. But behind the understanding of propagandist technique lies the sense of spiritual conviction."

Through the chairman, the Inter-American Commission of Women has received unparalleled honors during the first sixteen months of its existence. Miss Stevens, for example, has been asked and has agreed to give six lectures on the juridical status of women before the American Academy of International Law of Havana at its inauguration ceremonies in February 1930. She has also accepted an invitation to represent the commission on the North American committee formed for the celebration of the four hundredth anniversary of the delivery by Francisco de Vitoria of his famous disquisition *De Indis* [On the Indians; a defense of their rights against Spanish colonists] at Salamanca in 1532.

The latest in the long list of honors which have been given Doris Stevens is her appointment as secretary of sessions of the Institut du Droit International which will meet in Briarcliff in October. This is the first time that this body of distinguished international jurists have so honored a woman, and Miss Stevens' appointment comes as an impressive recognition of her dazzling work as chairman of the Inter-American Commission of Women.

One of the most interesting phases of the work of the commission is the response which it receives from all over the world; from individuals, organizations, and governments themselves. The Cuban government, for example, has assigned a suite of rooms to the commission, in the beautiful new Palace of Peace and Justice which is now under process of construction in Havana. Included in the cornerstone of this building are the eight speeches delivered by women before the Sixth Pan-American Conference—the seed from which the commission has sprung. The government of Salvador recently passed a decree, which was immediately signed by the president approving the creation of the commission, and pledging support to its programs of laying the foundations for establishing equality between men and women in the American republics.

Venezuela sent Sra. de Pérez Díaz, commissioner from that country, to the United States, at government expense immediately after her appointment so that she might familiarize herself with the work being inaugurated. The Argentine commissioner, Sra. Lopez de Nelson, has also visited Washington and conferred with the chairman. Miss González of Panama has been able to help greatly with the work of research. The chairman has been in continuous correspondence with the other commissioners, who have begun research in their respective countries.

The Pan American Union has been the headquarters of the commission, the director general having generously assigned the chairman a place in the Columbus Room.

During the summer of 1928, Mrs. Helen Archdale, distinguished British feminist, and her daughter Betty Archdale, student leader in the nationality campaign, gave invaluable help to the commission in the work of research, information, and inauguration of the work. Mlle. Fanny Bunand-Sevástos, young French feminist from Paris, also rendered valiant service during the early part of 1929, and will soon be back in Washington to help carry on the work of the commission. During the summers of 1928 and 1929, Muna Lee (in private life, Mrs. Luis Muñoz Marín), director of the Bureau of International Relations of the University of Puerto Rico, has acted as director of the Bureau of Public Relations of the Inter-American Commission of Women. Miss Elsie Ross Shields, executive secretary of the commission since its establishment, has been responsible for its translations in Spanish, French, Portuguese and Greek. Miss Rosalmira Colomo of Mexico has been assisting with the work of the commission since March 1929.

Commissioners and members of the volunteer staff have spoken before many groups and over the radio, explaining the work of the commission; and have written innumerable special articles for leading periodicals here and abroad. The effort put forth in giving out such information about the work has been repaid a thousand times by the immediate and enthusiastic response. Distinguished editors, men and women of letters, jurists, and feminists from all over the world have sent encouragement, congratulations and approval. The responses range from India to Greece, and from Canada to the Argentine.

There can no longer remain in the mind of anyone privileged to witness the swift development of this splendid feminist activity, any lingering doubt as to whether a Pan-American movement can flourish in spite of barriers of race [ethnicity] and language. The Inter-American Commission of Women is proving every day that such barriers are imaginary; like the wall in the fairy story which is there only so long as one believes it to be there, but which can be walked through and brushed aside by the ardent spirit with an invincible ideal.

Pan-American Magazine, October 1929

José de San Martín

There are two ways of measuring the greatness of José de San Martín: by the magnitude of his achievement, or by the magnitude of his renunciation. The former is an index to the second. It was no dreamer with his visions yet to be realized who slipped out unseen through a hidden doorway from the festivities at Guayaquil; went down to the sea; and set sail, out through the harbor gates, beyond the palms and the rocks, beyond every opportunity of personal wealth or power. The man who made so tremendous a renunciation so quietly had long since left footprints imperishable as granite in the Andean snows, and had molded nations and set them down, free agents of their own destinies. It is a story which lends itself magnificently to rhetoric; and yet is, perhaps, most impressive when told simply. The facts in San Martín's case are more convincing than any comment that can be made upon them. So let us tell over the outline of the facts.

Born in Yapeyú, a small town of the government of Buenos Aires, and educated in Spain, José de San Martín entered the Spanish army and served with distinction in the Peninsula against the French. In 1811 he laid down his rank of lieutenant colonel, became associated with the revolutionary juntas, and, in the following year, went to Buenos Aires and definitely threw his active support to the side of those who were striving to make of Argentina an independent nation. In January, 1813, he won the battle of San Lorenzo; and with the prestige of this decisive victory fresh upon him, determining to make the cause of the independence of Argentina enlarge itself to embrace the independence of Hispanic America, he assumed command of the army in Upper Peru in 1814. His plan was to overcome the Spanish power in Chile and then strike at Spain in Peru. After two years of almost geometrical preparations, with every step in time and place precisely mapped out in advance, he crossed the Andes, won the battle of Chacabuco, and, after reverses of arms, that of Maipú; thereby making possible the further victories of Boyacá and Ayacucho, and insuring the freedom of the Pacific Coast. Declining to be head of the government in Chile, after the Peruvian victories he became the Protector of Peru.

In the meantime Bolívar, victorious in northern South America and eager, as was San Martín, to unify and consolidate American forces against the Spanish power, proposed a meeting with San Martín, heartily acceded to by the latter. They met at Guayaquil, had a conference of several hours of which the details were long secret, and are still for the most part supposititious, and parted: San Martín to go thereafter into self-imposed exile, relinquishing every claim to power; Bolívar to continue his grandiloquent effort to become head of the Confederation of South America; and both to die amid poverty and the seeming defeat of every purpose to which they had dedicated themselves. That is the story. One may find it after that fashion in the encyclopedias. I would add nothing, but amplify a few details.

San Martín, though born in a small provincial town of the southernmost portion of South America, was a Spaniard rather than an American in temperament—a Spaniard after the fashion of the north of Spain; with the gravity, the keenness of wit and the absence of humor, the severity, the harshness even, which are the amalgam of a dry sweetness of temper and intuitive gentleness strangely at variance with an almost frigid reserve. Nobility is more native to such temperaments than graciousness; and suavity and tact are almost completely alien to them. San Martín could renounce; he could never have compromised. Educated in Spain, like Bolívar; a European officer, like Miranda; he was in every essential respect different from both. If we looked for his counterpart it would not be among his fellow-revolutionaries in the histrionic years which gave birth to new republics, but farther back, and farther away—to Seneca, perhaps; almost, indeed, to Hannibal.

Once he gave himself unreservedly to the cause of American independence, he knew no half measures and no limits. His dream was—as Bartolomé Mitre, his biographer, succinctly phrases it—"to Americanize the Argentine Revolution," and then, after revolt had spread like wildfire to every part of the continent, to let the different countries pursue each its own way, unhampered, every one a nation in itself. Emancipation, freedom, self-determination: his was the individualist ideal, as opposed to the program of liberation, absorption, and conquest which became Bolívar's dream. Of the two, it was San Martín's work that was to endure. Bolívar the general will not be shaken from his splendid place in the hall of heroes; but Bolívar, the political leader, was indeed a plower in the sea. San Martín, seeming to fail, had foreseen more clearly not merely the needs of the new republics, but the inevitable form which they would assume, as a crystal assumes its shape, by the compulsion of inner force. Not Bolívar's Union of American States with a one-man overlordship for life, but San Martín's free republics, people South America today, and may determine the course of the world's wealth and its balance of power in the twenty-first century.

Yet, having said the foregoing, one should add that its truth in nowise diminishes the importance of the work of Bolívar. San Martín's idea triumphed, comments his biographer, but Bolívar's effective action converted it into historic fact. These men, at opposite poles of character, complemented each other; and both were necessary to South America, in whatever form South American destiny chose to evolve itself.

To consider San Martín's initial triumph, the passage of the Andes, justly compared by Lajouane to that of the Alps by Hannibal and by Napoleon, is to find it both a psychological and a military master-stroke. In the popular parlance of today, it was the best possible publicity for the Revolution; it made the whole of South America "revolution-conscious"; one of those unprecedented feats which stir the public mind and transform a principle overnight into a battle-cry. It was the first great offensive against the Spanish power; and an incontrovertible proof of the discipline and devotion of the American troops. San Martín's own terse proud message is the best summary of the trip, whose difficulties and hardships are too obvious for comment: "The Army of the Andes has the glory of stating that in twenty-four days we have made our campaign, crossed the highest mountains of the globe, and freed Chile!"

History affords no better example of the tremendous effect of unexpected dynamic action; only that other masterpiece of sublime self-confidence on the part of a Spanish captain in America, Cortés' burning of the ships, is comparable to it in dramatic and emotional vividness.

The story of San Martín's great battles, however, is not so much a pageant of blood and glory as a proof of the military importance of mathematics. It is a story of concentration and calculation. With that courage far beyond display which takes itself for granted, a tall man with a bold profile, somewhat hoarse of voice, very deliberate in gesture, restive under any attempt on the part of another to come too close to his person or his mind, the general strides northward, his steps recorded by his victories, unchanged himself in the land which he was transforming. And as he went, he proclaimed his purpose of making South America a continent of free republics. It is with justice that Mitre called the monumental life, "The History of San Martín and of South American Emancipation" [*Historia de San Martín y de la emancipación sud-americana*, 1888; *The Emancipation of South America*, tr. William Pilling, 1893]. The man and his mission had become one.

Confident in that mission, he went to the interview at Guayaquil which was to change his personal destiny but could not alter his achievement. It was the liberator of the Southern half of the continent and the ruler of Peru who met Bolívar in the equatorial palm-fledged town; just the setting a dramatist would have chosen for such a meeting between two such men: an earthquake-shaken land, set about with volcanoes, wherein the conquering Revolutionary General from the north awaited the conquering Revolutionary General from the south, to decide the course of history in the Western Hemisphere.

There were no reporters. It was the greatest scoop in history—no two such protagonists had ever before met to decide questions affecting so great a territory nor so many people. But only a comparatively few soldiers and civilians knew of the meeting; and no one was present at the conference. It was preceded by spectacular celebrations in the little city. San Martín arrived on his modest sailing vessel, went to the hall where the crowd awaited, and there was met by Bolívar. The two generals embraced—"for the first and last time," an eyewitness commented with ironic under-emphasis. They had not met before. One can imagine the reservations in the mind of each as his eyes measured his coadjutor and antagonist. Bolívar, gallant, histrionic, splendid of port and gesture, the western hero; San Martín, stern, reserved, dedicated to one aim and that a selfless one. The prettiest girl in Guayaquil stepped from the crowd and placed on San Martín's head a gilt and enameled laurel wreath; a kind of gesture which he disliked with Asturian contempt for playing to the gallery. He lifted off the wreath, muttered something about preserving it in memory of the occasion and the giver but finding himself unaccustomed to laurels and undeserving of them; and turned to Bolívar.

The two spoke together as they walked about the hall. Their first talk lasted for an hour and a half; it was followed the same afternoon by a half-hour visit from Bolívar to San Martín's quarters by way of courtesy. The "Interview" took place on the following day, July 27, 1822. No one knows what was said. The two came out together, and neither made any comment on what had passed. That night there was another festivity honoring the two Generals. At the height of the merrymaking, San Martín slipped out, unnoticed, called his personal attendants, and set sail. His self-imposed exile in Europe followed. He lived there for years with his beloved daughter, in a little country house which the generosity of a Spanish friend made possible for him, his garden bright with the blue and purple and red wild flowers of which he had brought the seed from South America. Twenty-eight years later, on August 17, 1850, he died, a poverty-stricken old man, blind and lonely, in Boulogne-by-the-Sea.

And the free republics of South America are the footnotes to his life.

The greatness of his renunciation at Guayaquil is without historical parallel. There were, at this interview, only three possible decisions: the triumph of San Martín's plans, the triumph of Bolívar's; or a conflict between the two which would have meant the annihilation of the work of each. There was of course another solution—division of the power of the continent—which was impossible of consideration because San Martín could only conceive of free republics choosing their own manner of development.

When it became evident that his plan and Bolívar's could not be harmonized, and that a conflict between them would mean the downfall of the work of both, San Martín made the simple decision of stepping out of the way. His work had been done; he was secure of its permanence. He would have no personal reward; but the work would endure. It was all that he really cared for. If he felt personal bitterness—as being human, he must have—it remained personal and private. He uttered no criticism and no protest. His work had been for the freedom of America. America was free. Let honors go where they might, honor itself was intact. And so, the greatest conqueror of them all, whose final and supreme conquest was of himself, General José de San Martín passed from South America into the history of mankind.

Pan American Magazine, December 1930

Juan de Castellanos in the Perspective of 350 Years

As he lay dying in 1607 at Tunja in New Granada, far from Madrid and publishers, the aged priest, Juan de Castellanos, who had come to the Indies as a soldier close to seventy years before, "ordained, besought and encharged" his nephew Alonso de Castellanos to look after the monumental and diversified work, *Elegías de varones ilustres de Indias* [Elegies about Illustrious Men of the Indies]. Although license for publication in Spain had been issued, Castellanos, not even sure who there had the manuscript, urged that "at least, in view of the fact that Part I has been published separately, there be published the Second, Third and Fourth Parts and the Narrative about Sir Francis Drake in the Indies from his first harassments to his death at Puerto Bello." As a matter of fact, the Drake Narrative—*Discurso del capitán Francisco Draque* [Narrative about Sir Francis Drake]—was not to appear until 1921, when it was printed as a separate volume in Madrid. (When Part II of the complete manuscript was approved in Spain *"con comisión del consejo"* [with the court's approval], the Drake *Discurso* had been censored from the section on *Historia de Carthegena* [History of Cartagena].)

Elegías de varones ilustres de Indias is a series of independent but related verse narratives. Some of them Castellanos calls "Elegies" and others "Eulogies." They recount discovery, conquest, and settlement; much of which Castellanos himself witnessed, in the Caribbean Islands, Venezuela, and New Granada. For the rest, he interviewed participants and eyewitnesses whenever he could find them; and he depended largely on that excellent source, Oviedo [Gonzalo Fernández de Oviedo, *Historia general y natural de las Indias* (General and Natural History of the Indies), 1535]. It is interesting to observe how in many instances Castellanos takes a basic account of Oviedo, but adds details as he is able to pick them up, to fill in the gaps or otherwise interpret or vivify the narrative. The *Elegías* relate a Conquistador's adventures to the time of his death, and close with his epitaph in Latin; the *Elogios* celebrate exploits in which one personage has a principal but not necessarily dominant part. Considered as a whole, under the collective title, the total length of approximately 150,000 lines has caused the work to be generally termed "the longest poem in Spanish." Castellanos himself does not seem to have regarded it as a single poem, which, obviously, it is not.

The *Elegías de varones ilustres de Indias* was first published in its entirety at Caracas, in 1932, on occasion of the centennial of Bolívar's death, in a handsome two-volume definitive edition edited by Dr. Carraciolo Parra.

Otherwise, the bibliographical record is as follows:

Part I was published at Madrid during Castellanos' lifetime, in 1589. It deals with Christopher Columbus; Rodrigo de Arana; Francisco Bobadilla and Diego

Colón; Juan Ponce de León and the conquest of Boriquén, San Juan, or Puerto Rico (they are all the same); Diego Velázquez de Cúellar, governor of Cuba; Francisco Garay and the description of Jamaica; Diego de Ordaz and his Uyapari River excursion; Antonio Sedaño and the Isle of Trinadad; Jerónimo Ortal, governor of Paria, and his entrance by the Orinoco; the Islands of Cubagua and Margarita, that little land especially beloved by Castellanos, with mention of Pedro de Ursúa and Lope de Aguirre.

However, a full three and a quarter centuries were to elapse before the reprinting of Part I, when it was included, together with Parts II and III, in Rivadeneyra's *Biblioteca de autores españoles* [Library of Spanish Authors]. The five Elegies, one "Relation," and two Eulogies of Part II treat principally of Venezuela, Cabo de la Vela, and Santa Marta. Part III, "two-thirds written in *octava rima* and the other third in free verse," so Castellanos says, deals with Cartagena, Popayán, Antioquía, the Chocó and adjacent regions, from discovery until 1588, "in which year the poet ended his work."

In 1879 before the long-lost manuscript of Part IV had been rediscovered, Dr. Miguel Angel Caro published his analytical commentary on Castellanos. This study was to become the Prologue to the edition published in Bogatá in 1955.

Part IV was first published in 1886, in Madrid. "Almost entirely in free verse," it consists of the history of New Granada, with especial attention to Santa Fe de Bogatá, Tunja, and Vélez, from the time of Gonzalo Jiménez de Quesada to 1952.

All the *Elegías* were reprinted in 1914 in the fourth volume of a new edition of the *Biblioteca de autores españoles*. Seven years later, as already noted, the Drake Narrative was published separately.

It is strange to realize that the complete text of *Elegías de varones ilustres de Indias* has been in print for only twenty-six years; that in fact, for more than two centuries after the death of Castellanos, in spite of his last injunctions and whatever efforts his nephew may have put forth, Part I alone had been published. Yet with all this neglect, with not inconsiderable efforts of literary critics to drum the work as a whole out of literature instead of into it, the manuscript was so packed with fact and incident, with revealing minutiae as well as significant episodes, that serious research of the region and the era could not afford to ignore it.

For the reading public by and large, however, the name of Castellanos for upward of three hundred years has signified, when it signified anything, a dispiriting wasteland of mediocrity. They had not read it, of course: but that is what most critics said.

Nevertheless, if at long last the general reader will brave the intimidating proportions of the text; if, indeed, he will view the work not as one huge narrative poem but rather as what it truly is, a collection of many narratives; if he will not be overawed by the expanse and arboreal density of that forest, but enters in to observe the variety of the trees and undergrowth and wild things there, the sudden fireflies and darting birds, the surge and resurge of human conflict through its glades: then Castellanos will receive from posterity the only thing he ever wanted of it—the attention due a stirring story, truthfully told; not for its eloquence, nor its genius, but for the honest plodding persistence that covers a lifetime hendecasyllable by hendecasyllable just as the author—and we ourselves—live a lifetime hour by hour.

In Guatemala, another old soldier, Bernal Díaz del Castillo, was eighty-four when he began setting down the story of the conquest of Mexico as he had seen and lived it [*Historia verdadera de la conquista de la Nueva España* (True History of the Conquest of New Spain)]. It may be, as is often said, that the appearance of López de Gómara's scholarly armchair history [*Historia general de las Indias* (History of the Indies), 1552] spurred him to write. Bernal Díaz himself stated as sufficient reason his wish to tell the heroic adventures and great events in which he and his comrades participated, because he had nothing to leave his children and descendants except "this my true story, and they will presently find out what a wonderful story it is." Not published until 1632, it soon achieved, and has retained, the approval of critic and of reading public.

After long service in Chile, Alonso de Ercilla, poet, courtier, and conquistador, forty-odd years younger than Bernal Díaz, had begun writing the rolling sonorous octaves of *La Araucana* [The Araucaniad], a full twenty-one years before the old foot-soldier toiled at setting down his True History; and had commenced publishing the epic in 1569. Praise of his work was immediate, general, and has proved enduring. Cervantes admired Ercilla, and Voltaire in the *Essay on Epic Poetry* compared him to Homer.

Bernal Díaz has been magnificently translated into English. English translations of *La Araucana* have been undertaken by various hands. Insofar as the present commentator has been able to ascertain, no English translation of Castellanos except her own has ever been embarked upon.

Both Ercilla and Castellanos employed the heroic measure of *octava rima*, though the former's technique is far smoother and richer than the latter's. Both writers reveal not only a chivalrous recognition of Indian valor but a sympathetic evaluation of the Indian point of view. Both—though Castellanos even more than Ercilla—are enamored of the American environment. As the respective poetic merits of their two works, appraisal is easy: Ercilla's was the greater genius and the abler pen, as none recognized more readily than Castellanos himself. *La Araucana*, of which some fifty editions have been issued, was acclaimed as a masterpiece when published and it is still read and praised by many to whom *Elegías de varones ilustres de Indias* is merely an uninviting title. Castellanos, as a matter of fact, is read chiefly by the historian, the philologist, and the anthropologist, who continue to find placer gold in that meandering clay-colored stream. To mention only two names, Irene A. Wright and Fernando Ortiz, both distinguished collaborators in the Congress of Americanists, are among the many scholars who cite Castellanos frequently and appreciatively.

Miss Wright in *Further English Voyages to Spanish America* quotes him on the inadequacies of the city walls and defense preparations at Santo Domingo; the scarcity of powder in that city when under siege by Drake; the lack of warning when Drake approached the raising of the English colors on Government House; Drake's seizure of Spanish shipping in port; the testimony of captive Spanish sailors concerning *el capitán Draque.* Miss Wright quotes Castellanos' pen-picture of Drake with its unreluctant and ungrudging appreciation of an enemy's quality:

> He has a cordial manner, a ruddy Face,
> And is somewhat under medium height,
> Though well-proportioned; shows a courtly grace
> In parley, where he bears him like a knight.
> His wit is quick; many talents he displays;
> What thing he puts his hand to, comes out right.
> In war especially, as all aver,
> Seldom or never is he known to err.

Dr. Ortiz in *Cuban Counterpoint* notes the employment by Castellanos of *tercios* as the name for tightly packed bales of cotton, and of *ingenio* in the sense of powerful hydraulic sugar-mill; and cites his comments on plantations. Among the philologists, Pedro Enríquez Ureña and Augusto Malaret are among the authorities who have dealt exhaustively many times with the value of Castellanos in the study of Spanish, both as it was spoken by the conquistadors and as it was continuously enriched by the introduction or adaptation of Indian terms. In this connection, we may recall Pedro Enríquez Ureña's estimate of Castellanos: "Not only do the events he reports belong to the New World, his very language is a clear mirror of Spanish as it came to be spoken in the Caribbean zone during the latter half of the sixteenth century."

Castellanos, in truth, is not a poet of genius; perhaps not a poet at all: the question continues to be argued. He is a diligent versifier—there can be no question about that—who writes with a high seriousness, not infrequently enlivened by humor or irony. Upwards of 15,000 stanzas of *octava rima* could not be produced by a writer who held his theme or his medium lightly. One does not forget the laboring author when reading them—Castellanos' art was not great enough to obliterate visible traces of his toil—but one does have a feeling that he wrote with pleasure, working the many-colored skeins of his recollections into the stiffened pattern of his rhymes.

Ercilla in *La Araucana* splashed a big canvas with heroic scenes of noble Indians meeting noble Spaniards in a melee of arms, blood, and glory. While Castellanos gives us a far larger and far more detailed spectacle, his is not so much a museum piece by an artist as a cyclorama by a craftsman. His work has its noble protagonists too, and its heroic conflicts, but also has a down-to-earth, everyday quality which is far more akin to Bernal Díaz than to Ercilla. Castellanos, likewise, felt an impassioned determination to rescue as many as possible of his old companions from oblivion. He reveals their qualities and evokes them one by one:

> A teeming and prolific pen there needs
> To paint the history of such derring-do;
> Such strength and courage and such valorous deeds,
> Such doggedness in seeing hardships through;
> The tale in sooth all natural law exceeds;
> Such things before, man's memory never knew.
> Balthasar de Maldonado, he alone
> Would need a book to make his prowess known.
>
> And all of them were valiant beyond belief,
> Modest, adaptable, and friendly men,
> Submissive and obedient to their chief,
> Not seditious, mutable, nor vain;
> Toiling on tirelessly without relief,
> Facing adversity with no complaint;
> Better proof of this one could not ask
> Than Juan Valenciano ever at his task.
>
> Juan López, how he labored! Eke Macías!
> Likewise Rodríguez Carrión Mantilla!
> And Pedro Corredor! And Juan de Frías!
> And Diego Montañez! Juan de Pinilla!
> Paredes Calderón! Francisco Díaz!
> One Martín from the Islands! One Chinchilla!
> Paniagua! Pero Ruíz Herrezuelo!
> And, who still lives today, Pedro Sotelo!
>
> And how the rest all toiled, no words can say;
> Not that their deeds forgotten are nor vain,

But to recount them would too much delay
Getting on with this story of the New Reign . . .

Though these were heroes, he tells us, their lot was unglamorous:

They ate not dishes spiced with cinnamon
Nor any sort of dainty nor of cake.
Hard weapons made the mattress they slept on,
And their surest rest was to stay awake.
The buckler was their pillow stuffed with down;
For cushions, rocks and hillocks must they take.
And for a snack, the best they ever boasted,
Two handfuls of corn kernels badly toasted.

Next month—the specific date is August 12 [1958]—brings the celebration in the Commonwealth of Puerto Rico of the 450th Anniversary of Juan Ponce de León's arrival as first governor of the Island in 1508. In honor of the anniversary let us note that the *Elegía a la muerte de Juan Ponce de León* [Elegy on the Death of Juan Ponce de León], which deals with Ponce's long governorship and his expedition to "finish discovering Florida"—his own phrase—where he was to receive his death wound from an Indian arrow, was esteemed by Menéndez y Pelayo as "the section most pleasing to read" in all of Castellanos' massive work. In it are many vignettes of landscape and numerous personality sketches; many revealing anecdotes, and evocative detail. Here is Ponce's arrival at Puerto Rico from Santo Domingo:

Juan Ponce, having readied men and store,
Under the powers given to his hand,
Made the journey without delaying more,
With interpreters from Hayti in his command,
And since on St. John's day he went ashore,
San Juan de Puerto Rico he called that land.
The men that he brought with him on this day
Stepped forth on sandy beaches of a bay.

It showed itself to be a friendly place,
Fit for the purposes that brought them there.
Great hordes of Indians, wonder on their face,
Thronged forward, on the stranger men to stare.
Peaceful they looked, without the slightest trace
Of diffidence, nor any dread nor care.

> Likewise King Agueybaná came to meet them,
> His aged mother by his side to greet them.
>
> Indians came flocking to the beach they knew,
> They called out to the people Ponce brought.
> Rejoiced they were the stranger-folk to view,
> With satisfaction were their faces fraught;
> And Juan Ponce was rejoicing too,
> Inviting them, through the interpreters he brought,
> To come up closer, that knowing one another,
> Each should be to each a neighbor and a brother.

This idyllic situation, of course, was to change all too soon; and Castellanos faithfully describes the mutable aspects of relations between Borínquen and Spaniard. Moreover, he was never one to overlay with pastoral scenes or Arcadian fancies the grim intrusive inescapable fact. For instance, he has never an ameliorating word for mosquitoes. Guanica in Puerto Rico, he says, had a beautiful location by the sea, but "The settlers found it ill-advised to stay, / Since vast hordes of mosquitoes were their plight, / —Never was there such a plague as they!" Again at Santo Domingo: "Except mosquitoes, they lacked everything: / They were beset by enormous hordes of those."

Bees Castellanos regarded very differently; especially those admirable swarms of the Guachaca that hived in the huts of the Indians, had no poison in their sting, and produced a delectable honey which he found less liquid than the Castillan, but finer-flavored.

Castellanos had an eager curiosity, an active mind. Details of daily living interested him, and individual particularities. The sports of the Indians, their food, their politics, the psychological effect on them of discovery and conquest: all this was to him material deserving careful consideration. He examined each item in its time and place with the same lively interest and the same careful scrutiny, if not always with due regard to proportional importance. Note, for example, his description of a favorite game of the Borínquen Indians:

> The game they play is with a bouncing ball,
> Good-sized, and fashioned from some yielding gum,
> Time and time again, come one, come all,
> Round their plaza, or batey, they run;
> Striking the ball—they must not let it fall—
> Hip, thigh, shoulder, hand, or knee, each one.
> In this the only end to be descried
> Is that the ball pass from the opposing side.

It has been said that the Indians in Puerto Rico were totally unacquainted with rubber. I leave it to the anthropologists to prove that the ball was not rubber, and to explain why the Caribs could not have brought balls of rubber to the island on their frequent incursions.

Castellanos gives another picture in far greater detail of a people much more addicted to a variety of sports, the indigenes whom Ponce found in Florida. These Floridians, as described by Castellanos, do not sound wholly unfamiliar to twentieth-century ears:

> These folk of Florida are a comely crew,
> Robust, agile, vigorous, and bold.
> In every proportion grace and strength they shew,
> And bow and arrow they are skilled to hold.
> Their stance at ease is dexterous and true,
> And as to fighting, naught need they be told;
> Old men and young alike join in the fray,
> Likest wild animals leaping at their prey.
>
> No siren swims so daringly as they,
> Nor is so dexterous in heavy seas;
> Any of them would deem it merely play
> Among ferocious fish to sport at ease.
> On the high sea they often kill a while,
> Sharing the carcass later as they please;
> However the monster plunge in the sea's trough,
> The Indian is not thwarted, nor shaken off . . .
>
> Their occupations are to hunt or fish,
> And in these two sports they display most skill;
> Beyond the two, there is little that they wish.
> Boys and youths and men, that is all their will.
> Work of any sort is not their dish.
> Few of them there are who delve and till.
> In their hands you see by day or night,
> Clubs, bows, arrows, axes for the fight.
>
> Verdure paints this land a changeful green,
> From afar, it seems enameled in that hue;
> And yet to your amazement is seen
> To bear but little sustenance, on close view.
> That for the most part it is flat demesne

Without any high point, is quite true,
On every side, unto the horizon's lines
Is a multitude of walnut trees and pines.

Menéndez y Pelayo, who somewhat gives the impression of admiring Castellanos in spite of himself, deplored the fact that the latter had elected to write in verse. Castellanos, it may be noted, bending under the enormous burden of so many eight-line stanzas, reached practically the same conclusion. "It wouldn't be so hard to find my way out of this labyrinth," he complains mildly, "if those who had persuaded me to enter in would be content to let me weave my cloth with prose; but instead, enamored (and justly so), of the mellifluous verse with which Don Alonso de Ercilla celebrated the war in Chile, they have insisted that I sing the same measure, which is *octava rima.*"

He adds, however, that on so long a journey some variation of posture is desirable, to prevent the traveler from being over-wearied; wherefore Part IV of his work is largely in *"versos sueltos"* [free verse]. While he tried his hand at the "free verse," he had to contend with two old comrades-at-arms. The poet-soldier, Lorenzo Martín, argued violently against the new technique, and Gonzalo Jiménez de Quesada, poetry-loving conquistador, also condemned it energetically. In the *Historia del nuevo reino de Granada* [History of the New Kingdom of Granada] Castellanos draws a lively and humorous picture of how the three of them, old men and old soldiers that they were, sat up late of nights to argue over the merits and demerits of the "new-fangled, adopted" measures (*"metros . . . advendeizos, adoptivos"*). Incidentally, he slyly reports the whole discussion for us in the disputed *verso suelto.*

But for Castellanos the medium of narration was never so important as the narrative itself, though he established for his own guidance in both matter and meter equally stern standards of integrity. He tells us he had grieved because chroniclers of Peru and New Spain consistently neglected the West Indies where, "though there was not so much prosperity and grandeur, occurrences and events worthy of remembrance had not been lacking." It was while he and his friends discussed this neglect that they began insisting for him to be the chronicler, since he had participated in a great part of the Caribbean story and had heard firsthand accounts of most of the rest. In the end, Castellanos says, these arguments became convincing when he considered how rapidly those living participants were disappearing and how no historian would have eyewitness knowledge when they were gone. At best, the sources would be secondhand, and perhaps imperfectly assimilated.

"At least," he asserted proudly long afterwards, as he finally neared the end of *Elegías de varones ilustres de Indias,* "posterity (for whom principally all this has been written) will be sure that the principal condiment required by history is not lacking here; and that is truth."

That quality of truth, more than any other, makes his multiple narrative catch at our interest and hold it. We become fascinated by the superabundant detail which Castellanos supplies regarding time, place, and circumstance so remote from ours, and yet, we come to realize as we read, related to our own twentieth-century life and problems by such variety of slender but enduring threads. The very garrulousness of his work is a kind of genius. As we are swept along the rolling tide of its thousands of stanzas, we cease to demand of Castellanos that he be what he neither was nor thought himself to be, a great poet endowed with creative imagination and skilled in technique. Rather, let us accept him with enjoyment for what he knew he was: a wanderer who, despite his toils and sears, is eager to relate before the swift-coming nightfall the story of his long adventurous day.

Paper presented at the Thirty-Third International Congress of Americanists, San José, Costa Rica, July 20–27, 1958; all translations by Muna Lee

Two Seventeenth-Century Pen-Women

✦ Anne Bradstreet of Massachusetts and Sor Juana Inés de la Cruz of Mexico ✦

It is a happy event in the calendar of the hemisphere when so distinguished a group as this audience meets in recognition of inter-American cultural relations under auspices of the Pan American Union in this House of the Americas wherein—by virtue of that fact—we are all welcome and all at home.

In such an environment, what could be more fitting than for us to consider two great pen-women from the American past, one from seventeenth-century Massachusetts; the other, from seventeenth-century Mexico. These two were Mistress Anne Bradstreet, daughter of one colonial governor of Massachusetts and wife of another, and Sor Juana Inés de la Cruz, a Mexican nun who, to many of us who love her work this side idolatry, was and is still the greatest woman poet whom this whole of America has produced. I say that at the beginning, to make it clear that in comparing their personalities and their lives, I am not implying, nor could any serious critic imply, any equality of their genius. Sor Juana Inés is one of the great lyric poets of all time. Anne Bradstreet wrote seven thousand lines of verse and most of it is derivative, unremarkable, sometimes even soporific, although her best is very good indeed; and her real achievements in poetry have not been duly recognized for almost three hundred years. But in greatness of spirit, generosity of outlook, love for learning as a path toward truth; in their quick responsive delight in the everyday wonder of the world and their deeply devout faith in the goodness of God, Anne Bradstreet and Juana Inés de la Cruz—the one a Puritan, the other a Roman Catholic—were very close akin.

Remarking upon the brevity of human life, Anne Bradstreet wrote, "And though thus short, we shorten many ways, / Living so little while we are alive"; and Sor Juana said, "Angels are higher than men because they understand more."

Their backgrounds were very different: Anne Bradstreet was of gentle English birth, and she studied under eight tutors before marrying at the age of sixteen. Two years later she accompanied her husband and her father to Massachusetts Bay. In her diary she set down her reactions to the strange land which seemed to her young eyes so harsh: "I found a new world and new manners," she said bleakly; but, perhaps to her own surprise, she was to achieve fulfillment and happiness in that environment which had loomed so grim. This would be due in large part to a marriage which seems to have been one of the happiest in history. Simon Bradstreet, who stood resolutely against his fellow-colonists when they were urging war with New

York and war with the Indians, and who was equally steadfast in refusing to yield to the delusion of witchcraft when most of the colony was jittery on the subject, was an intellectual and political leader of his day; and his wife's writings in both prose and poetry reflect not only their mutual devotion but the encouragement and strength which each gave the other. Their many distinguished descendants include Oliver Wendell Holmes and Wendell Phillips.

Anne's writings show also an interest in child care and a sound knowledge of child psychology which seem to belong more to our day than hers. Recalling the painfully formal portraits of those poor seventeenth-century tots, bound and sheathed from chin to heel in heavy ornate garments, we are refreshed to find Anne Bradstreet writing: "A prudent mother will not clothe her little child with a long and cumbersome garment: she easily foresees what events it is likely to produce; at the best, falls and bruises, or perhaps somewhat worse." And again, still in the modern manner, she says: "A wise father will not lay a burden on a child of seven years old which he knows is enough for one of twice his years." And she was writing these things in a period when little girls of six were taught to sew by hand their fathers' fine cambric shirts, stitch by infinitesimal stitch. We may deduce that Simon's shirts were confected by Anne and not by their small daughters.

They had eight children, Simon and Anne, four boys and four girls. When the time came for them to make their own homes and live their own lives, that time that somehow always seems to come as an unforeseen event to every mother, Anne wrote, half-proudly, half-sadly:

> I had eight birds hatched in the nest,
> Four cocks there were, and hens the rest,
> For cost nor labor did I spare,
> 'Till at last they felt their wing,
> Mounted the trees and learned to sing.

Anne Bradstreet's volume of poems, published under the title *The Tenth Muse Lately Sprung Up in America*, appeared in London in 1630 when she was thirty-eight years old, and received considerable praise. It was in fact the poet Milton's nephew who bestowed on her the title of the Tenth Muse. That book, however, did not contain her best poem, "Contemplations," which was not to appear until a second edition was published in 1678, a half-dozen years after Anne's death.

In "Contemplations" we can see not only how much she had been influenced by Spenser, Sidney, and contemporary French poets, but what good use she made of the techniques thus learned. And in one stanza we find a thought which Shelley was to express a generation later, "O Wind, / If Winter comes, can Spring be far behind?" Anne Bradstreet wrote:

When I behold the heavens in their prime
And then the earth (though old) still clad in green,
The stones and trees insensible of time,
Nor age nor wrinkles on their front are seen;
If Winter comes, and greenness then do fade,
A Spring returns, and they're more youthful made.
But man grows old, lies down, remaining where once he's laid.

In "Contemplations" we find much evidence of Anne Bradstreet's love for nature—we find this also in the still surviving crewel chair backs which she embroidered with squirrels and stags and flowers. And in her lines evidence also of her desire to write, her love to write, and her harassing doubts as to whether her writing is really any good. For example:

Silent, alone, where none or saw or heard,
In pathless paths I lead my wandering feet,
My humble eyes to lofty skies I reared,
To sing some song, my mazéd Muse thought meet,
My quiet Creator I would magnify
That Nature had thus deckéd literally,
But ah and ah again, my imbecility!

However much Anne may have been a severe critic of her own work, she was quick to resent those who whispered (or said aloud) that women should not write, could not write, and that if they did write well, it is either an accident or else some man must have been the real author if truth were known. To such calumny Anne retorted hotly:

I am obnoxious to each carping tongue
Who says my hand a needle better fits.
A Poet's pen all scorn I thus should wrong,
For such dispute they cast on female wits,
If what I do, prove well, it won't advance,
They'll say it's stolen, or else it was by chance.

Those lines were probably written just about the time that Juana Inés in Mexico, lovely, witty, and seventeen years old, was being quizzed by an awesome board of forty of Mexico's most illustrious men in order to ascertain whether she really was the prodigy of learning which she seemed to be. They questioned her on literature, history, theology, philosophy, science. The Viceroy, who had arranged the hearing in order to set every doubt at rest, announced delightedly after it was all over, and the wise men had admitted that Juana's learning was everything, and more, than it had been reputed to be, "She defended herself like a royal galleon surrounded by shallops!"

She had not been born at the viceroyal court, nor had her early home been one of culture and comfort like Anne Bradstreet's. Juana Inés de Asbaje—who was to become Sor Juana Inés de la Cruz by which name she is known in the literature of the world—was born in a farmhouse near a little mountain village fifty miles away from Mexico City.

She seems to have had extraordinary ability from her infancy. Before she was six she had learned how to read, write, count, and do the elaborate, intricate embroidery of the period. When at the age of eight she went to live with her grandfather in Mexico City, she seemed to absorb learning as a flower absorbs the dew. No, that is the wrong metaphor and she would have scorned it; because, while she learned easily, she worked hard, and very consciously, at acquiring as full an education as was to be had. Sometimes she did not learn fast enough to meet her own exigent standards. On such occasions she would cut off five inches of the long beautiful hair which was her pride. She explained that it was not right that her head should be adorned with hair when it lacked the more beautiful adornment of knowledge.

In her early teens she was already proficient on many musical instruments and had assembled a small, but workable, astronomical observatory of her own. Her fame spread throughout the city, at that time, as at this, one of the most delightful capitals of the world, and the Vicereine, the Marquesa de Mancera, made Juana Inés one of her ladies-in-waiting. The young girl was a great favorite at the viceroyal court. Her charm, her wit, her beauty, the poetry which she seemed to produce so effortlessly ("when I was a child," she once said, "I thought everybody wrote poetry!"), her high spirits and her *simpatía* [cordialness] enchanted all beholders.

And at sixteen she gave up the world and entered a convent. Pedro Salinas, the great Spanish poet who more than once spoke from this platform before his untimely death, said of Sor Juana that her most vital, her essential characteristic, was love of knowledge, an ardent passion to find the wise truth; and he added that within the original meaning of the word *philosophy*—lover of wisdom—Sor Juana's can be most accurately described as a philosophical soul. Salinas said too that Sor Juana was an anomaly in seventeenth-century Mexico; that her rightful environment would be either a Renaissance court or a city of the United States today. But Sor Juana herself found in the convent enlarged opportunities for studying her own soul and God's world, and her many-facultied educational processes never dwindled. She was as much interested as was Anne Bradstreet in the small circumstances of every day life. She simply could not be bored. Observing convergent lines of walls and roofs in her cell, she speculated on the mathematics of lines. Watching children spin tops at play, she theorized about physics. In the convent kitchens she kept her eyes open while her hands were busy.

Here for example is a jotting from her notebook [this appears in her "Reply to Sister Philotea"]: "I observe that an egg holds its shape when it is fried in lard or oil, but it goes to pieces in syrup. I observe that in order to keep sugar fluid, one need only pour into it a little bit of water mixed with some citrus fruit. I observe that the yoke and white of an egg are so different that one of them will mix well with sugar as will the other, but together they will not . . . If Aristotle had known how to cook, he would have written much more."

Sor Juana wrote poetry, plays and verse. Some of her verse, besides being charming and deftly wrought, was as sparkling and witty as the liveliest contemporary newspaper column, and like such a column, dealt rapier-thrusts at her adversaries. She was as impatient as was Anne Bradstreet with men who found fault with women. In one of her most-quoted poems, which, while not great poetry, is lively argument, she exclaims:

> Stupid men, who do not realize,
> Scolding women in and out of season
> That they are themselves the reason
> Of the faults they criticize!

She never believed that learning was good as an end, but as a means. "Many study in order to be ignorant," she declared, "a fool in many languages instead of only one." But she made an impassioned defense of the right of intelligence to be trained. "Without logic," she asked, "how could I know the structure of the Holy Scripture? Without rhetoric, how could I understand its figures of speech, its hopes and phrases? Without physics, how could I comprehend so many scientific questions about the nature of sacrificial animals in which so many manifest things and many other elements are symbolized? How could I describe to my satisfaction whether Saul's restoration to health by the sound of David's harp was due to inherent virtue and natural power of music, or to some supernatural force that God had willed to place in David?"

Her greatest venture—which had repercussions far beyond the convent walls and indeed, beyond the Atlantic—was her brilliant criticism of one of the great theologians of her time, Padre Antonio de Vieyra, confessor of the King of Portugal and the Queen of Sweden [her criticism written in 1690 was of his sermon preached in 1650]. Such boldness by a nun in engaging in argument with one of the greatest figures of the day brought restrictions and censures. Her own part in the ensuing controversy was climaxed by her famous "Reply to Sister Philotea" [pseudonym of the Bishop of Puebla], a piece of aesthetic and philosophical polemic as to the nature and pursuit of learning which shook the Mexican intellectual world to its foundations. As a consequence of the controversy and the criticism, Sor Juana gave up her writing, even her books. Her 4,500-volume library she had sold for the benefit of the poor, along with her musical and astronomical instruments. She devoted herself to caring for the sick, and soon thereafter when the plague invaded Mexico, she herself became infected and at the age of forty-four she died.

[Lee concluded this talk by reciting a few of her translations of Sor Juana's poetry; see pages 126–27 for samples. To preface them, she noted that like Anne Bradstreet, Sor Juana was hailed as the "Tenth Muse"—that when she (also) was thirty-eight, her poems were first published in Spain in a volume whose title-page called her "the Unique Poetess, the Tenth Muse."]

Address before the Biennial Convention of the National League of American Pen-Women, Pan American Union, Washington, D.C., April 10, 1954

Flowering in a Phrase

A scant half-dozen times in my own experience, human beings have in single sentences given the essence of themselves; utterances leaving on the hearer a never-to-be-diminished sense of having stood for one moment at life's center, whereon all dreams and tendencies converge. Five of these sentences I heard as they were uttered, casual doors leading inward; one antedates my time. That one was Don Román Baldorioty de Castro's retort, winged with divine guile, to a heckler in the Spanish Cortes when, as delegate of Puerto Rican slave-owners, Don Román demanded of Spain that slavery be abolished in Puerto Rico, with or without compensation to the owners. Don Román was my mother-in-law's godfather, and I have the story from her.

There was at the moment strong opposition in Spain to the Puerto Rican demand, and the attitude of the Cortes was unfriendly. When Baldorioty de Castro rose to speak, tall and commanding, brown from the tropical sun overlaying bronze of remote Indian ancestors on his face, a mocking voice called from the opposition, "How *dark* the day is getting!"

Don Román smiled benevolently.

"Be patient, my friend," he counseled; "for as I speak, it will grow brighter and brighter."

Hispanic and oratorical, but perfect to its occasion, that is not unlike another epigram theatrical too, but none the less the *mot juste* for that; the auto-portrait of a hackdriver in a town among the hills of northern Mississippi. William Faulkner's town, as a matter of fact. The man himself was that not unfamiliar figure in the South, the son of an old family who had seen the family fortunes dwindle and vanish, and, taking to drink, had himself sunk to the lowest depths. From those depths he had pulled himself up to the seat of the town's one hack in great demand for dances, weddings and funerals. He was completely un-sorry for himself, no hypochondriac, no neurasthenic. Apparently he liked his hack.

"I used to lead society," he remarked with a flick of his whip; "but now I drive it."

Back in the mists of childhood, at the beginning perhaps of recognition of potential agony of the spirit, is the mulatto house-boy at Grandfather Lee's. His name was Bob Owens and when I was five he must have been about eighteen. (He was to die a year or so later from tuberculosis.) Everybody liked Bob Owens; soft-eyed, soft-spoken, always doing the thing that needed to be done before it was requested. Not far from Grandfather's were mineral springs and a big frame hotel which drew visitors from Jackson and Vicksburg and even from New Orleans. Every year there was a grand ball to open the season; not a dance, but a ball. Thirty years have not healed the heartbreak in Bob Owens's voice as he watched the surrey-load of flowered silks and black coats drive off one evening to the ball at the Wells:

"If I could jes' be white for tonight, jes' for this one night!"

And there was a man who stood at a door in a state asylum for the insane and watched a chattering psychology class from a Midwestern university file past him. Flippant sophomores, we were resolved not to be impressed as his eyes searched each face in turn; but when the Doctor who was herding us asked, "How are you today, Charley?" we caught his answer's utter definiteness once and forever:

"I'll know her when she comes."

In the Indian Territory before it was a part of the state of Oklahoma, on the day when a public school was opened for the first time in Hugo down near the Texas border, a pioneer farmer came in to the drugstore with his grandchildren to buy books; and he fell to talking about the wondrous thing an education is. He himself, it appeared, had lived far from schools as a boy, and would have had no opportunity to attend in any case; but he knew that learning was good, and now that he was seventy-two and his sons were taking on the hard labor, he had time at last to learn how to read: his grandchild was teaching him. Schoolbooks were piled on the counters. There was an air of excitement through the store; and a smell of fresh print and new cloth bindings mingled with the familiar drugstore odors of menthol and drying flypaper and faint effluvia of chocolate syrup. The old farmer fingered the books and said with proud satisfaction:

"It won't take long for me to learn to read 'em now; I'm getting along fast: I already know A and O."

Of course there are other phrases—a life accumulates so much bric-à-brac. There are shattering phrases, lovely phrases, phrases witty and ironic which exactly hit off a person or a situation; phrases like Luis's comment on an office-holder who flaunted public opinion and yet writhed horribly under criticism, "The fact that the governor is always in hot water doesn't mean that he is hardboiled!"

But all that is something else, the comment from without. Another's estimate has never the rich completeness of the sudden word from the inner self.

Commonweal, July 13, 1934

Eugenio María de Hostos

→ After One Hundred Years ←

In 1839 in the United States, Van Buren was in the last year of his unpopular presidency and the turbulent political campaign of 1840 was brewing; so that it is highly improbable that it occurred to anyone that the really significant event of that year in the States was the first application of the screw propeller to an ocean steamer. In 1839 in England, the twenty-year-old Queen Victoria announced her engagement to Prince Albert and seemed not overly concerned with the proletarian riots and violence all over the country, greater that year than ever before or since. In 1839 in Prussia, Frederick William the Third, a sick old man, was ending the forty-third and ultimate year of his reign and nearing the close of his life. In Spain in 1839, General Espartero quelled the Carlists, and through the Treaty of Vergara became the most powerful figure of the peninsula, in opposition to the Queen Mother, María Cristina. In 1839 in France, Molé, puppet Prime Minister of Louis Philippe, went down to defeat in the elections. In 1839 Brazil, restless and dissatisfied, was being governed by a regency for the fourteen-year-old Prince Pedro. Juan Manuel Rosas still dominated in Argentina in 1839; General Páez ruled Venezuela with a firm hand; and Joaquín Prieto was the strong conservative president of Chile. Santa Anna continued to control Mexico; but the dictatorship of General Santa Cruz over Peru was ended in 1839 when he tried to extend it to Bolivia as well. In Colombia—or New Granada—uprisings which began in 1839 soon acquired the proportions of civil war. Boyer was the military dictator of Haiti and Santo Domingo in 1839; although the revolutionary spirit which would create the Dominican Republic was already stirring. In 1839 the ill-starred Federation of Central American States disintegrated after a troubled existence of some two decades, and the five states severally became independent. In Cuba in 1839 the notorious O'Donnell had just been installed as Captain-General; while in Russia, Nicholas I was beginning to feel the effects of university reaction toward the very freedom of thought and extension of learning which he pretended to control. The first war of China with Great Britain broke out in 1839; in Japan, where there was a famine, feeling ran high against the food monopolies of the merchants' guilds; and in Italy Mazzini entered into relations with the revolutionary committees in Malta and Paris, in an effort to liberate the Italian people from foreign and domestic tyranny.

And in 1839 in Puerto Rico, Eugenio María de Hostos was born in the little city of Mayagüez on the western coast.

At the time, nothing could have seemed more unlikely than that one hundred years later, the republics of the western hemisphere should unite in honoring that birth-date in recognition of multiple service in many countries to the universal cause of freedom and the development of the human spirit.

If the year of birth seemed unpropitious, the place was apparently even more so. In Puerto Rico, during the preceding year, the Conspiracy of 1838 to proclaim the constitution of Cádiz had been put down with an iron hand; and martial law was to remain in effect on the Island for the succeeding thirty years. The Spanish poet Salas Quiroga, appointee to an insular post, summed up his impressions of Puerto Rico for that very year, 1839, in one devastating line: *"Puerto Rico es el cadáver de una sociedad que no ha nacido"* [Puerto Rico is the corpse of a society that hasn't been born]. There was little contact of the Island with the outer world; not even direct communication with the mother-country, Spain: shipping and mails went irregularly to Havana and thence to Cádiz. Indeed, the Puerto Rican poet and dramatist Alejandro Tapia, Hostos' contemporary, goes so far as to say that Puerto Rico in 1839 was still in the sixteenth century.

Hostos received his first schooling in Puerto Rico, his secondary instruction in Bilbao, and at the age of eighteen entered the Law School of the Central University of Madrid. In the capital, he was one of that brilliant group which included Giner de los Ríos, Salmerón, Azcárate, Castelar, Pí y Margall, Ruiz Zorrilla, Valera, and Leopoldo Alas. Pérez Galdós has perpetuated in one of his vivid *Episodios nacionales* [National Episodes] an early, characteristic appearance of Hostos as the champion of academic liberty. Galdós, a youth of twenty at the time, himself witnessed the incident (later recorded in his novel, *Prim*), which took place on St. Daniel's night, 1865. There was bloodshed that night in the streets of Madrid. The students were up in arms against the government's attempt to suppress the free speech of university professors. Long after midnight, says Galdós, "in the main hallway of the Athenaeum, two flocks of nighthawks still hovered. The largest and noisiest was in a huddle in the corner next the Senate door. There an Antillean named Hostos, a brilliant and forceful young man of very radical opinions, analyzed the earsplitting racket."

The young man of radical opinions was to expend his brilliance and his force during the remaining years of his life in threefold dedication to the ideals of humanitarianism, education, and liberty. Hostos had long since been a prophet honored in his own country and abroad when in 1908, five years after his death, upon publication in Paris of the second edition of his lessons in constitutional law, that same Athenaeum in Madrid hung his portrait upon its walls; the Scientific Society of Chile held a memorial session in his memory; and the legislature of his native Puerto Rico authorized the publication of his complete works at government expense; a project held up then by executive veto but since again passed unanimously and put into effect by the present legislature, so that the twenty volumes of the complete works, now in press, are to be distributed shortly [*Obras completas* (Complete Works), 1939]. Meanwhile, the League of Nations, largely upon initiative of the Chilean poet Gabriela Mistral, has published selected essays of Hostos in French translation [*Essais*, 1936] as one of the volumes in the Ibero American Collection sponsored by its Committee on Intellectual Cooperation; a collection designed for distribution among the great libraries of the world in order to make known the vigorous new literature of Ibero America. In further tribute, the expenses of printing the Hostos volume were defrayed by the governments of Chile, Venezuela, and the Dominican Republic; and by the admirers of Hostos in Puerto Rico.

This book of *Essais* includes the fine study on *Hamlet*, generally considered the best in the Spanish language; the linked essays on social morality which Henríquez Ureña declares to be the author's most representative work; two addresses on teaching delivered to teachers whom he had trained through textbooks he had written under a school-law which he had drawn up; excerpts from his *La cuna de América* [The Cradle of America] with its pictures of pre-Colombian America, of Columbus' departure from Spain, of the voyage and the man; and four travel-sketches, with lively reminiscences of Santos, Rio de Janeiro, the Andes, and Patagonia.

Throughout his life Hostos advocated the establishment of a Federated Antillean Republic to be composed of Cuba, Haiti, Santo Domingo, and Puerto Rico. Never an enemy of Spain, though detesting the Spanish colonial policy, Hostos "traced a vast plan of Hispanic union within which should be included the islands, the peninsula, and the Hispanic portions of the continent." In preparation for this Federated Republic, he wished to secure the judicial and economic autonomy of the three Antilles, to be succeeded duly by a democratic confederation representative in form.

Believing that a free Cuba would be followed inevitably by a free Puerto Rico, and that by Federation, Hostos began in 1863 the work for Cuban independence which was to continue without pause until 1898. When in 1870 a law was passed by the congress of the republic of Colombia giving the bases of a working alliance between the Spanish American republics for furthering the independence of Cuba and Puerto Rico, Hostos undertook his travels on behalf of independence; travels which, encircling South America, and requiring half a life-time, left a record permanently inscribed in the laws and the educational systems of the countries wherein he labored.

In Santo Domingo, Hostos founded and directed the first Normal School, wrote textbooks, and drew up school legislation. The Dominican historian Américo Lugo declares that what deserves to be called a national literature did not begin until after the fructifying presence there of Eugenio María de Hostos.

In Peru he founded a newspaper which, advocating Cuban independence, did not limit itself to that theme: through its columns Hostos waged successful campaigns on behalf of shorter hours and higher wages for Peruvian workers, and roused public opinion against the exploitation of Chinese laborers in the mines. When the Peruvian government was considering the project for the Oroya railroad, Hostos, pointing out editorially clauses contrary to the public interest, had the satisfaction of refusing $200,000 offered him by the would-be incorporators ostensibly "for the Cubans," as well as of seeing the offending clauses deleted.

In Chile, through another newspaper campaign incidental to his major theme of independence, Hostos won for Chilean women full recognition of their right to enter the university and to obtain professional training in law and medicine.

In Argentina, Hostos defended energetically in the press the Transandine railway project, which he had been first to propose. And when the railway did come into existence, the first locomotive that crossed the Andes bore the name of Eugenio María de Hostos.

In Venezuela, in Chile, in his native Puerto Rico, he contributed to raising the standards and developing the systems of public education.

Brazil, Colombia, Peru, Argentina and Chile knew him also as a brilliant journalist, never swerving from his campaign for Cuban and Puerto Rican independence, and always conscious of the responsibility, as of the power of the press.

In view of this tremendously productive and inspiring life, it is not too much to say of Eugenio María de Hostos, as he himself said of Hamlet, in his famous essay, that he was "a moment of the human spirit"; not a moment of gloom and vacillation, but a moment of resolution and courage not to be extinguished even by the hazard of birth in an impoverished sea-girt Caribbean colony, in that harassed and threatening year 1839.

Address before the delegates to the Biennial Congress of the World Federation of Education Associations, at the unveiling of the bronze plaque commemorating the Hostos Centenary—as authorized by the Eighth Pan-American Conference—by the statue of Eugenio María de Hostos on the campus of the University of Puerto Rico, Rio Piedras, Puerto Rico; *Books Abroad*, 1940

Birds, Beasts, and Flowers, and Indians

Unknown birds in the west with their beautiful wings.

—Archibald MacLeish

The pages in which the first Europeans who visited the new world of America described what they saw are still alive with wonder and delight. They seemed to feel a kind of showman's pride even in the fierceness of the alligators. Pineapples of the tropics and small wild strawberries of the north are described with gusto again and again by voyagers who had eaten stale ship's food too long. Pleasure in the shapes and colors and flavors of such strange exotic vegetables as potatoes and corn and tomatoes, pleased interest in the flowers and trees and grasses, and more—much more—in the bright birds, bright fruits, and great green-glowing fireflies are repeated in page after page of Spanish, English, and French by men who either never looked on one another's faces or else looked in enmity, but all of whom gazed amazed and entranced on the wonders of America. The Indians too were described repeatedly, according to the nature of the observer; and so were new stars in the soft, low-hanging skies and strange fishes in the deep-colored waters, and tall trees with woods of many uses, and leaves and barks and roots that eventually would medicine a world. And time after time is described the sweet smell of America, that fresh wild fragrance wafted far out over the ocean long before land came into sight.

In a letter to the Pope describing a colorful heap of tropical fruits—"violet inside and white outside . . . red inside and white outside . . . red outside and white outside . . . purplish . . . yellowish . . . violet skin and white pulp," Peter Martyr observes:

> I am aware that in enumerating these species I shall provoke envious people, who will laugh when my writings reach them, at my sending such minute particulars to Your Holiness, who is charged with such weighty interests and on whose shoulders rests the burden of the whole Christian world. I would like to know from these envious, whether Pliny and the other sages famous for their science sought, in communicating similar details to the powerful men of their day, to be useful only to the princes with whom they corresponded. They mingled together obscure reports and positive knowledge, great things and small, generalities and details; to the end that posterity might, equally with the princes, learn everything together, and also in the hope that those who crave details and are interested in novelties, might be able to distinguish between different countries and regions, the earth's products, national customs, and the nature of things . . .

The great popularity of later books repeating and amplifying such details is proof that Peter Martyr was right as to popular interest in every item of information from the New World. Here are several such items from among the thousands avidly received:

[From Peru in 1532] It appears to me that in no part have sheep like those of the Indies been found or heard of. . . . These sheep are among the most excellent creatures that God has created, and the most useful. . . . In the mountainous parts . . . no tree will grow, and if the cotton was sown it would yield nothing, so that the natives, unless they obtained it by trading, could have no clothing. To supply this need, the Giver of all good things, who is God our Lord, created . . . vast flocks of these animals which we call sheep. . . . The natives call these sheep *llamas*. . . . Some are white, others black, and others grey. Some of them are as large as small donkeys, with long legs, broad bellies, and a neck of the length and shape of that of a camel. . . . Truly it is very pleasant to see the Indians of Callao go forth with their beasts, and return with them to their homes in the evening, laden with fuel. They feed on the herbage of the plains, and when they complain they make a noise like the groaning of camels. (Pedro Cieza de León in *The Chronicle of Peru, Part I, Travels.*)

[From the West Indian Islands in 1585. In Cates's description of Sir Francis Drake's voyage there is the following excellent description of coconuts and bananas, here called cochos nuts and plantans] The saide cochos hath a hard shell and a greene huske over it, as hath our walnut, but it farre exceedeth in greatnesse, for this cochos in his greene huske is bigger than any mans two fistes: of the hard shell many drinking cups are made here in England, and set in silver as I have often seen. Next within this hard shell is a white rine resembling in shewe very much even as any thing may do, to the white of an egge when it is hard boyled. And within this white of the nut lyeth a water, which is whitish and very cleere, to the quantitie of halfe a pynt or thereabout, which water and white rine before spoken of, are both of a very coole fresh tast, and as pleasing as any thing may be. I have heard some hold opinion, that it is very restorative. The plantan groweth in cods, somewhat like to beanes, but is bigger and longer, and much more thicke together on the stalke, and when it waxeth ripe, the meate which filleth the rine of the cod becommeth yellow, and is exceeding sweet and pleasant. (*A Summarie and True Discourse of Sir Francis Drake's West Indian Voyage*, in Hakluyt.)

[From Paraguay and the present Argentina, in 1587] Cotton likewise growes vpon small shrubs and great trees like to little apples, which doe open and yealde forth this webbe; which being gathered, they spinne to make stuffes. It is one of the things at the Indies of greatest profite, and most in vse, for it serves them both instead of flaxe and wooll to make their garments. It groweth in hote

soyle . . . the greatest store of any place that I know is in the province of Tu-
cumán, in that of Santa Cruz de la Sierra, and at Paraguay, whereas cotton is
their chief revenue. . . . At the Indies whereas this cotton growes, they make
cloth, which both men and women vse commonly, making table napkins
thereof, yea and sailes for their shippes. (Father José de Acosta's *Natural and Moral
History of the Indies.*)

As for the Indians, there is probably no more heartfelt note than this, about
Brazilian savages, in Roger Barlow's *Brief Summe of Geographie* published in 1541:
"They have diverse other wild fruits good to eat and the country is good, but the
people be so beastly that they put them self to no manner of labour but to study
how to take their neighbours for to eat them."

American Story: Historical Broadcast Series of the NBC Inter-American University of the Air, 1944;
all translations by Muna Lee

Translating the Untranslatable

→ Can Poetry Stand the Change? ←

When Victor Hugo was asked if it is not very difficult to write a poem, he is said to have replied, "It is either very easy or it is impossible!" That answer is perfectly applicable to a translation of poetry—a successful translation. No one has expressed this more exactly than one of the most felicitous of translators, Helen Waddell, who has rendered into English poetry the Latin lyrics of medieval poets and wandering scholars in two volumes in which "Joyously return again / Singing-birds in chorus."

In explaining the basis for selecting the poems translated, Miss Waddell acknowledges that "the omissions here may well seem unaccountable. There are five lyrics from Fortunatus, but not the two that are his immortality: Hrabanus Maurus is here, but not his pupil and far greater poet, the ill-starred Gottschalk. . . . I tried to translate them, and could not. . . . A man cannot say, 'I will translate,' any more than he can say, 'I will compose poetry.' In this minor art also, the wind blows where it lists." But, Helen Waddell adds proudly, "In one thing the translator is happy: he walks with good companions." Companions, it should be added, of his own choosing. The translation of poetry offers no material advantage—no inducement, indeed, beyond the pleasure of the task. No sane person would expect to make a living wage by writing poetry, although he might cherish hopes of that remote eventuality, fame. But the translator of poetry, likewise without expectation of money, has even less of fame. On the contrary, the better, the more successful, he is as a translator, the less perceptible his own part in the finished work: it is the author who speaks, who is heard and acknowledged; and that is as it should be. The translator is an agent, a medium, a passive vessel; his triumph is to achieve a translation so little his own possession that nothing, not even consciousness of the translator's presence, comes between the author and his new audience in another language.

Parturition, however easy and natural, may be expected to be painful. Victor Hugo was not denying the birth pangs of poetry when scoffing at the supposed difficulties. In that, the writing of poetry is almost wholly different from translation—which, indeed, is not so much parturition as adoption. The tension of making a poem is very unlike the relaxation of translating a poem already created by someone else. In both, there may be high excitement; but in the one, the excitement is striving to lift to the utmost of one's reach; in the other, it is the excitement of enticing beauty to another habitat nearer home.

It is not strange, then, that in spite of the lack of conspicuous rewards almost every creative writer (as well as hordes with no creative gifts) is constantly trying his hand at translation. Cicero and Quintilian long ago recommended the practice as beneficial literary exercise. Voltaire—than whom no one could have been temperamentally less fitted for the task—tried translating Shakespeare, with lamentable results. The genius of each was too great, and too unlike the other's, for success to have been possible. Lesser talents have been applied far more profitably to lesser works. In fact, the failures in translation are hardly less spectacular than the triumphs. And of all forms of literary endeavor, the translation of poetry has, perhaps, been responsible for most time misspent and labor wasted. (That clomp-clomp that offends your ears is all too often the heavy unangelic footfall of translators fearless where they tread.)

Yet *"traduttore, traditore"* [translator, traitor] is not always an adequate summing-up of the translator's zeal, even when his work falls short of perfection. The controlled ecstasy of Keats' sonnet "On First Looking into Chapman's Homer" would be an enduring monument to the new planet and his own wild surmise even if there were no "Ode on a Grecian Urn" to attest it further.

In a recent after-dinner conversation with other delegates to a UNESCO conference, the Consul General of Iran remarked that often a translation was so far superior to the original as to bestow on the latter a literary fame it would hardly have won by itself. He mentioned as an example Edward FitzGerald's adoption, adaptation, and appropriation of Omar Khayyam's *Rubaiyat*, and added that Persian literature presents a curiously satisfactory analogy in reverse translation. It seems that an early nineteenth-century Persian writer translated an English Gothic novel, not one of the well-known examples of its school; in fact, of those taking part in the conversation, all of whom had at least an average acquaintance with English literature, none had ever heard of the original work or its author. The novel nevertheless was so beautifully translated that it became a gem of Persian literature, as familiar and beloved in Iran now as the *Rubaiyat* is in English-speaking lands. Often, the Consul General concluded, an Iranian on his first visit to London, eager to pay tribute at a literary shrine, will inquire about the house in which that classic was written, only to be met with blank looks and discover that both novel and writer are utterly forgotten in the land of their origin.

Is it possible to be really faithful to the original text in both form and spirit? Or must the translator forgo the one for the sake of the other, his immediate problem always being which to choose, rendition of the language or rendition of the meaning? These are questions that every conscientious translator must sometimes ponder, though they are rarely presented as such a choice between extremes as the inexperienced might suppose. Readers not themselves translators often express wonder that a poem can be carried over from one language to another with the poetic pattern intact, rhyme scheme and all. It is sometimes viewed as a remarkable achievement that a Spanish sonnet should be transformed into a sonnet in English, with its fourteen lines no more, no less, its octet still rising, its sestet still retreating, as free and as orderly as a wave; or that Spanish *décimas* [ten octosyllabic verses rhyming *abbaaccddc*] should become ten-lined English stanzas, rhymes marching properly in place. The fact is that if a translator can translate the poem at all, and if he knows his poetic technique and loves the craft as well as the art of verse, he often finds that a fixed pattern facilitates his task. It is not necessarily more difficult to put a sonnet thought into English lines than into Spanish. Rather, it often helps to have the sonnet already mapped, so to speak. It helps, that is, if the thing can be done at all; for sometimes, despite the best of will and skill, it cannot.

Writing more than a century and a half ago, Alexander Fraser Tytler [Woodhouselee] listed in his *Essay on the Principles of Translation* three general laws: that the translation give a complete transcript of the ideas of the original work; that the style and manner of writing in a translation be "of the same character with that of the original"; and that a translation have "all the ease of original composition." Ease, however, Tytler warned, must never "degenerate into licentiousness . . . the ease of Billingsgate and Wapping."

What makes for easy translation? Take two examples, both easy to translate: Poe and Whitman. Edgar Allan Poe is clearly one of the most "translatable" poets in literature. Yet he is also one of the most patterned, one whose melody is not only part of the poem; sometimes it *is* the poem, which, lacking the music, would cease to exist. A poem by Poe put into prose is hardly a poem and is decidedly not Poe; but how easily, how melodiously, the rolling numbers sweep sonorous into French or Spanish or German, sound and sense indissoluble. And how completely the translations remain recognizably, unmistakably Poe.

Whitman, on the other hand, translates easily because the pattern counts for comparatively little. The idea is the thing, and it seems to make its own rhythms as it flows outward and onward in whatever language. Whitman's poetry is not molded by, but itself shapes, any vessel into which it is poured.

The poet difficult, next to impossible, to translate—Juan Ramón Jiménez, for example—is the one who has not only his own style and his own message, but an idiom so personal that words may mean one thing to him and something quite different to the rest of the world, or may have connotations so peculiarly his that no approximation in other speech can render the hovering thought. Translation can cast no light on poetry that is darkened, not illuminated, by its own images. (Yet even such poetry has its translators, and sometimes the translations do achieve a miracle. In the case of Helen Waddell, it is a recurrent miracle.)

Quite apart from translations which are not properly such because of failure to give the spirit, the meaning, and the approximate form of the original, it is surprising to find how wide the divergence may be between two good renditions by different hands of the same original. No matter how well a poet-translator knows both languages, no matter how thoroughly he is imbued with the spirit of the original nor how faithful to it, what he sets down in translation will be as different from the version of another poet-translator equally endowed as (to be brutally frank) both are from the original. English literature, which abounds in good translations, proves time and time again that the translator's personality will inevitably, and despite his best intention, give color and inclination to his work.

Respective renditions by Austin Dobson and George Santayana of Théophile Gautier's "L'art" [Art] strikingly illustrate the translator's coloration. Both versions are memorable achievements, as translation and as English poetry; but how different they are, within the larger fidelity to essential image and general pattern. Take two of the finest stanzas as examples. Gautier wrote:

> Point de contraintes fausses!
> Mais que pour marcher droit
>   Tu chausses,
> Muse, un cothurne êtroit.

Dobson gives:

> O Poet, then forbear
>   The loosely-sandalled verse,
> Choose rather then to wear
> The buskin—strait and terse.

This, in Santayana's hands becomes:

> No idle chains endure;
> Yet, Muse, to walk aright,
>   Lace tight
> Thy buskin proud and sure.

Again, the original reads:

> Tout passe. L'art robuste
> Seul a l'éternité
>   Le buste
> Survit à la cité.

Dobson has:

> All passes. Art alone
>   Enduring stays to us;
> The bust outlasts the throne,
>   The coin, Tiberius.

Santayana renders it:

> All things return to dust
> Save beauties fashioned well.
>   The bust
> Outlasts the citadel.

A look into a translator's workshop may help us understand something of his problems and his method. Walter Owen, of Buenos Aires, whose long, devoted service to translation was fittingly recognized last March 29 [1954] by the unveiling of his bust at the Glasgow school he attended, affords us an opportunity. In the preface to his version of Book I of *La Araucana* (1945), Mr. Owen offers as an example his own progressive rendering of the opening stanza [of this epic by Alonso de Ercilla about the Spanish conquest of the Araucanian peoples of Chile, originally published in the late sixteenth century]. Ercilla wrote:

> No las damas, amor, no gentilezas,
> De caballeros canto enamorados,
> Ni las muestras, regalos y ternezas
> De amorosos afectos y cuidados;
> Mas el valor, los hechos, las proezas
> De aquellos españoles esforzados,
> Que a la cerviz de Arauco no domada,
> Pusieron duro jugo por la espada.

His first, and approximately literal draft translation, he says, was:

> Not ladies, love, nor courtesies
> Of amorous knights I sing,
> Nor tokens, sweets, and favours
> Of love's delights and cares.
> But the valour, deeds, and exploits
> Of those stalwart Spaniards,
> That on Arauco's untamed neck
> Placed by the sword a rigorous yoke.

The sense is there, Mr. Owen points out; the matter. The expression is not adequate. "But the rhythm and ring and martial tramp of Ercilla are absent. The epic note is wanting; the bird of poetry has escaped our net of English words." And then he shows us a translator at work.

Since Ercilla followed traditional models, notably Homer and Virgil, Mr. Owen decides on a classic invocation ("Sing, Muse!"), but is faced with the necessity of adhering to Ercilla's list of what the Muse is not to sing. Several of the prohibited items can be loosely grouped as "Venus," especially if she be accompanied by Cupid—at which Mr. Owen has a happy inspiration and calls the latter not Cupid but "her chuck": "Sing, Muse! but not of Venus and her chuck." A similar process transmutes Ercilla's *caballeros enamorados* [literally, knights in love] into "Nor amorous jousts in dainty lists of love"; and since gallant cavaliers naturally lay siege to Beauty, Ercilla's *"muestras, regalos y ternezas / De amorosos afectos y cuidados"* becomes "Favours and forfeits won in Beauty's siege, / By soft assaults of chamber-gallantry" which ends the negations and brings the translator to encharge the Muse affirmatively. "But of the valiant deeds and stratagems," Mr. Owen confesses, was his first revision but quickly straightened out into "But of the valiant deeds and worthy fame."

In the next line, *"españoles"* is a key word, but "Spaniards" in English is a trochee, and difficult. Reluctantly the translator decides to omit "Spaniards" here and "bring in the national note" later on; so the line becomes "Of those who far on surge-ensundered shores"—with the phrase giving a sense of the sixteenth-century remoteness of "those" who fought in Arauco. The next line came "easy and unforced" as "Placed by the sword the rigorous yoke of Spain" which—on second thought—Mr. Owen wryly decided was "a riggish jig of letters," not to mention the ambiguity of "placed by the sword." He then hit on "to Spain's stern yoke"; but was still faced by the necessity of getting the sword in again, and of employing six English syllables for the purpose. He meditates: "A set-phrase suggests itself here: 'the arbitrament of the sword'; slightly worn by use, but one that can serve our turn by a slight change. 'By war's arbitrament'—now we have our six syllables; a good ending for the stanza, with the last three syllables cracking like a whip-lash that flickers on that grim yoke in the fore-part of the line."

Thus Walter Owen arrived by pleasant stages at his final version:

> Sing, Muse; but not of Venus and her chuck,
> And amorous jousts in dainty lists of love,
> Favours and forfeits won in Beauty's siege
> By soft assaults of chamber gallantry;
> But of the valiant deeds and worthy fame
> Of those who far on surge-ensundered shores,
> Bent the proud neck of Araucania's race
> To Spain's stern yoke, by war's arbitrament.

Criticism and advice, both abundantly good and abundantly bad, are never lacking to the translator. "What work nobler than transplanting foreign thought?" asked Carlyle. It is true that the advice is frequently contradictory (and, for that matter, the criticism too). For the one school, Francklin advises with respect to an author: "Soften each blemish, and each grace improve, / And treat him with the dignity of love"—while Roscommon counsels sternly: "Your author always will the best advise; / Fall when he falls, and when he rises, rise"; which Andrew Marvell makes even more explicit:

> He is translation's thief that addeth more,
> As much as he that taketh from the store
> Of the first author. Here he maketh blots
> That mends; and added beauties are but spots.

Perhaps the translator's proud humility has never been more adequately stated than by Fray Luis de León, when he said: "Regarding what I compose, each will judge as he wish; regarding what is translated, let him who would be judge first find out what it is to translate elegant poems from a foreign language into one's own without adding nor taking away idea; preserving wherever possible the imagery of the original, and its grace; and making the poems speak Spanish not like upstarts and foreigners but like those born and native to it. I do not say that I have done this; I am not so arrogant; but that I have tried to do so I confess. And let him who says that I have not succeeded attempt it himself, and then it may be that he will esteem my work more highly, to which I bent myself only to show that our tongue receives well all that is entrusted to it and is neither hard nor scanty, as some say, but waxen and abundant for those who know how to deal with it."

As for criticism, the most welcome that any translator could receive is such an accolade as Dr. Alberto Lleras Camargo once bestowed with characteristic generosity: "For me, this is not only a sample of how I would like to write English, but an example of how I would desire to be translated."

Américas, September 1954

Governments Invest in Culture

"Today, science has brought all the different quarters of the globe so close together that it is impossible to isolate them one from another," Franklin D. Roosevelt wrote the night before he died, in an address which was to be his last message. "Today we are faced with the pre-eminent fact that, if civilization is to survive, we must cultivate the science of human relationships—the ability of all peoples, of all kinds, to live together and work together in the same world, at peace."

The cultural relations of a people are its efforts toward mutual acquaintance and the mutual understanding that such acquaintance brings. The world's bitter experience of war in our time has made it clear that peace is no chance growth but must be planned. It seems to be a conviction generally accepted by the governments which have furthered long-term programs, that among the measures used to build up peace none has proved more successful—that for the same investment of mind and treasure none has proved nearly so successful—as the cultural relations program, in spite of the undeniable fact that it has been used on occasion to further political and military interests as well as the interests of peace. Nevertheless, the degree in which these programs of cultural relations have contributed to solidarity among peoples is a matter of record. The part of that historic record transcribed in this volume includes instances from many governments and languages. It is a significant fact that every country which has carried on a government program of cultural relations with other countries over a period of years sets a high value on such relationships. It is significant too that these programs are not slackened but intensified in periods of national crisis—whether a crisis of war, impending or actual, or a national crisis of any other nature responsive to foreign opinion.

It is relevant to note that "cultural" as an adjective entered the English language fairly recently. It is first recorded by the Oxford Dictionary from the year 1875, when Whitney spoke of "a mere incident of social life and of cultural growth." "Culture," however, appeared as early as 1420 when the *Palladium on Husbandry* said—in a reference that might have been to international programs of mutual intellectual advantage but was in fact to the tilling of the soil—"In places there thou wilt have the culture." By 1510, Sir Thomas More could speak figuratively of "the culture and profit of theyr myndes," but it was not until more than two and one-half centuries later, in 1867, that the word was employed to mean a particular form or type of intellectual development, and not till 1876, a year after "cultural" first appeared on the printed page, did Matthew Arnold use the noun: "Culture, the acquainting ourselves with the best that has been known and said in the world," in the sense corresponding to that of the adjective in our title.

Communication is the feature that definitely marks off man from other creatures; according to John Dewey: "It is the condition without which culture would not exist." Any program of cultural relations is a program of communication. A nation's culture is the sum total of its achievement; its own expression of its own personality; its way of thinking and acting. Its program of cultural relations abroad is its method of making these things known to foreigners. Such a program is in fact a self-portrait into which go all a people's creative ability and technical skill and which it wishes the rest of the world to recognize as a speaking likeness.

Cultural relations neither duplicate nor replace diplomatic and commercial relations among the countries of the world, though they may both strengthen and facilitate these other relationships by giving them a basis of friendly understanding. For the cultural relationship is essentially that of friendship from people to people, from the citizenry of one country to the citizenry of another, through such channels of mutual acquaintance as make friendship rewarding between individual and individual.

International programs of cultural relations take many forms and are carried on through both official and unofficial agencies. Numbers of them are directed toward some specific ideological or political objective. In this volume, only official government programs are considered; and of these, only long-range programs established by the governments with the avowed purpose of making their own peoples' culture more widely known and better understood. Multilateral programs, carried on by a number of nations, as is the case of cultural organizations within the framework of the League of Nations, the United Nations, and the American republics, do not come within the scope of a work dealing with cultural relationships set up with other countries by individual governments. And in the latter instance, programs born of an immediate crisis, those of wartime information or of specific ideological propaganda, are considered here only in those aspects that overlap and coalesce with the cultural relations program as such.

Within the limits defined, the present study considers such cultural relations programs as developed by ten governments. Several programs have been presented in considerable detail from their initiation to 1946, the year of writing; those of France, Germany, Great Britain, the United States. For the rest—as in the case of the other American republics, the Soviet Union, and Japan—the pattern is indicated and the present picture sketched. Although the authors have made an historical analysis of twenty-nine such government programs, they make no pretension of having examined all; if the list were complete, it would be a roll call of the world.

The bilateral cultural programs outlined in the following pages are of relatively recent origin, dating from the latter part of the nineteenth century. France and

Germany had fairly extensive programs of cultural expansion abroad before the First World War. Between 1918 and 1939, such German and French activities were greatly increased and most of the other European governments were following suit. Great Britain, however, did not recognize the need for "national interpretation" abroad until 1934, when she established the British Council for Relations with Other Countries. The United States government initiated a program in 1938, with creation of the Interdepartmental Committee on Cooperation with the Other American Republics and of the Division of Cultural Relations in the Department of State.

While the several national programs differ greatly, there seem to be some points common to most.

1. From the beginning, most programs of cultural relations abroad have been initiated and controlled or supervised by the Ministry of Foreign Affairs or the Foreign Office, in whose budgets a large proportion of the funds for carrying them is placed. In only a few cases were they initiated by the Ministry of Education, although this Ministry usually cooperates closely with the Foreign Office cultural projects abroad. By and large, the programs have become an important arm of foreign policy.

2. Each country has a strong belief in the importance of its own culture and a desire to have other countries know and appreciate this culture.

3. Each country believes that the improvement of cultural relations leads to better economic and political relations.

4. Each country centers much of its effort in the teaching of the national language (French, German, English) in foreign lands as a basis for better cultural and economic relationships.

5. Each country, having decided to develop a program of cultural relations with other nations, has given it strong moral and financial support. All have recognized the need for a permanent program of cultural relations abroad to carry out certain of their foreign policies.

The cultural activities carried on abroad by governments commonly include the establishment and support of cultural centers or institutes and schools in foreign countries; the interchange of technical experts, professors, teachers, students, and leaders in various fields of intellectual and artistic expression; the exchange of books and other printed materials, lectures, concerts, and exhibitions. The newer media, motion picture and radio, are used increasingly. It is important to note that the cultural relations activities carried on through official channels are planned in the main to encourage and to supplement rather than to displace the international activities of private organizations, institutions, and individuals.

In outlining in the following chapters the historical development of the programs in ten governments—France, Germany, Japan, the U.S.S.R., Great Britain, Argentina, Brazil, Chile, Mexico, and the United States—official documents such as reports, laws and decrees, and parliamentary debates, have been used almost entirely. Through official statements of the authorities responsible for the development of the program in each country, the policy, the kinds of activities undertaken, the scope of the activities, the budgets, and even the values placed on the program by the governments concerned are made clear. In other words, it is the deliberate purpose of the authors, using the documentation available, to have each country explain the development of its own cultural relations program with other countries. It should be added that the conclusions reached in the final chapter are based not only on the studies of the programs of the ten countries included in this volume, but also on the authors' comparable studies of the programs of nineteen additional countries.

Organized for national interpretation abroad by the various governments, these programs, in spite of common elements, reflect clearly differences in national character and in cultural background. This fact becomes apparent in examining and comparing the cultural programs carried on by the ten nations dealt with in the ensuing chapters.

Cultural activities of countries not given special attention in this book are too numerous even to be counted definitively. The Spanish Basques, for example, during World War II, circulated in several languages copies of the wartime autobiography of José Antonio de Aguirre, president of Euzkadi in exile. They established contacts with nationals of Basque ancestry—however remote—in the Hispanic American republics. At the University of Montevideo in Uruguay they created a Chair of Research on the Basque Language. The government of the Netherlands while in exile and at war included in its radio programs—in Dutch, in English, in Spanish—cultural as well as war news. It showed in London motion pictures on Holland at war, on the Netherlands colonies, on the drainage of the Zuyder Zee. It engaged in the United States, in provision for the needs of peace, medical specialists to help rehabilitate Nazi-disorganized Dutch universities. The wartime Netherlands Ambassador at Mexico City gave lectures illustrated by slides on "Dutch Colonization as a Phenomenon of Civilization" and similar topics. A cultural institute (Instituto de Alta Cultura Brasil-Holanda) was inaugurated at Rio de Janeiro. Documentary films, with Indonesian tongues dubbed in, were prepared for the Pacific area, including long-range educational films on the Indonesian Islands for peacetime showing. A former Netherlands Minister of Over-Seas Territories was sent out in the spring of 1945 on a South American tour "to extend existing relations not only commercial but cultural"; and the Minister of Education journeyed over the United States to observe and report upon methods in education. Reciprocal relationships were established through many channels—music, folklore, transla- tions, visiting lecturers—between the republic of Venezuela and the little islands of Aruba and Curaçao in the Netherlands West Indies.

Such reportage as the foregoing could be expanded and extended indefinitely. Taken together, it all amounts to irrefutable proof of how valuable, how necessary, the cultural approach of understanding between peoples has proved, even under the hard test of war. In wartime, as in time of peace, no other investment seems to give so large a proportional return as the investment in international solidarity through a cultural relationship.

Obviously, in two-hundred-odd pages it would be impossible to consider in detail, or even to outline, the cultural relations programs of all foreign countries. The authors of this volume, in presenting somewhat detailed historical studies of the longest established and most extensive programs and in giving the pattern of a number of others in Europe, the Americas, and Asia, have not made, nor desired to make, an objective evaluation, but, on the contrary have confined themselves to presentation of the several programs as envisaged by the governments carrying them on, a presentation emphasized by direct citation of official statements and documents. In other words, the purpose here is to set forth the several programs with their underlying philosophies and with the estimates, according to their sev- eral exponents, of the results achieved through them. The wealth of relevant ma- terial in the various national archives is no less surprising than the fact that hitherto relatively little such information from official sources on cultural relations has ever been made available in any language to the general public. The governments them- selves, however, through official channels have always been profoundly interested in all details of the development of their own cultural programs and, from the be- ginning, have observed narrowly the programs of other governments; a fact abun- dantly attested especially in the records of parliamentary debate. Much evidence in support of this statement is quoted in the following pages, in direct translations by the authors of the present volume, from parliamentary proceedings and other state documents.

A study of the following chapters will show, without editorializing on the part of the authors, that a program of national interpretation may be largely non- political in character in its international aspects, or may be directed toward ends demonstrably political. In their plans for world domination, for example, the to- talitarian states have relied on cultural activities abroad to pave the way for a com- plete dictatorship over the lives of foreign peoples. On the other hand, the democ- racies have used cultural programs to develop the free and friendly relationships between their own and other peoples which lead to mutual understanding and re- spect and to that intangible, good will, which is a recognized asset in all relation- ships, individual and collective, whether political, economic, or cultural. But one invariable fact becomes increasingly evident to any observer of such developing programs in action, or to any student of historical documentation relating to them; namely, that they produce results. In view of their increasing use as an arm of foreign policy by governments throughout the world, no nation can afford to ignore these programs or to underestimate their importance.

Chapter 1 of *The Cultural Approach: Another Way in International Relations* (with Ruth Emily McMurry), 1947

Appendixes

Bibliography

Acknowledgments

Index

Appendix A

Letter from Muna Lee (1915)

This letter, handwritten and dated November 29, 1915, was sent to H. L. Mencken from Lawton, Oklahoma, where Muna Lee was teaching at the time. (H. L. Mencken Papers 1905–56, New York Public Library, New York, N. Y.) With characteristic self-deprecating humor, modesty, and gratitude to Mencken, she describes her earliest efforts to publish as well as her beginnings as a poet. This was the start of their correspondence in which, for nearly two decades, he encouraged her to write.

My dear Mr. Mencken:

It was very kind of you to ask about my work. Your questions are easily answered, for there is really nothing interesting to tell you. I have never even considered printing a book. During the year, I have submitted work to five magazines—*The Smart Set, Poetry, Others, The Woman's Home Companion, Judge* (an ill-assorted list, but I don't know where verse should be sent). Miss Monroe [*Poetry*] accepted some of my work; Mr. Kreymborg [*Others*] and Mr. Carruth [*Woman's Home Companion*] returned the verses submitted, but have requested to see others; *Judge* sent me a printed rejection slip. The little three-line stanza you printed in September [October issue] was my first accepted composition, and was also the first work I had ever sent to a magazine, excepting several specimens which I sent you last spring, at Mr. McClure's suggestion, and which you promptly returned, as I had expected.

As for how long I've been writing—always, it seems to me. Since very early childhood, at any rate. I shall be twenty-one in January.

It seems wonderful to me that my verses have given you pleasure—that they could give pleasure to anyone. Thank you for telling me.

Yours sincerely, Muna Lee

Appendix B

Letter from Gloria Muñoz Arjona (1965)

On the occasion of the death of Muna Lee, her daughter-in-law, Gloria Muñoz
Arjona of San Juan, Puerto Rico, sent an impassioned condolence letter dated
April 13, 1965, to Lee's sister, Virginia Reppy of Stamford, Connecticut. The body
of it is presented here. Doña Gloria's devotion has also been expressed over the
years in her dedicated guardianship of Lee's papers and other memorabilia.

It is a real sad thing that my almost only letter in almost twenty years must be because
of our beloved Muna's death. If I had known she was so ill, I would have traveled to
Washington in December and stayed with a friend of ours in Baltimore, in order to
spend those last days in that non-comparable-to-anything family harmony which
makes people who are leaving us so happy. But nobody told me. As you know, I was in
Spain with my children, for my PhD, in Madrid. I came back in June. I saw Muna that
last summer. Then I saw her many times in December [in Puerto Rico]. I didn't know
she was having that recurrence, until she came back with Munita in February, when I
thought to myself she was really ill. And then, almost immediately, she passed away.

We shall never have enough tears, nor of the quality she deserved, to cry for
Muna. It is not that she passed away. It is the cruelty of life or destiny, the world of
illusions and dreams that was torn down by her illness, the nothingness of her
dreams about Puerto Rico and her house, friends, family gatherings, etc. Yet she
was so brave, so tall in her way, so different, so really brave. That has comforted us
a little: the remembrance of her unique example.

She was—in my opinion—the real, authentic, old American of the best tradi-
tion, someone who can understand all people's different lives and traditions, and
love them, protect them, sponsor them. For she was one thing very difficult to be:
the incarnation of love. There is not one single moment in my family or place in
this house which does not bring Muna before our eyes. My children adored her,
had for her the highest estimation, admiration, that one person can have for an-
other. She will be among us forever. I'll try to write something in memoriam—and
publish it—and will send you a copy. Newspapers have said a lot of deserved good
things. Next week I'm having a play done for the *Fiesta de la Lengua* [Festival of the
Spanish Language; celebration of Cervantes] and will dedicate it to her memory.

Appendix C

Letter from Francis Klafter née Lee (2000)

Born in Hugo, Oklahoma, in 1909, Frances Klafter is a sister—and the sole surviving sibling—of Muna Lee. Here is her response to an early draft of the present biography, which she expressed to the author in a letter written in June 2000. She refers to an incident in which her sister was a victim of the McCarthy-era witch hunts. This incident took place in 1953. On March 9, Muna was suspended from the State Department, pending the outcome of a hearing before its Loyalty Security Board. Among other charges she was accused of associating with her sister and brother-in-law, then government workers in Washington who were alleged to be "active communists." Three weeks later, on April 1, the suspension was ended when the board found no reasonable doubt as to her loyalty. A sad note, also reminiscent of that era, was that the board recommended that she discontinue her limited contacts with her sister and brother-in-law.

Not only was my sister Muna a very fine poet and a brilliant leader, she was a warm, generous, and loving person. She was completely devoted to her family—her original one, her own children, her parents (particularly her mother) and all of her siblings. She was particularly loving to her sister Virginia (Virginia Reppy whose husband was a law professor at New York University and later dean of a small, private law school). Her closeness to Virginia and dependence on her for companionship and personal support was extraordinary, and rather amazing considering that she was a person of much more consequence in the world than was Virginia.

Muna was also particularly devoted to my brother, Bill, for whom she had a lot of compassion because, although my father was a very lovable man, he became a man incapable of assuming his responsibility as the main family breadwinner and an unfair part of the burden fell on my brother Bill. So Muna tried to help him and even took him to Puerto Rico for one year of college [in 1928].

Furthermore, she was surprisingly devoted to my younger sister and me. At the time the family was the most economically hard-pressed and she herself was helping financially all she could, she never failed to send us beautiful presents for Christmas. Even later, when she worked at the State Department and I was a rather too prominent radical government worker, she showed affection and interest in me despite the danger to her job of associating with someone with my left-wing politics in the days of loyalty oaths and red-baiting.

Bibliography

ARCHIVAL COLLECTIONS

Carrera Andrade, Jorge, Collection (correspondence). Frank Melville Jr. Memorial Library. Stony Brook University. Stony Brook, N. Y.

Frost Ballantine, Lesley, Papers, 1905–80 (correspondence). University of New Hampshire Library. University of New Hampshire. Durham, N. H.

Grant, Frances R., Papers (correspondence). Rutgers University Libraries. Rutgers, the State University of New Jersey. New Brunswick, N. J.

Lalley, J. M., Papers, 1895–1981 (correspondence). Milton S. Eisenhower Library. Johns Hopkins University. Baltimore, Md.

Lee, Muna (federal personnel file; documents, 1941–65). National Archives and Records Administration. St. Louis, Mo.

Lee, Muna, Papers, c. 1908–65 (private collection of family). Instituto Rafael Arjona Siaca. San Juan, P.R.

Lee de Muñoz Marín, Muna, Reading Her Poems in the Recording Laboratory, April 25, 1960 (sound recording). Archive of Recorded Poetry and Literature. Library of Congress. Washington, D.C.

MacLeish, Archibald, Papers, 1907–81 (correspondence). Library of Congress. Washington, D.C.

Mencken, H. L., Papers, 1905–56 (correspondence). New York Public Library. New York, N. Y.

Muñoz Marín, Luis, Papers, 1926–28 (correspondence). New York Public Library. New York, N. Y.

Porter, Katherine Anne, Papers, 1890–1980 (correspondence). University Libraries. University of Maryland. College Park, Md.

Roosevelt, Theodore, Papers, 1780–1962 (correspondence). Library of Congress. Washington, D.C.

Skinner, Constance Lindsay, Papers, 1873–1939 (correspondence). New York Public Library. New York, N. Y.

Society of Woman Geographers, Records of the, 1925–98. Library of Congress. Washington, D.C.

Spencer, Martha Linsley, Collection (correspondence). Watkinson Library. Trinity College. Hartford, Conn.

WORKS BY MUNA LEE
Poetry

"I–VII" ("I thought love would come gloriously"). *Others* 2 (May-June 1916): 224–25.

"Acacia Island." *New Yorker* 6 (March 15, 1930): 20.

"Addendum." *Smart Set* 54 (January 1918): 124.

"Afternoon Ramble." *Carillon* 4 (January 1933): 3.

"After Reading in the Spanish Mystics." *America* 33 (August 8, 1925): 404.

"Albatross." *New Yorker* 6 (April 12, 1930): 27.

"Alcatraz." *Poetry* 45 (November 1934): 80–81.

"Apology." *Saturday Review of Literature* 1 (December 20, 1924): 393.

"Arcady." *Smart Set* 48 (April 1916): 1.

"As Helen Once." *Current Opinion* 75 (July 1923): 95.

"Assignation." *Carillon* 5 (October 1933): 2.

"Atavian." *New Yorker* 7 (August 22, 1931): 18.

"Bereavement." *Smart Set* 48 (February 1916): 82.

"Blindman." *North American Review* 222 (December 1925): 284.

"Blue-Eyed Grass." *Everybody's Magazine* 42 (May 1920): 121.

"But Still—." *Smart Set* 51 (February 1917): 257.

"By the Caribbean One Remembers the Prairie." *University of Oklahoma Magazine* 18 (November 1929): 2.

"The Cabbage Field." *Smart Set* 54 (March 1918): 62.

"Caribbean Marsh." *New Yorker* 8 (January 7, 1933): 25.

"Caribbean Noon." *New Yorker* 10 (October 20, 1934): 98.

"Carib Fantasy." *New Yorker* 6 (December 27, 1930): 41.

"Carib Garden." *New Yorker* 9 (January 13, 1934): 70.

"Carib Summer" ("Garden Episode"; "Song before Outcry"; "Protest against Security"; "Epithalamium"; "Ballad"). *Poetry* 41 (October 1932): 19–22.

"Champion." *American Mercury* 29 (May 1933): 98.

"Choice." *Liberator* 3 (October 1920): 33.

"Christmas Eve." *New Yorker* 8 (December 24, 1932): 35.

"Concerning All the Poets of All the World." *Smart Set* 53 (September 1917): 35.

"Deliverance." *American Mercury* 29 (May 1933): 98.

"Deserted Orchard." *New Yorker* 9 (April 29, 1933): 49.

"Dialogue." *American Mercury* 15 (September 1928): 20.

"Dies Irae." *New York Herald Tribune Books* (May 5, 1929): 6.

"Division." *America* 39 (August 4, 1928): 399.

"Don Henry." *New Republic* 65 (January 7, 1931): 65.

"Explanation." *New Yorker* 7 (July 4, 1931): 20.

"The Fall of the Year." *Smart Set* 56 (October 1918): 165.

"The Flame-Trees." *Measure* 16 (June 1922): 7.

"Flight." *America* 41 (May 11, 1929): 111.

"Footnotes" (I–IX). *Poetry* 7 (January 1916): 175–78.

"Frankly Prose." *Smart Set* 56 (November 1918): 268.

"From a Book of Phrases" ("November"; "Memory"; "Dreams"). *Smart Set* 53 (December 1917): 85.

"Genesis." *Smart Set* 52 (June 1917): 36.

"Gifts." *Current Opinion* 75 (July 1923): 95.

"Go Out across the Hills." *Smart Set* 51 (February 1917): 308.

"Hill of Thistles." *Southwest Review* 10 (January 1925): 56.

"Indian Pipe." *New York Herald Tribune Books* (January 6, 1929): 4.

"Islander." *New Yorker* 9 (July 8, 1933): 12.

"It Is Only Then." *Smart Set* 51 (April 1917): 162.

"I Who Had Sought God" (Yo que tan ciegamente, tr. Salomón de la Selva). *Pan-American Magazine* 27 (July 1918): 154.

"Keen in Cold Weather." *Commonweal* 21 (December 14, 1934): 195.

"Last Word." *America* 39 (June 23, 1928): 259.

"Life of Itself." *Current Opinion* 73 (October 1922): 528.

"Locust Grove." *Southwest Review* 10 (January 1925): 56.

"Love Song." *Smart Set* 54 (April 1918): 88.

"Lyric to the Sun." *Commonweal* 22 (May 31, 1935): 118.

"Mistress Mary." *Carillon* 5 (October 1933): 3.

"Mushroom Town" ("The Drug-Store"; "Electors"; "August"; "Murderers"; "The Carnival"; "Mrs. Hastings"; "Methodist Revival"; "Prairie Sky"). *American Mercury* 1 (April 1924): 459–62.

"Night of San Juan." *New Yorker* 7 (September 5, 1931): 20.

"Of Writing Verse." *Literary Digest* 85 (April 11, 1925): 34.

"An Old Grief." *Smart Set* 52 (July 1917): 128.

"An Old Story." *America* 39 (April 28, 1928): 63.

"On Bayou Chicot." *Delineator* 97 (October 1920): 95.

"On Discovering Land." *American Mercury* 15 (September 1928): 20.

"On Not Writing about Mauna Loa." *New York Herald Tribune* (March 4, 1936): 15.

"The Perfect Song." *Smart Set* 50 (October 1916): 35.

"Planet." *Commonweal* 10 (September 11, 1929): 479.

"Porto Rican Hacienda." *Commonweal* 12 (June 11, 1930): 162.

"Portrait." *North American Review* 222 (December 1925): 284.

"Prairie Lily." *Southwest Review* 10 (January 1925): 56.

"Protagonists." *Carillon* 3 (Summer 1932): 19.

"Puerto Rican Moonrise." *Commonweal* 18 (May 26, 1933): 102.

"Rich Port." *American Mercury* 19 (January 1930): 108.

"San Cristóbal." *Double Dealer* 4 (July 1922): 24.

"Security." *New Yorker* 7 (January 16, 1932): 18.

"Sentence." *Poetry* 45 (November 1934): 80.

"She Makes a Suggestion to Herself." *New Yorker* 6 (September 20, 1930): 22.

"Shout to Be Whispered." *Carillon* 5 (October 1933): 3.

"So Many Things." *Southwest Review* 12 (October 1926): 11.

"So Many Ways." *Poetry* 22 (June 1923): 125.

"Song." *Smart Set* 58 (February 1919): 38.

"A Song at Parting." *Smart Set* 49 (May 1916): 252.

"Song for a Harp." *Smart Set* 51 (January 1917): 192.

"Song of an Old Love." *Smart Set* 54 (February 1918): 116.

"Songs." *Poetry* 22 (June 1923): 124.

"Songs of Many Moods" ("A Song of Happiness"; "Mahhavis"; "Shadows"; "Wind-Blown"; "Compensation"). *Poetry* 10 (August 1917): 228–31.

"Stalactite." *New Yorker* 10 (June 23, 1934): 24.

"The Stars Are Colored Blossoms." *Smart Set* 50 (November 1916): 270.

"These Are But Words." *Poetry* 20 (August 1922): 235–41.

"Tropic Dawn." *Poetry* 35 (March 1930): 321.

"The Tryst." *Smart Set* 52 (May 1917): 363.

"Twilight Song." *Smart Set* 50 (December 1916): 32.

"Two Love Songs" ("Out of my turbulent days"; "I had believed love vast and tragic"). *Smart Set* 53 (October 1917): 78.

"Unbroken Spell." *New York Herald Tribune Books* (January 6, 1929): 4.

"The Unforgotten." *Smart Set* 48 (January 1916): 194.

"The Unforgotten" (not same as above poem). *America* 38 (February 18, 1928): 467.

"The Vigil." *Smart Set* 47 (October 1915): 45.

"Villanelle." *America* 39 (September 8, 1928): 518.

"A Villanelle of Forgetfulness." *Contemporary Verse* 2 (July 1916): 16.

"Villanelle of His Preferences." *Commonweal* 7 (November 23, 1927): 714.

"Visitant." *New Yorker* 9 (March 18, 1933): 13.

"Wayfarer." *New Yorker* 7 (December 19, 1931): 18.

"West Indian Plaque." *New Yorker* 10 (September 29, 1934): 16.

"When We Shall Be Dust" (Cuando en el cementerio, tr. Salomón de la Selva). *Pan-American Magazine* 27 (July 1918): 154.

"Why." *Current Opinion* 73 (October 1922): 528.

"You love [. . .]." *Others* 3 (March 1916): 64–65.

Verse Translation

Abril, Xavier. "Dawn"; "Elegy to the Invented Woman." In *Anthology of Contemporary Latin-American Poetry*, edited by Dudley Fitts, 373, 377. New York: New Directions, 1942.

Adán, Martín. "Nativity." In *Anthology of Contemporary Latin-American Poetry*, edited by Fitts, 477.

Arévalo Martínez, Rafael. "Clean Clothes"; "Give Yourself Wholly." In *Anthology of Contemporary Latin-American Poetry*, edited by Fitts, 485–87.

Arrieta, Rafael Alberto. "January Night . . ." In *Anthology of Contemporary Latin-American Poetry*, edited by Fitts, 465.

Bazil, Osvaldo. "Idyl." *Poetry* 26 (June 1925): 147.

Bécquer, Gustavo Adolfo. "Song." In *Hispanic Anthology*, edited by Thomas Walsh, 500–501. New York: Putnam's, 1920.

Blanco, Antonio Nicolás. "Intimate Prayer." *Poetry* 26 (June 1925): 143–44.

Blanco-Fombona, Rufino. "At Parting." In *Hispanic Anthology,* edited by Walsh, 617–18.

———. "Escape"; "By the Sea." *Poetry* 26 (June 1925): 153–54.

Bustamente y Ballivián, Enrique. "Telegraph Pole." In *Anthology of Contemporary Latin-American Poetry,* edited by Fitts, 125–27.

Carrera Andrade, Jorge. "Ballot for Green"; "Movements of Nature"; "Clock." *Poetry* 59 (February 1942): 256–57.

———. "Sierra"; "Sunday"; "Reaping the Barley"; "It Rained in the Night"; "The Guest"; "Vocation of the Mirror"; "Stroke of One"; "Klare von Reuter"; "Second Life of My Mother." In *Anthology of Contemporary Latin-American Poetry,* edited by Fitts, 3–17.

Cerna Sandoval, O. "Lover." *Golden Book* 2 (November 1925): 621.

Chocano, José Santos. "Horses of the Conquistadores." *Poetry* 26 (June 1925): 139–42.

Darío, Rubén. "Litany for Our Lord Don Quixote." *Poetry* 26 (June 1925): 135–37.

———. "Philosophy"; "Unhappy He . . ." In *An Anthology of Spanish Poetry from Garcilaso to García Lorca,* edited by Angel Flores, 221–22. Garden City, Conn.: Anchor (Doubleday), 1961.

Díaz Mirón, Salvador. "The Dead Man." *Poetry* 26 (June 1925): 133.

Dublé Urrutia, Diego. "[*From*] The Mines." *Poetry* 26 (June 1925): 121–22.

Escudero, Gonzalo. "Overtones." *Poetry* 26 (June 1925): 131.

Fernández Moreno, César. "On Certain Things." *Poetry* 26 (June 1925): 118.

Fiallo, Fabio. "Full Moon." *Poetry* 26 (June 1925): 148.

———. "Nostalgia." In *Hispanic Anthology,* edited by Walsh, 591–92.

Florit, Eugenio. "On Someone's Death." In *Anthology of Contemporary Latin-American Poetry,* edited by Fitts, 31–33.

"Folk-Songs of the Pampas." *Poetry* 26 (June 1925): 138.

Franco, Luis L. "Goat-Pen." In *Anthology of Contemporary Latin-American Poetry,* edited by Fitts, 183.

Gómez Jaime, Alfredo. "Problem." *Poetry* 26 (June 1925): 127.

González Martínez, Enrique. "The Owl and the Swan." *Bookman* 49 (June 1919): 398.

Hernández Miyares, Enrique. "The Most Fair." *Poetry* 26 (June 1925): 128.

Herrera y Reissig, Julio. "Night"; "Interment"; "The Quarrel"; "Heraldic Decoration." *Poetry* 26 (June 1925): 149–51.

Ibarbourou, Juana de. "Bond." *Poetry* 26 (June 1925): 151–52.

Jaimes Freyre, Ricardo. "Aeternum Vale." *Poetry* 26 (June 1925): 119.

Juana Inés de la Cruz, Sister. "To Her Portrait." *Bulletin of the Pan American Union* 60 (September 1926): 890–91.

Lloréns Torres, Luis. "Bolívar." *Poetry* 26 (June 1925): 146.

López, Luis C. "Village Night." *Poetry* 26 (June 1925): 126–25.

Lugones, Leopoldo. "Journey." *Poetry* 26 (June 1925): 118.

Magallanes Moure, Manuel. "Table Talk." *Poetry* 26 (June 1925): 122.

Mata, Andrés. "Soul and Landscape." *Poetry* 26 (June 1925): 154.

Mistral, Gabriela. "Ecstasy." *Poetry* 26 (June 1925): 120–21.

———. "The Little Girl That Lost a Finger." In *Anthology of Contemporary Latin-American Poetry,* edited by Fitts, 39.

Moro, César. "Vision of Moth-Eaten Pianos Falling to Pieces"; "The Illustrated World." In *Anthology of Contemporary Latin-American Poetry*, edited by Fitts, 383–87.

Muñoz Marín, Luis. "Proletarians"; "Pamphlet." In *Anthology of Contemporary Latin-American Poetry*, edited by Fitts, 207–9.

Oribe, Emilio. "Song to the Glory of the Sky of America." In *Anthology of Contemporary Latin-American Poetry*, edited by Fitts (1947), 579–85.

Palés Matos, Luis. "San Sabas." *Poetry* 26 (June 1925): 144–46.

Peña Barrenechea, Enrique. "Man's Road." In *Anthology of Contemporary Latin-American Poetry*, edited by Fitts, 531–33.

Peralta, Alejandro. "Andean Crossing." In *Anthology of Contemporary Latin-American Poetry*, edited by Fitts, 153–55.

Pereda Valdés, Ildefonso. "Cradle Song to Put a Negro Baby to Sleep." In *Anthology of Contemporary Latin-American Poetry*, edited by Fitts, 471.

Poveda, José Manuel. "Withdrawal." *Poetry* 26 (June 1925): 128–29

Rosado Vega, Luis. "To the Unknown Goddess." *Poetry* 26 (June 1925): 132–33.

Sabogal (Diéguez), José. "To Franklin Delano Roosevelt." *Books Abroad* 20 (1946): 36.

Salóm, Diwaldo. "I Know Not." *Poetry* 26 (June 1925): 129.

Sánchez, Luis Aníbal. "Brother Dog." *Poetry* 26 (June 1925): 130.

Silva, José Asunción. "Nocturne." *Poetry* 26 (June 1925): 123–25.

Spinetti Dini, Antonio. "Parable of Generosity." In *Anthology of Contemporary Latin-American Poetry*, edited by Fitts, 501.

Storni, Alfonsina. "Running Water." *Poetry* 26 (June 1925): 117.

Suasnavar, Constantino. "Numbers." In *Anthology of Contemporary Latin-American Poetry*, edited by Fitts, 221–23.

Torres Bodet, Jaime. "Core"; "Love." In *Anthology of Contemporary Latin-American Poetry*, edited by Fitts, 99–101.

Urbina, Luis G. "Clear Night." *Poetry* 26 (June 1925): 132.

Valencia, Guillermo. "[*From*] Anarchs." *Poetry* 26 (June 1925): 125–26.

Valle, Rafael Heliodoro. "Thirsting Amphora." In *Anthology of Contemporary Latin-American Poetry*, edited by Fitts, 483.

Vallejo, César. "Dregs." In *Anthology of Contemporary Latin-American Poetry*, edited by Fitts, 411–13.

Varallanos, José. "Mob of Mountains." In *Anthology of Contemporary Latin-American Poetry*, edited by Fitts, 151.

Villalobos, Asdrúbal. "Provincial Moment." In *Anthology of Contemporary Latin-American Poetry*, edited by Fitts, 211.

Xammar, Luis Fabio. "The Spring." In *Anthology of Contemporary Latin-American Poetry*, edited by Fitts, 469.

Prose

"Address Made by Muna Lee of the National Woman's Party, Porto Rico Branch, and the University of Porto Rico, in Behalf of Equal Rights Treaty before Unofficial Plenary Session of the Sixth Pan-American Conference." In *National Woman's Party*

Papers, 1913–1972, edited by Thomas C. Pardo. Reel 38. Glenn Rock, N. J.: Microfilming Corporation of America, 1977.

"Alva Belmont, Feminist." *Equal Rights* 16 (January 10, 1931): 391–92.

"Brother of Poe." *Southwest Review* 11 (July 1926): 305–12.

"Building the Irreplaceable Bridge." *Modern Mexico* 19 (March 1947): 10–11, 24.

"Can't Book Reviewers Be Honest?" *Books Abroad* 20 (1946): 370–72.

"A Charming Mexican Lady." *American Mercury* 4 (January 1925): 105–8.

"Clara Guthrie D'Arcis and the Three L's." *Equal Rights* 17 (August 8, 1931): 211.

"Closer to Blood Than to Ink." Review of *Residence on Earth and Other Poems*, by Pablo Neruda, tr. Angel Flores. *Saturday Review of Literature* 30 (April 26, 1947): 34.

"Conquistador for Science." *North American Review* 226 (August 1928): 129–40.

"Constance Lindsay Skinner: Primitive and Modern." *Equal Rights* 17 (March 18, 1931): 84.

"Contemporary Spanish-American Poetry." *North American Review* 219 (May 1924): 687–98.

"Cuban Literature." Review of *Historia de la literatura cubana*, by Juan J. Remos y Rubio. *Americas* 3 (April 1947): 493–501.

"Cultural Interchanges between the Americas." *Pan-American Magazine* 42 (October 1929): 89–95.

"An Ecuadoran Observes His World." Review of *Registro del mundo*, by Jorge Carrera Andrade. *Poetry* 59 (February 1942): 278–82.

"Eugenio María de Hostos: After One Hundred Years." *Books Abroad* 14 (1940): 124–28.

"Flowering in a Phrase." *Commonweal* 20 (July 13, 1934): 285.

"Getting Acquainted." *Puerto Rico World Journal*. April 19, 1943.

"Harriet Monroe: Poet and Pioneer." *Equal Rights* 18 (August 27, 1932): 235–36.

"An Indian Territory Childhood." Parts 1–2. *University of Oklahoma Magazine* 18 (November 1929): 3–9.

"An Indian Territory Childhood." Part 3. *University of Oklahoma Magazine* 18 (January 1930): 33–45.

"The Inter-American Commission of Women: A New International Venture." *Pan-American Magazine* 42 (October 1929): 105–14.

"José de San Martín." *Pan American Magazine* 43 (December 1930): 386–91.

"Juan de Castellanos and Puerto Rico." Paper presented at the Eighth Congress of the Instituto Internacional de Literatura Iberoamericana, August 21–31, 1957, San Juan, P.R. In *La gesta de Puerto Rico* (The Epic of Puerto Rico), by Juan de Castellanos, 21–31. San Juan, P.R.: Ediciones Mirador, 1967.

"Juan de Castellanos in the Perspective of 350 Years." *Proceedings of the Thirty-Third International Congress of Americanists, San José, Costa Rica, July 20–27, 1958*. Vol. 2, 859–72. San José: Lehmann, 1959.

"Latin America for U.S. Children." *Américas* 6 (September 1954): 32–34.

"Leonora Speyer, Poet." *Equal Rights* 16 (January 31, 1931): 412–13.

"Let Women Make Their Own Choice." *Equal Rights* 17 (April 11, 1931): 76–77.

"Like a Tale of Old Romance." *Smart Set* 49 (August 1916): 111.

"Luis—and an Episode." *Smart Set* 58 (April 1919): 117–20.

"Narciso Lopez." *Pan American* 10 (November 1949): 8–11.

"Neruda in Translation." Review of *Selected Poems*, by Pablo Neruda, tr. Angel Flores. *Poetry* 65 (January 1945): 225–27.

"Notes from a Feminist's Travel Diary." *Equal Rights* 18 (March 26, 1932): 59–60.

"Notes from a Feminist's Travel Diary." *Equal Rights* 18 (May 21, 1932): 125–26.

"Our Alfonso Reyes." *Books Abroad* 19 (April 1945): 113–16.

"A Painful Example." Review of *Prosas profanas*, by Rubén Darío, tr. Charles B. McMichael. *Poetry* 22 (June 1923): 165–68.

"Pan-American Women." *Nation* 126 (March 14, 1928): 294–95.

"Paulina Luisi, Internationalist." *Equal Rights* 18 (August 6, 1932): 213–14.

"Pio Baroja." Review of *The Quest*, by Pio Baroja, tr. Isaac Goldberg. *Double Dealer* 5 (March-April 1923): 120–22.

"Pitfalls of a Translator." *Inter-American* 4 (November 1945): 12–14, 37.

"Poetry Every Day." *Four Talks on Writing, Delivered at the Southern Literary Festival, 13–16*. Blue Mountain, Miss.: privately printed, 1947.

"Poets of the Tropics." *Double Dealer* 4 (November 1922): 221–24.

"The Port-Au-Prince Bicentennial." *Record* 6 (1950): 1–4.

"Puerto Rican Women Writers: The Record of One Hundred Years." *Books Abroad* 8 (January 1934): 7–10.

Review of *Algunas cartas de Don Diego Hurtado de Mendoza, escritas 1528–1552*, edited by Alberto Vázquez and R. Selden Rose. *Hispania* 31 (February 1948): 107–11.

Review of *Balduino Enrico: asedio de la ciudad de San Juan de Puerto Rico por la flota holandesa*, by Fernando J. Geigel Sabat. *Hispanic American Historical Review* 15 (February 1935): 85–86.

Review of *Diary of the Alarcón Expedition into Texas, 1718–1719*, by Fray Francisco Céliz, tr. Fritz Leo Hoffman. *Hispanic American Historical Review* 16 (February 1936): 77–79.

Review of *The Geology of Puerto Rico*, by Howard A. Meyerhoff. *Hispanic American Historical Review* 14 (August 1934): 340–42.

Review of *The Pathless Grove: A Collection of Seventeenth Century Mexican Sonnets of Sor Juana Inés de la Cruz*, tr. Pauline Cook. *Hispania* 34 (August 1951): 316–17.

Review of *Three Tragedies*, by Federico García Lorca, trs. Richard L. O'Connell and James Graham-Luján. *Hispania* 32 (November 1949): 556–57.

"Some Backgrounds of Latin-American Education." *Americas* 8 (July 1951): 53–58.

"Some Early Cultural Relations in the Caribbean." In *The Caribbean: Peoples, Problems, and Prospects*, edited by A. Curtis Wilgus, 117–22. Gainesville: University of Florida Press, 1952.

"Some Experiences with the Hispanic-American Press." *Matrix* 27 (August 1942): 5.

"Spain and U.S. Writing." Review of *The Spanish Background of American Literature*, by Stanley T. Williams. *Américas* 7 (October 1955): 41–42.

"Translating the Untranslatable: Can Poetry Stand the Change?" *Américas* 6 (September 1954): 12–15.

"Walt Dehner: Artist at the University of Puerto Rico." *Magazine of Art* 35 (January 1942): 16–21.

"Winning of San Juan Hill." *Review of Reviews* 83 (April 1931): 72–73.

"The Woman's Party Stands Guard." *Equal Rights* 16 (October 4, 1930): 278–79.
"Women and the World Court." *Equal Rights* 18 (April 9, 1932): 75–76.
"Women Voters and the University of Porto Rico." *Equal Rights* 16 (February 2, 1930): 4–5.

Books (Key: F, fiction; NF, nonfiction; P, poetry; T, translation)

American Story: Historical Broadcast Series of the NBC Inter-American University of the Air (NF). New York: Columbia University Press, 1944.

Art in Review: Reprints of Material Dealing with Art Exhibitions Directed by Walt Dehner and Acquisitions in the University of Puerto Rico, 1929–1938 (NF). Río Piedras: University of Puerto Rico, 1937.

The Cultural Approach: Another Way in International Relations (NF). With Ruth Emily McMurry. Chapel Hill: University of North Carolina Press, 1947; Port Washington, N. Y.: Kennikat Press, 1971.

Death Follows a Formula (F). By Newton Gayle (Maurice Guinness and Muna Lee). New York: Scribner's, 1935.

Death in the Glass (F). By Newton Gayle (Maurice Guinness and Muna Lee). New York: Scribner's, 1937.

Equal Rights Approved by American Institute of International Law (NF). Washington, D.C.: Inter-American Commission of Women, Pan American Union, 1931.

Four Years beneath the Crescent (T/NF). By Rafael de Nogales. New York: Scribner's, 1926; Reading, England: Taderon Press, 2003.

A History of Spain (T/NF). By Rafael Altamira. New York: Van Nostrand, 1949.

Murder at 28:10 (F). By Newton Gayle (Maurice Guinness and Muna Lee). New York: Scribner's, 1936.

On Being Good Neighbors (T/NF). By Mariano Picón Salas. Washington, D.C.: Division of Intellectual Cooperation, Pan American Union, 1944.

Pioneers of Puerto Rico (NF). Boston: Heath, 1944.

Sea-Change (P). New York: Macmillan, 1923.

Secret Country (T/P). By Jorge Carrera Andrade. New York: Macmillan, 1946.

The Sentry Box Murder (F). By Newton Gayle (Maurice Guinness and Muna Lee). New York: Scribner's, 1935.

Sinister Crag (F). By Newton Gayle (Maurice Guinness and Muna Lee). New York: Scribner's, 1938.

WORKS ABOUT MUNA LEE

Aitken, Thomas, Jr. *Poet in the Fortress: The Story of Luis Muñoz Marín.* New York: New American Library, 1964.

Bernier-Grand, Carmen T. *Poet and Politician of Puerto Rico: Don Luis Muñoz Marín.* New York: Orchard, 1995.

Blackman, M. C. "Muna Lee, Poet Was Wife of Luis Munoz Marin." *New York Herald Tribune* (April 4, 1965): 38.

Blotner, Joseph. *Faulkner: A Biography.* Vol. 2. New York: Random House, 1974.

Brodsky, Louis Daniel. *William Faulkner, Life Glimpses.* Austin: University of Texas Press, 1990.

Dear Editor: A History of Poetry *in Letters,* edited by Joseph Parisi and Stephen Young. New York: Norton, 2003.

Deutsch, Babette. "Lyrics from Ecuador and New England." Review of *Secret Country,* by Jorge Carrera Andrade, tr. Muna Lee. *New York Times Book Review* (February 16, 1947): 4.

Dolmetsch, Carl R. *The Smart Set: A History and Anthology.* New York: Dial Press, 1966.

Dorgan, Cornelia James. "Muna Lee of the Americas." *Matrix* (June 1944): 13.

Elliott, L. E. "Women's Progress towards Equal Rights: Feminist and World Treaties." *Pan-American Magazine* 41 (December 1928): 205–14.

Espinosa, J. Manuel. Review of *Pioneers of Puerto Rico,* by Muna Lee. *Americas* 1 (April 1945): 518–20.

Gregory, Horace. *The House on Jefferson Street.* New York: Holt, Reinhart and Winston, 1971.

Guyton, David E. "Potluck with the Poets"; "Biographical Sketch." *Four Talks on Writing; Delivered at the Southern Literary Festival.* Blue Mountain, Miss.: privately printed, 1947.

Haddox, Barbara. "Muna Lee—An Envoy for the Americas." *Ohio State Journal,* May 18, 1944.

Hughes, Elaine. "Lee, Muna: 1895–1965." In *Lives of Mississippi Authors, 1817–1967,* edited by James B. Lloyd, 291–93. Jackson: University Press of Mississippi, 1981.

———. "Lee, Muna." In *Notable American Women: The Modern Period,* edited by Barbara Sicherman and Carol Hurd Green, 413–14. Cambridge, Mass.: Harvard University Press, 1980.

Jiménez-Muñoz, Gladys. "Deconstructing Colonialist Discourse: Links between the Women's Suffrage Movement in the United States and Puerto Rico." *Phoebe* 5.1 (1993): 9–34.

Kroll, Ernest. "Muna Lee (1895–1965)." *Texas Quarterly* 20.4 (1977): 152.

MacLeish, Archibald. *Archibald MacLeish: Reflections,* edited by Bernard A. Drabeck and Helen E. Ellis. Amherst: University of Massachusetts Press, 1986.

Marable, Mary Hays, and Elaine Boylan. "Muna Lee (Mrs. Luis Muñoz Marín)." *Handbook of Oklahoma Writers,* 67–69. Norman: University of Oklahoma Press, 1939.

"Miss Lee Ends Distinguished Years at State." *Department of State News Letter* (March 1965): 41.

"Miss Muna Lee." *Ole Miss 1913,* 39. Oxford: University of Mississippi, 1913.

"Muna Lee, 70; Poet, U.S. Cultural Official." *Washington Post* (April 4, 1965): B14.

"Muna Lee, Writer, Ex-U.S. Aide, Dies." *New York Times* (April 4, 1965): 87.

Niles, Blair. "'If You Hear of a Good War, Go to It.'" Review of *Four Years beneath the Crescent,* by Rafael de Nogales, tr. Muna Lee. *New York Herald Tribune Books* (June 20, 1926): 18.

"Pan-American Literary Ties Urged on U.S." *New York Herald Tribune* (November 30, 1941): 40.

Puerto Rico: A Guide to the Island of Boriquén. New York: University Society, 1940.

Reid, Mary. "Muna Lee: Poet and Feminist." *Holland's, the Magazine of the South* 59 (April 1940): 6, 25.

The Republic of Letters in America: The Correspondence of John Peale Bishop and Allen Tate, edited by Thomas Daniel Young and John J. Hindle. Lexington: University Press of Kentucky, 1981.

Review of *The Cultural Approach: Another Way in International Relations,* by Ruth Emily McMurry and Muna Lee. *American Historical Review* 53 (January 1948): 371.

————. *American Political Science Review* 42 (February 1948): 141–42.

————. *American Sociological Review* 13 (April 1948): 235.

Review of *Four Years beneath the Crescent,* by Rafael de Nogales, tr. Muna Lee. *American Review of Reviews* 74 (July 1926): 110.

————. *Boston Evening Transcript* (June 5, 1926): 5.

————. *New York Times Book Review* (June 20, 1926): 18, 28.

Review of *A History of Spain,* by Rafael Altamira, tr. Muna Lee. *Hispania* 33 (May 1950): 179–80.

————. *Hispanic American Historical Review* 30 (May 1950): 218.

————. *Nation* 169 (December 3, 1949): 550.

————. *Western Political Quarterly* 3 (December 1950): 637–38.

Review of *Murder at* 28:10, by Newton Gayle. *New Statesman and Nation* 11 (February 29, 1936): 315–16.

Review of *Sea-Change,* by Muna Lee. *Boston Evening Transcript* (September 29, 1923): 3.

————. *New York Times Book Review* (June 10, 1923): 12.

Review of *Secret Country,* by Jorge Carrera Andrade, tr. Muna Lee. *Hispania* 29 (November 1946): 627–29.

————. *Yale Review* 36 (Autumn 1946): 150.

Rosenthal, M. L. "By an Ecuadorean Poet." Review of *Secret Country,* by Jorge Carrera Andrade, tr. Muna Lee. *New York Herald Tribune Weekly Book Review* (April 6, 1947): 2.

Swett, Margery. "Words That Fly Singing." Review of *Sea-Change,* by Muna Lee. *Poetry* (October 1923): 51–54.

Walsh, Donald Devenish. "Spanish American Literature in 1946." *Hispania* 30 (February 1947): 20–26.

Wamsley, Esther Sue. "A Hemisphere of Women: Latin American and U.S. Feminists in the IACW, 1915–1939." Ph.D. diss., Ohio State University, 1998.

GENERAL WORKS

Beyond the Ideal: Pan Americanism in Inter-American Affairs, edited by David Sheinin. Westport, Conn.: Greenwood Press, 2000.

Bishop, John Peale. "The Poetry of Jorge Carrera Andrade." *Secret Country,* by Jorge Carrera Andrade, tr. Muna Lee, v–xi. New York: Macmillan, 1946.

Donaldson, Scott, in collaboration with R. H. Winnick. *Archibald MacLeish: An American Life.* Boston: Houghton Mifflin, 1992.

Kreymborg, Alfred. *Troubadour: An American Autobiography.* New York: Sagamore Press, 1957.

MacLeish, Archibald. *The American Story: Ten Broadcasts.* New York: Duell, Sloan and Pearce, 1944.

McClure, John. *Airs and Ballads.* New York: Knopf, 1918.

Mencken, H. L. *The New Mencken Letters,* edited by Carl Bode. New York: Dial Press, 1977.

Meriwether, James B. *A Faulkner Miscellany.* Jackson: University Press of Mississippi, 1974.

Miller, Francesca. *Latin American Women and the Search for Social Justice.* Lebanon, N. H.: University Press of New England, 1991.

The Mississippi Poets, compiled by Ernestine Clayton Deavours. Memphis, Tenn.: Clarke, 1922.

Mississippi Verse, edited by Alice James. Chapel Hill: University of North Carolina Press, 1934.

Monroe, Harriet. "Pan-American Concord." *Poetry* 26 (June 1925): 155–58.

Muñoz Marín, Luis. *Memorias: autobiografía pública.* San Juan, P.R.: Universidad Interamericana de Puerto Rico, 1982.

National Woman's Party Papers, 1913–1972, edited by Thomas C. Pardo. Glenn Rock, N. J.: Microfilming Corporation of America, 1977.

"NBC University of the Air Opens Course in Literature." *NBC* (February 1944): 1.

Review of *The Americas Look at Each Other,* by José Agustín Balseiro, tr. Muna Muñoz Lee. *Library Journal* 95 (February 1, 1970): 507.

Torres-Ríoseco, Arturo. *The Epic of Latin American Literature.* Berkeley: University of California Press, 1970.

Note: A copy of Muna Lee's complete federal personnel file, which contains information about her work for the U.S. Department of State from 1941 to 1965, can be obtained (free of charge) from the National Archives and Records Administration; the request for her "official personnel folder" must include her social security number, 577–34–8281, along with proof that she is deceased (e.g., a copy of her obituary published in the *New York Times* on April 4, 1965), and should be addressed to: Office of Personnel Management, OPF/EMF Access Unit, P.O. Box 18673, St. Louis, MO 63118.

Acknowledgments

Special gratitude is expressed to the family of Muna Lee for approval to reprint these works and all others whose original publication data are noted elsewhere in these pages. Grateful acknowledgments are made to all publishers, organizations, and other persons for permission to reprint Lee's previously published work:

POETRY

"Acacia Island," "Albatross," "Atavian," "Carib Garden," "Caribbean Marsh," "Deserted Orchard," "Night of San Juan," "Stalactite," "Visitant," and "Wayfarer" were originally published in *The New Yorker*.

"April Wind," "Choice," "The Confidante," "Gifts," "I Have Had Enough of Glamour," "Imprisoned," "Lips You Were Not Anhungered For," "Mid-Western," "The Seeker," "A Song of Dreams Come True," "The Stars Are Colored Blossoms," "Survival," "The Thought of You," "Tropic Rain," and "A Woman's Song" were published by Macmillan in *Sea-Change*.

"Lyric to the Sun" © 1935 Commonweal Foundation; "Planet" © 1929 Commonweal Foundation; "Porto Rican Hacienda" © 1930 Commonweal Foundation; "Puerto Rican Moonrise" © 1933 Commonweal Foundation—reprinted with permission.

VERSE TRANSLATION

"Andean Crossing," "Dregs," "Elegy to the Invented Woman," "The Illustrated World," "The Little Girl That Lost a Finger," "Love," "Man's Road," "Mob of Mountains," "On Someone's Death," "Pamphlet," "Parable of Generosity," "Proletarians," "Provincial Moment," "Sierra," and "Vision of Moth-Eaten Pianos Falling to Pieces": From *Anthology of Contemporary Latin-American Poetry*, edited by Dudley Fitts, translated by Muna Lee de Muñoz Marín, copyright © 1947 by New Directions Publishing Corp. Reprinted by permission of New Directions Publishing Corp.

"Biography for the Use of the Birds," "The Guest," "Nameless District," "Nameless Islands," "Place of Origin," "Sunday," and "Vocation of the Mirror" were published by Macmillan in *Secret Country*.

"Brother Dog," "Horses of the Conquistadores," and "Running Water" originally appeared in *Poetry* (Chicago).

PROSE

"Brother of Poe" was originally published in *Southwest Review.*

"Contemporary Spanish-American Poetry" was originally published in *North American Review.*

"Cuban Literature" was originally published in *Americas* and is reprinted courtesy of the Academy of American Franciscan History.

"Eugenio María de Hostos: After One Hundred Years" and "Puerto Rican Women Writers: The Record of One Hundred Years" are reprinted courtesy of *World Literature Today.*

"Flowering in a Phrase" © 1934 Commonweal Foundation, reprinted with permission.

"Governments Invest in Culture" is from *The Cultural Approach: Another Way in International Relations* by Ruth Emily McMurry and Muna Lee. Copyright © 1947 by the University of North Carolina Press, renewed 1975 by Donald L. McMurry. Used by permission of the publisher.

"Harriet Monroe: Poet and Pioneer"; "Notes from a Feminist's Travel Diary"; and "Paulina Luisi, Internationalist" are reprinted courtesy of the National Woman's Party, Sewell-Belmont House, Washington, D.C.

"Pan-American Women" is reprinted with permission from the March 14, 1928, issue of *The Nation* magazine.

"Translating the Untranslatable: Can Poetry Stand the Change?" is reprinted from *Américas,* a bimonthly magazine published by the General Secretariat of the Organization of American States in English and Spanish.

Acknowledgments are also made of the works by other authors, excerpts of which appear in the present biography: Newton Gayle's *Murder at 28:10* © 1936 Scribner's. Horace Gregory's *The House on Jefferson Street; A Cycle of Memories* © 1971 Holt, Rinehart and Winston.

In addition, an acknowledgment is made of the following work that is reprinted in its entirety: "Muna Lee (1895–1965)," by Ernest Kroll, from *Texas Quarterly* 20.4 (1977): 152. Copyright © 1977 by the University of Texas Press. All rights reserved.

Index

"Elegy to the Invented Woman" (Abril), 150

employment, discrimination against women in, 32–33

equal rights, 26–27; Equal Rights Amendment, 27, 61, 197; "Equal Rights Approved by American Institute of International Law," 33–34; Equal Rights Treaty, 33–34, 193–94; NWP and Sixth Pan-American Conference, 190–92; as poetic subject, 34–35

Equal Rights (magazine), 40

Ercilla, Alonso de, 236, 263–64

"Eugenio María de Hostos: After One Hundred Years," 252–55

the everyday in poetry, 18, 58

exploration, 53, 71–72n32

familial relationships, 5, 37–42, 276–77; children and motherhood, 14–16, 18, 32, 37–38, 57, 66

Faulkner, William, *vii*, 59–60

feminism: Caribbean women and, 48–49; Sor Juana as "first feminist," 65; "Notes from a Feminist's Travel Diary," 200–202; Pan-Americanism and, 19; as poetic subject, 246; Sixth Pan-American Conference, 27–29; Society of Woman Geographers, 53; suffrage, 5, 26–27, 200; women poets translated by Lee, 20–21; women's right to work, 32–33; women writers promoted by Lee, 20–21, 23, 203–7; World Woman's Party, 41. *See also* equal rights; National Woman's Party (NWP)

Fiallo, Fabio, 19

figurative language, 163

Fitts, Dudley, 43–44

"The Flame-Trees," 15

Florit, Eugenio, 145, 213

"Flowering in a Phrase," 250–51

flowers as poetic images, *xviii*, 4–5, 8–9, 15, 24, 38, 42, 163–64

folk-poetry, 165

food, 216–17

"Footnotes" series, 7–8

forms, poetic: *cantares*, 165; free verse, 9–10; *octava rima*, 237–42; *redondilla*, 178–79; sonnets, 16–17, 166–67, 179, 180–81; translation and preservation of, 260–61; *villancicos*, 179–80

Four Years beneath the Crescent (Nogales), 25

"Frontier" (unfinished autobiographical novel), 40, 72n35

Frost, Robert: inspiration for first poem, 62; Latin American poets and, 170

Gautier, Théophile, 262–63

Gayle, Newton (pen name of Lee and Guinness), 39

geography, 53

"Gifts," 116

Glines, Ellen, 204–5

Goldberg, Isaac, 219

Gómez de la Avellaneda, Gertrudis, 211

Gómez Tejera, Carmen, 204

Góngora, Luis de, 178

González Martínez, Enrique, 169

"Governments Invest in Culture," 266–71

grandmothers, 37–39, 42

Gregory, Horace, 24

"The Guest" (Carrera Andrade), 139

Guillén, Nicolás, 213

Guillén Zelaya, Alfonso, 169

Guinness, Maurice, 39

Gutiérrez Nájera, Manuel, 212

Guyton, David, 5, 161

"Hacienda," 80

"Harriet Monroe: Poet and Pioneer," 197–99

Heredia, José María, 211

Hernández Catá, Alfonso, 214

Hernández Miyares, Enrique, 213

Herrera y Reissig, Julio, 173–74

Hispanic Anthology, 19

Hispano, Cornelio, 170

A History of Spain (Altamira), 58–59

honeymoon, 14

"The Carnival," 104; "A Charming Mexican Lady," 176–82; "Choice," 115; "Compensation," 11; "The Confidante," 118; "Conquistador for Science," 39; "Contemporary Spanish American Poetry," 20, 165–75; "Cuban Literature," 208–15; *The Cultural Approach*, 57–58; "Cultural Interchanges between the Americas," 216–21; "Deliverance," 36, 89; "Deserted Orchard," 92; "Dies Irae," 81; "Dregs" (Vallejo), 44, 156; "The Drugstore," 100; "The Duelists," 103; "Electors," 101; "Elegy to the Invented Woman" (Abril), 150; "Equal Rights Approved by American Institute of International Law," 33–34; "Eugenio María de Hostos: After One Hundred Years," 252–55; "The Flame-Trees," 15; "Flowering in a Phrase," 250–51; "Footnotes" series, 7–8; *Four Years beneath the Crescent* (Nogales), 25; "Frontier" (unfinished autobiographical novel), 40, 72n35; "Gifts," 116; "Governments Invest in Culture," 266–71; "The Guest" (Carrera Andrade), 139; "Hacienda," 80; "Harriet Monroe: Poet and Pioneer," 197–99; *A History of Spain* (Altamira), 58–59; "Horses of the Conquistadores" (Chocano), 133–35; "I Have Had Enough of Glamour," 113; "The Illustrated World" (Moro), 152; "Imprisoned," 36–37, 117; "In Behalf of the Equal Rights Treaty," 28–29, 193–94; "An Indian Territory Childhood," 72n35; "The Inter-American Commission of Women: A New International Venture," 222–29; "I Who Had Sought God," 13, 17; "José de San Martín," 230–33; "Juan de Castellanos in the Perspective of 350 Years," 234–43; "Like a Tale of Old Romance," 10; "Lips You Were Not Anhungered For," 110; "The Litany for Our Lord Don Quixote" (Darío), 168; "The Little Girl's Lost Finger" (Mistral),

45; "Love" (Torres Bodet), 128–29; "Luis—and an Episode," 72n35; "Lyric to the Sun," 38; "Magdalen," 7; "Man's Road" (Peña Barrenechea), 155; "Mid-Western," 119; "Mob of Mountains" (Varallanos), 146; "Moonrise," 82; *Murder at 28:10*, 39–40; "Mushroom Town" sonnet series, 99–108; "Nameless District" (Carrera Andrade), 46–48, 142; "Nameless Islands" (Carrera Andrade), 136–37; "Night of San Juan," 85; "Nightpiece," 97; "Nocturne" (Silva), 21–22, 184–85; "Notes from a Feminist's Travel Diary," 200–202; numbered verses, 9–10; "Of Writing Verse," 78; *On Being Good Neighbors* (Picón Salas), 52; "On Going Ashore," 83; "On Not Writing about Mauna Loa," 38–39; "On Someone's Death" (Florit), 145; "Pamphlet" (Muñoz Marín), 14–15, 44, 131; "Pan American Day in the Park," 34–35; "Pan-American Women," 29–30, 190–92; "Parable of Generosity" (Spinetti Dini), 153–54; "Paulina Luisi, Internationalist," 195–96; *Pioneers of Puerto Rico*, 52; "Place of Origin" (Carrera Andrade), 141; "Planet," 79; "Poetry Every Day," 58, 161–64; "Prairie Sky," 107; "Proletarians" (Muñoz Marín), 44, 130; "Provincial Moment" (Villalobos), 149; "Puerto Rican Women Writers: The Record of One Hundred Years," 203–7; "Reality" (Silva), 184–85; "The Revival," 106; "Rich Port," 31–32, 77; "The Rose" (Sor Juana), 127; "Running Water" (Storni), 20–21, 125; *Sea-Change*, 16–19, 63; *Secret Country* (Carrera Andrade), 46–48, 53–56; "The Seeker," 17, 63, 122; "Sierra" (Carrera Andrade), 45–46; "Silvio, I abhor you . . ." (Sor Juana), 64; "A Song of Dreams Come True," 13–14, 121; "Songs of Many Moods" series, 13; "Song to the Glory of the Sky of America" (Oribe), 46; "Stalactite," 91; "The

THE AMERICAS